CHRISTIANS, MUSLIMS, AND JESUS

Christians, Muslims, and Jesus

Mona Siddiqui

YALE UNIVERSITY PRESS
NEW HAVEN AND LONDON

For information about this and other Yale University Press publications please contact:
U.S. Office: sales.press@yale.edu   yalebooks.com
Europe Office: sales@yaleup.co.uk   www.yalebooks.co.uk

Set in Adobe Caslon Pro by IDSUK (DataConnection) Ltd
Printed in Great Britain by TJ International Ltd., Padstow, Cornwall

Library of Congress Control Number 2013934407

ISBN 978-0-300-16970-6

A catalogue record for this book is available from the British Library.

10 9 8 7 6 5 4 3 2 1

FSC www.fsc.org MIX Paper from responsible sources FSC® C013056

For Allen

Contents

Acknowledgments

I would like to thank Malcolm Gerratt from Yale University Press who first approached me about a book on Jesus in the Islamic tradition. Although the ground shifted somewhat from our initial conversations, his encouragement and enthusiasm allowed me to embark on a far more challenging project. Thus, this book reflects an academic as well as a personal journey. I would also like to express my gratitude to the Sir Halley Stewart Trust whose faith in my research and generous financial award bought me time off from university duties during the critical early stages; I am very grateful to the trustees. Although I did not discuss the contents of this book with any colleagues in particular, I owe so much to so many who have inspired my interest in Christian–Muslim relations over the years. As for my husband, Farhaj, and my sons, Suhaib, Zuhayr and Fayz, who have been on this journey with me in their own ways, your unfailing respect for my work has always been invaluable; thank you!

INTRODUCTION

I have been engaged in Christian–Muslim relations for most of my academic life. While this was not initially a particular research area of mine, my involvement in 'dialogue' over the years inspired in me a much deeper interest in the theological themes and conversations between the world's two largest faiths. Dialogue itself is a contested term, but for me it has always been about learning, my desire to know more about Christian theology, and through this to be challenged in my own Muslim faith. As a Muslim woman, often a lone voice in what is still a largely male-dominated academic field, I have always felt an ethical imperative to stay involved. This interest has also been reinforced by the knowledge that there are still very few Muslims throughout the world who have a theological interest in Christianity. However, it would be fair to say that even if the current impetus behind the growth of dialogue is more politically rather than theologically motivated, the various disciplines of dialogue are growing as many realise that to be religious today, one has to be aware of the inter-religious.

There are many ways to look at the history of Christian–Muslim engagement throughout the centuries. Both these religions are lived religions with complex histories of conflict and coexistence which have influenced and continue to influence mutual perceptions and understandings. Furthermore, both religions experienced internal schisms brought about by theological and political conflicts. In Christianity this became manifest mainly through the Eastern Orthodox, Roman Catholic and Protestant traditions, and in Islam principally through the Sunnī and Shī'a sectarian divide, although many other groups followed. Outside institutional structures, some claim that mystical dimensions retained a distinct approach to the search for God.

Scholarship in this area has focused mainly upon the historical, sociological, theological and political interaction between Christianity and Islam. In recent years Christian scholars have made a huge contribution in translation work, making accessible Arabic writings of Muslim scholars from the eighth century onwards. This kind of work has been invaluable in acquiring a much deeper insight into the richness of theological debate between Christians and Muslims.

This book, however, is different and there are two fundamental purposes behind it. The first is that the book is to some extent my own journey exploring the views, doctrines and conversations Christians and Muslims have held on the figure of Jesus Christ, in particular even when Muḥammad is used as a point of comparison. This Christological basis therefore is where all the chapters are heading in their own ways, rather than providing a general history of Christian–Muslim relations or a historical or political overview. How did Christians discuss the unique nature of Jesus and how did Muslims respond? What were the theological nuances in the doctrinal debates from the eighth century onwards and how do the poetical references to Jesus reflect a particular kind of empathy? Can the theology of the cross have any meaning for a Muslim today? The selection of names and quotes around these questions is of course to some extent subjective and absolutely not exhaustive. But in the selection of material, I am confident that I have included some of the most significant figures in both Christianity and Islam who reflected on the status and meaning of Jesus in conversation with one another or in reaction to one another.

The second purpose is to offer the reader an adequate sense of what the primary sources are saying about Jesus, so that the book functions as a 'sourcebook' as much as a personal reflection on Jesus and related themes. Thus there are almost two methodologies with some overlap. In Chapters 1, 4, 5 and 6, I have selected particular themes for discussion and to show how they have been and could be compared today. Using a variety of sources, I look at the topics of prophecy, divinity, Mary, evil, sin, redemption, love and law as conversation themes about Jesus between Christianity and Islam. Chapter 6, the conclusion, is my personal reflection on the cross, on how Jesus' death on the cross remains for many Christians the centre of their faith, and on what the cross says to me as a Muslim.

Chapters 2 and 3 have a slightly different style. In these chapters I have used primary sources from Eastern and Latin Christianity as well as the writings of Muslim scholars and poets from the eighth century onwards to show the kind of polemics and reflections on Jesus between Christians and Muslims. Much of the doctrinal debate focused on how to understand God through concepts such as the Word, Incarnation and Trinity. The scholarly ingenuity on both sides means that the discourse is theologically very technical at times. God and his nature through scriptural revelation or the Incarnation remain the central focus, but an appreciation of the nuance and logic in these debates can only be acquired if the citations are long enough to reflect the flow of arguments. This is crucial, for it is important to know what was actually said by theologians on both sides about Jesus' nature, as well as by Christians for Muslims, and what was said about Muḥammad by Christians in their comparisons with Jesus. While I have tried to minimise long citations, it is essential that it is their words which are read rather than my own interpretation or paraphrase. These two chapters are important for our understanding of how certain doctrines continued to shape mutual understanding and mutual suspicions. Even though many of the early texts cited here appear as complete, edited treatises of real dialogues, it is difficult to say with any certainty how the authors of these imagined disputations really felt about each other's faiths. In other words, we can get glimpses into various dialogical worlds, but these worlds were not static. Thus, it is most probable that many of the views expressed underwent modification over the years for a variety of political, theological and sociological reasons.

The overall aim of the book is not any concerted effort to dispel misunderstandings and recriminations, although if that is a consequence of the book, it is a most welcome consequence. The aim is to show more clearly what Christians and Muslims were saying in conciliatory as well as polemical terms in response to each other's beliefs about Jesus. The book can therefore be seen as a historical overview of what the scholars *said* rather than what ordinary Christians and Muslims *did*. The exploration of these themes has used Islamic and Biblical terms as I feel it is important for Muslims to know and be challenged by some of the New Testament terminology. There has been a sustained inner life to this engagement shaped and inspired *by* the faithful *to* the faithful. A revered prophet or God Incarnate, Jesus is central to continued theological engagement, yet Christology seems to be a difficult subject for discussion between Christians and Muslims in dialogue today. It is as if the divinity and humanity of Christ cannot be a basis for any scholarly discussion by Muslims because it represents everything Islamic monotheism has struggled against, the ultimate stumbling block in dialogue. This has then had the unfortunate consequence of closing off any real empathy with what Christ means in the life of Christians. Without real empathy, Christian–Muslim dialogue remains a dialogue on the surface, a light encounter as opposed to a rich, mutually shared experience which can continue to inspire new avenues for exploration. My own experience in dialogue and as a western Muslim has encouraged me to reflect in diverse ways on what kind of conversations Muslims and Christians can have which will enrich their personal faith as well as open new ways of thinking about traditional themes. I have been encouraged to write in this area owing to some of the moving, humorous and inspirational conversations I have enjoyed with colleagues from all over the world throughout my academic life. I very much hope that my style of writing here, a mixture of the personal and the objective, will draw the reader into accompanying me on this journey.

Note on presentation

The book tries to keep Arabic and other terms in transliteration to a minimum, but where these words are used in the main body of the text, they have been fully vocalised. When quoting from other sources, I have kept the spellings and diacritics of all names and transliterated terms as they are written in the sources; I have not modified them. As for scriptural translations, I have used various online translations of the Bible via Biblegateway.com. For the Qur'ān translations, I have relied on Yusuf Ali and Muḥammad A. Haleem (2004); in both cases, slight adjustments have been made for ease of reading where necessary. All dates given here are according to the Gregorian calendar.

CHAPTER 1

THE END OF PROPHECY

In Islam, prophecy and scripture are inextricably tied to divine communication, so that it is principally through Muḥammad and the Qur'ān that Muslims come to see God as a moral and eschatological reality. There is an understanding that throughout history God sends and humanity receives different forms of God's communication. It is in this receiving that humankind understands something of God, a God who both hides and reveals himself. Scripture is given first and written second. By contrast, scripture and prophecy play a secondary role in Christianity in the sense that through Jesus Christ, God no longer offers us a prophetic message pointing to an eschatological reality, but rather offers himself; the Incarnation is central to Christian theology. All of God's past wagers on previous prophets and messages culminate in this final act of his self-giving in the hope that 'they all shall know me' (Jeremiah 31:31).

Christianity did not begin as a bookish religion. The earliest written text about Jesus is Paul's First Letter to the Thessalonians, but there is no evidence that Paul ever met Jesus. The identities of the authors of the Gospels are unknown. Yet, while the authors of the Gospels probably did not think of themselves as writing scripture, their works cannot be regarded merely as human transcripts of what Jesus said and did. The Gospels' genre is analogous to ancient biographies, but they are more than biographies; they are also *kerygma*. If the life and message of Jesus is contained in the Gospels, the Gospels were written as testimonies to an event. Much of the Christian language about God affirms Jesus as God in self-revelation, and much of the Muslim language about God seeks exception to that Christian claim by Islam's particular insistence on divine unity and uniqueness which is perceived mainly through scripture. Islam makes reference to Christianity in various ways, but it lays emphasis on scripture and prophecy as defining modes of God's revelation. In this chapter I will reflect on how prophecy and divinity speak to us in both Christianity and Islam, but also on how the finality of prophecy means different things in both religions.

When I was growing up, my parents told us stories of the prophets as a way of conveying and elaborating the sacred tales contained in the Qur'ān. It was a way of explaining how God connects to human beings and how these stories always point to a presence and power beyond us. In later years I discovered that many of the prophets, including the great prophets of Israel, had scant mention in the Qur'ān. The actual stories with the romantic amplification of the Qur'ānic material were largely from the *Qiṣaṣ al-anbiyā'*, the particular genre of literature known as the 'Stories of the Prophets'. These were the embellished and intriguing narratives of the lives of prophetic figures who appeared in the Qur'ān, prominent characters who coincided almost entirely with the Judeo-Christian Biblical tradition. These prophetic tales fall in the category of hagiographical anthologies or 'collected lives'. The events in their lives always contained a moral dimension and the themes covered in this literary genre began with creation, recounted the lives of the various prophets, and concluded with the life and messengership of Muḥammad. The way in which these stories were told lifted the prophets and men of wisdom out of their historical time and into a universal time. In other words, these stories were not simply tales of ancient wisdom but contained a deeper essence and truth, a higher reality which made them relevant for all time. In a religious sense, this linear chronology formed a prehistory to Muḥammad's own prophecy and mission. While there are several collections of the *Qiṣaṣ al-anbiyā'*, one of the most significant collections was written by Abū Isḥāq al-Tha'labī (d.1035). In it al-Tha'labī explains how God had five reasons to reveal to Muḥammad the stories of the prophets who preceded him. Each of the five reasons explains at least one passage from the Qur'ān which confirms what has been stated. The following example taken from Brinner's translation clarifies al-Tha'labī's method:

> The fifth that he told him, the stories of the preceding prophets and saints to keep their memory and legacy alive, so that those who do well in keeping the saints' memory alive assure themselves thereby a speedy reward in this world, in order that the saints' good renown and legacy may remain forever, just as Abraham, the friend of God, desired the preservation of his good reputation and said, 'And let me have a good report with posterity' (Q26:84). For men are tales – it is said that no man dies but mention of him revives him.[1]

Recounting such tales did indeed make the prophetic messages meaningful in some way as well as bringing into a sharper focus the numerous Qur'ānic passages which mention human prophecy as God's chosen method of conveying his divine message in the course of history. There is no real philosophy or theory of prophethood in the Qur'ān, except that God's prophets and messengers are a sign of his mercy (*raḥma*) and the stories of previous prophets are mentioned as part of God's revelatory scheme:

> To every people was sent a messenger (Q10:47).
>
> We have sent you inspiration as we sent it to Noah and the messengers after him. We sent inspiration to Abraham, Isma'il, Isaac, Jacob and the tribes, to Jesus, Job, Jonah, Aaron, and Solomon, and to David we gave the Psalms (Q4:163).

Indeed, the Qur'ān contains many allusions to the prophets and messengers of the past and the fate of the communities who rejected the truths brought by God's chosen men. The didactic function of these prophecy (*nubuwwa*) narratives means that they can be seen as 'homilies on religious history' and their function is not just to relate the past but to warn the believers of the future.[2]

In Islamic thought, revelation is to be understood as a process of God communicating in the concreteness of events, re-igniting in people a new awareness of themselves and their relation to the world. In Islam, God has done this throughout history by sending messengers from Adam to Muḥammad who all bring the same primordial truth anchored in the heart of humanity, the oneness of God and human obligation to worship God. The messages come through prophets and messengers, some receiving revelation through scripture, while others are somehow inspired. What the Qur'ān conveys is the sense of an overriding continuity found in the repeated mention of the names of Old Testament prophets. But the Qur'ān does not quote earlier scripture directly, even though Biblical resonances are to be found in the text. The concept of prophecy is shared between Judaism, Christianity and Islam, though each has accorded prophecy varying time, significance and purpose. Jewish tradition regarded prophecy as the gift of the holy spirit (*rūaḥ nĕbû'â*). Moses was perhaps the first to define the phenomenon of a prophet as one who claims to speak with divine authority, although it can be traced much further back in the history of God's people. If a prophet was bringing the actual words of God to a people, to ignore the message was tantamount to ignoring God himself.[3] Such a position of authority had to be tested and false prophets were condemned, as in the words, 'A prophet who presumes to speak in my name anything I have not commanded him to say, or a prophet who speaks in the name of other gods, must be put to death' (Deuteronomy 18:20). Graham Houston writes that the story of Elijah illustrates how man could be truly 'a man of God' and that Elijah acted as a bridge between the Mosaic tradition and the writings of the prophets recorded in the major and minor prophets. He states, 'The major (such as Isaiah and Jeremiah) and the minor (such as Amos and Micah) were united in the conviction that they brought the word of the Lord to their people.'[4] This prophetic tradition is characterized by a claim to absolute verbal authority and an official sanction of divine communication in antiquity. Prophecy confirmed God's presence with his people. After Malachi (c.400 BC), the voice of authoritative prophecy was stilled. In speaking of the end of prophecy, Frederick Greenspahn wrote:

> The pseudonymity of intertestamental apocalyptic suggests that claims of direct revelation were by that time no longer credible, and indeed the biblical canon includes no prophetic works ascribed to figures who lived later than Malachi. This conforms to the rabbinic tradition that the holy spirit withdrew from Israel after the death of Haggai, Zechariah, and Malachi. Several texts from the intertestamental period also allude to an

> absence of prophecy, occasioning various theories about the circumstances and causes of its coming to an end.[5]

Old Testament prophets spoke for the Lord. 'Thus speaks the Lord,' they said, and their mouths were filled with the Word of God. They were inspired by God's presence as their response to some event, and the history of the religious community that was thus established has verified that response in the only possible and only appropriate way: in the religious life of the community which that Word established:

> The Prophet's Word, the Word of God, is also the Word of the people who accept it. They became and have remained, however inconstantly, the 'people of the Word.' God is in his Word, and his Word is in his people. It is this fact, for instance, which explains the Protestant Reformers' concern with the Word, both as a written testament and as the Spirit which, in the presence of faith, that testament contains. God is both the form and the content of his people's experience when they keep his Word, and that experience (so deeply mythopoeic) includes their whole world and their own persons. In the biblical sense of prophecy, a prophet is anyone in whom some event is suddenly revealed as 'a mighty act of God,' and who announces the presence of the Lord in that event. The event is now taken as a sign of God, and, accordingly, he comes to live in it as its fundamental meaning. His presence embraces both the sign and the prophet who takes up the sign in its sacred significance. Man and God are joined sacramentally in the sign.[6]

The prophecy of the Old Testament prophets was not just preaching but also proclamation. This proclamation announces the end of this age, and the call to repentance is God's very last offer. The prophetic gift was seen more and more as an eschatological phenomenon which would become a reality again only at the end of days, and then in a particular way.[7] Oscar Cullmann's analysis of prophecy explains how John the Baptist was seen as a living prophet like ancient prophets, so that we find in Luke 3:2, 'The word of God came to John'. But John was considered as an eschatological event as well, the Prophet of the end time. In the Synoptic Gospels, although John nowhere gives an explanation of his own person, he is either the forerunner of God or the forerunner of the Messiah.[8]

In Islamic theology, Jesus is the only prophet and messenger of end times, but he is also one of the twenty-five mentioned by name in the Qur'ān. The Qur'ān speaks of prophets and messengers as being those people whom God has elected for his divine purpose. Prophecy allows God to remain veiled and there is no suggestion in the Qur'ān that God wishes to reveal of himself just yet. Prophets guarantee interpretation of revelation and that God's message will be understood. It is generally accepted that not every prophet is a messenger, but every messenger is a prophet, though Hūd and Sālih are spoken of as 'sent' but not prophets. In this prophetic chronology Muḥammad became the seal of the prophets or the final messenger for Muslims, but even in this particular doctrine of prophethood his message is essentially the same as that of his predecessors. Once distilled to its fundamentals, the message is of the oneness, mercy and sovereignty of God. Thus, despite the unique place of Muḥammad in Muslim piety and veneration, Muḥammad's prophecy in the Qur'ān lies in the wider context and mission of previous prophecies. He is asked the same questions previous prophets were asked about God, and he is challenged and rejected by those who refuse to believe in the truth of his prophetic status and the truth of his words.

The Qur'ān does not itself contain any distinct doctrine of prophecy, except to distinguish prophecy (*nubuwwa*) from revelation (*waḥy*). But the phenomenon of revelation and its reception by a human soul and the 'office' of prophethood were themes explored by the Muslim philosophers centuries after Muḥammad's death. Philosophical ideas about Muḥammad's prophecy culminated at the beginning of the eleventh century in the prophetology of Ibn Sīnā, who developed a systematic explanation of the nature of Muḥammad's prophecy and saw Muḥammad as the most perfect of all prophets. Unlike his predecessor al-Farābī (870–950/951), who never explicitly refers to the prophet of Islam, Ibn Sīnā states that Muḥammad had fulfilled all a prophet should do as a lawgiver and in what he should convey in his revelation to create the most benefits for God's creation.[9] As Frank Griffel writes, 'In his psychology and his prophetology, Ibn Sīnā gives a distinctly Islamic expression to a theory that has its earliest roots in the works of Aristotle'. Griffel states:

> Prophecy in Ibn Sīnā consists of three elements: strong imaginative revelation, intellectual revelation, and a powerful practical faculty of the soul. Revelation of the kind received by Muḥammad requires the utmost degree of all these three properties. The true prophet, for Ibn Sīnā, is a philosopher. He may not have devoted much to learning, but his power of intuition puts his theoretical insight at par with the most advanced among the philosophers. Both of them achieve conjunction with the active intellect. Yet where the philosopher may teach his insights only to those who practise philosophy, the prophet

> can convey them in figurative language and thus make them accessible to all people.[10]

Although it is not within the scope of this work to analyse at any length the philosophical arguments on prophecy, it is important to single out the contribution of the foremost theologian-jurist of the medieval Islamic world, Abū Ḥāmid al-Ghazālī (1058–1111). Al-Ghazālī rejected the view that prophets teach only the masses and that philosophers are in no need of divine revelation. The benefits of prophets go well beyond their political activities and bringing laws, but rather 'the prophet's revelations are full of original information that human beings cannot acquire through the practice of reason'.[11] In his book *Prophecy in Islam*, Fazlur Rahman writes of al-Ghazālī's work *Maʿārij al-Quds*:

> Prophecy is a divine favour and gift which cannot be acquired by effort – although effort and acquisition are necessary to prepare the soul for the reception of revelation by acts of worship accompanied by exercise in thinking and by pure sincere deeds. Thus prophecy is neither a pure chance (without a natural desert) so that every creeping shuffling creature may be its recipient, nor is it attained by pure effort so that everyone who thinks may have it. . . . Just as humanity is not acquired by individual humans nor angelness by members of the 'species' 'angel', but their actions which flow from their specific natures will depend on their effort and choice . . . so prophecy which is the specific nature of the prophets is not acquired by them but their actions which flow from their specific form depend on their acquisition and choice in order to prepare themselves for revelation.[12]

Furthermore, there developed a particular doctrine that came to be associated with prophets which is protection from falling into sin or making mistakes. This came to be known as the doctrine of *ʿiṣma*, though it cannot be said even of Muḥammad that impeccability or sinlessness of the prophets is a doctrine supported by the Qur'ān. Yet in trying to address the question of how human prophets could receive divine revelation, Muslim theologians wrestled with the notion of human sin and fallibility. By the time of Al-Ashʿarī (tenth century), it became orthodox dogma that after assuming office it is not possible for prophets to commit any deadly or even minor sins.[13]

The Qur'ān speaks of 'taking a covenant' with five particular prophets, Muḥammad, Noah, Moses, Abraham and Jesus, as if the relationship of prophet to God is a long-term integrated project. Wadad Kadi talks of prophecy as an institution where all prophets are united through embodying wisdom and scripture:

> Whereas wisdom can be considered a characterization of the prophets and/or scripture, scripture must indicate an additional physical form in which prophecy is expressed, thus adding a dimension to its physical embodiment.[14]

The Qur'ān is concerned with both individual prophets and the nature of prophecy in the dialectic between human reception and divine message. In that sense Muḥammad is the same as previous prophets. He can only speak of that which is part of God's plan and only reveal that which God wishes him to reveal. His task was to reveal the new truth, but not to contest the old truths nor to distinguish between the messengers who preceded him:

> The Messenger has believed in what was revealed to him from his Lord and so have the believers. All of them believe in God, his angels, his books and his messengers, saying, 'We make no distinction between any of his messengers', and they say, 'We hear and obey and we seek your forgiveness, O Lord, for to you is the final destination' (Q2:285).

Thus, revelation in Islam sends us back to the unconditional proclamation of the oneness of God. Jane McAuliffe defines this continuity of message, 'For Muslims Islam is not simply God's final revelation but also God's first.'[15] All the prophets and messengers are chosen above others in their communities with their own messages, but all are regarded as human prophets. They are given varying epithets beyond the title prophet, but in their mission to transform the society around them, they themselves are never divinised. In this process Christ too is incorporated into humanity as reinforcing the truth of Islam, but his divinity is removed, with the consequent neutralization of the fundamentals of Christian Christology.

Revelation belongs to the history of the manifestation of God and is present in the history of those sent by God. Revelation communicates not only the truth of God in himself, but the truth of man and of history by telling humankind something different from what it knows. In this way, the Qur'ān sees itself as both the *furqān*, the criterion of right and wrong, and as a historical oral process recalling past history. The Qur'ān presumes that its immediate audience is familiar with the stories and beliefs in the scriptures of Jewish and Christian communities. Stories of Adam, his family and descent to earth, Noah and the great flood, Moses, the burning bush, and his trials against Pharaoh and the children of Israel, Joseph and his brothers, Job and his suffering, Jesus, his virgin mother, and his miracles, are all mentioned in the Qur'ān as real events, as truths about prophets and their communities and the course of God's intervention in human history. The listener is constantly urged to remember these historical occurrences, as for example, 'And remember we gave Moses the scripture' (Q2:53) and 'Remember we divided the sea for you; we saved you and drowned Pharaoh's people'(Q2:50). From this perspective, one of the major Qur'ānic themes is to convey the immediate presence of a past message and messenger. The Qur'ān asks us to remember, to recall these stories so that we are living them in present time as if these events have an immediate relevance in our lives. The stories may be rooted in another historical reality, but their moral relevance and immediacy means that this historical distance is not real, the recollection of these tales creates a truth which spans time and distance. When the Qur'ān tells the believers to 'remember', it is as if these events exist within a collective human memory so that the events in the lives of God's prophets and messengers become intertwined with our own lives.

Over sixty years ago Hamilton Gibb wrote of the theme of continuity in Islam's relationship to Judaism and Christianity, but pointed also to a new departure in Islam:

> The originality of Islam is nonetheless real, in that it represents a further step in the logical (if not philosophical) evolution of the monotheistic religions. Its monotheism, like that of the Hebrew Prophets, is absolute and unconditioned, but with this it combines the universalism of Christianity. On the one hand, it rejects the nationalist taint from which Judaism as a religion did not succeed in freeing itself; for Islam never identified itself with the Arabs, although at times Arabs have identified themselves with

> it. On the other hand, it is distinguished from Christianity not so much (in spite of all outward appearances) by its repudiation of the Trinitarian concept of the unity of God, as by *its rejection of the soteriology of the Christian doctrine* and the relics of the old nature cults which survived in the rites and practices of the Christian Church.[16]

The continuity of the same message, however, raises a particular tension. An example of this tension can be found in Q2:213, 'the people were one community and God sent to them prophets, preaching and warning', which has been the subject of various interpretations. Did this verse mean that all people were followers of one faith before the advent of prophetic missions, were they all polytheists to whom God had to send prophets as guidance, or were they all believers in the one God who then started to dispute amongst themselves and needed prophets to be reminded of the one true primordial message of which Islam is the culmination?

Although the Qur'ān is not more definitive about what one community means, many Muslim exegetes fleshed this out into a particular understanding – that the primordial religion of all people was Islam, meaning people who were God's servants in their submission to him, and that this started with Adam, considered to be the first Prophet, and it is this primordial Islam which is being referred to in the verses about Abraham:

> O people of the book, why dispute about Abraham when the Torah and the Injīl were not revealed till after him? Abraham was not a Jew nor a Christian, but he was upright (*ḥanīf*), surrendering to God (*muslimann*), and not one of those who associate with God (Q3:65 and Q3:67).

If Islam is the primordial religion, then the Prophet inherits the legacies of previous messengers who were all Muslim and teaching the same creed – belief in the one God:

> He has laid down for you as religion that which he charged Noah with and that which we have revealed to you, and that which we have charged Abraham with, Moses and Jesus (Q42:13).

This has become a well-known verse in interreligious contexts as well as in Muslim apologetics concerning Islam's inherent harmony with previous prophets and their messages. Even though in practical piety Muslims do not understand this linear concept of revelation to mean that the Qur'ān is the same as other scriptures, this is one of the many verses used to illustrate a Qur'ānic interreligious or dialogical theology. The Qur'ān is not unique as a book, because other prophets were also sent with a 'book', nor is the prophet unique in presenting this message of belief in one God, since other messengers also had the mission of warning against *shirk* or of associating another being with God and warning people of the hereafter. Muḥammad made no special claims for himself, for the divine purpose lay in the message first and the messenger second. The Qur'ān tells us that the earthly Qur'ān, the collection of verses into a book, has a prior existence. A complete Qur'ān is believed to be preserved on a Preserved Tablet (*lauḥ al maḥfūz*) in the realm of eternity. The Qur'ān mentions this in Q85:21–22, 'Indeed, this is a glorious Qur'ān, inscribed in a Tablet Preserved'. Classical scholars of the Qur'ān claim that the Qur'ān descended in three stages. In the first stage, it came from God to the Preserved Tablet, a Tablet which is also referred to as the Mother of the Book (*Umm al-Kitāb*).

For Muslims, this is an original heavenly book, the archetype in which all earthly revelations including the Qur'ān and also the Jewish and Christian scriptures have their origin. Secondly, the Qur'ān was sent from the highest heaven to the lowest heaven; thirdly, it was sent or 'revealed' via Gabriel (Jibrīl) to Muḥammad gradually over a period of twenty-two years. For most Muslims, then, worship entails seeing the earthly Qur'ān, bound between two covers, as an accurate transcript of the eternal Preserved Tablet. The speech of God is now the same as what is written in the physical book of God. It is through his speech that God reveals.

It should be noted here that since the nineteenth century and with an increased impetus during the last three decades, there have been several revisionist approaches to the origins, structure and timeline of the Qur'ān by a number of western scholars who have seriously questioned many of the traditional views on the history and compilation of the Qur'ān. The works of Günter Lülling (1974), John Wansbrough (1977), and Patricia Crone and Michael Cook (1977) have all posed challenges to the accepted Muslim accounts of Islam's origins as well as the genesis and construction of the Qur'ān which Muslims have today. Some have accepted Lülling's concept of an 'Ur-Qur'ān', that there existed an early textual archetype for the present Qur'ān. While there is some agreement that its function was to act as a source of religious and moral guidance for the believers, beyond this religious didactic role there is little agreement on other characteristics of the text. Some dissenting scholars follow John Wansbrough's argument that the Qur'ān we have today does not go back to an early prototype, 'but rather represents the fruit of a long and slow process of crystallization spanning two centuries or more, during which the Qur'ān as we know it was pieced together from disparate materials circulating in "the community"'.[17] By 'community' Wansbrough refers to the possible Jewish and Christian influences on the Qur'ān.

One other point of reflection is that the very notion of book is itself open to scrutiny and remains elusive. The self-referential style of the Qur'ān is one where it consistently refers to itself as a book, although it was not in any book form during the period of revelation. The Qur'ān is conveyed as oral recitations, unwritten at the time of revelation, yet it refers to itself as a piece of writing. It refers to itself as the Book of God (*kitāb Allah*), revelation (*tanzīl/waḥy*), wise book (*kitāb ḥakīm*), mercy (*raḥma*), guidance (*hudan*), distinguisher between right and wrong (*furqān*). Not only is the Qur'ān the most metatextual holy text in the history of world religions but, as Aliza Shnizer says, 'The sheer number of titles, descriptions and metaphors used by the Qur'ān to describe its own nature as a divine book revealed by God himself, is quite unique.'[18]

Yet, if the Qur'ān is God's final revealed truth in words, it also 'confirmed' the truth of previous revelation as embodied in the Jewish and Christian scriptures. As Dan Madigan shows in his study, *The Qur'ân's Self-Image*, the implication is that what the Arabs have now is what the Jews and Christians have had from some time earlier.[19] In other words, however one understands 'confirmation', the Qur'ān tells the new community of believers, 'If you are in doubt about what we have sent down to you, ask those who were reading scripture before you' (Q10:94).

Among those who were reading scripture before the revelation of the Qur'ān are the Christians. Christians, however, are never named directly in the Qur'ān but included within the group of people whom the Qur'ān calls the People of the Book (*ahl al-kitāb*) or 'scriptuaries', a general term to denote both Jews and Christians. The one name which is used some fourteen times to refer to

Christians is *nasārā*, the Arabic form of the name Nazarenes, the adjective which refers to people from Jesus' hometown of Nazareth in Galilee. There has been much scholarly speculation as to who are the Christians of which the Qur'ān speaks and which Christian group is specifically being referred to as the Nazarenes. In a detailed analysis, François de Blois writes that in the Greek Gospels Jesus is associated with the town of Nazareth and is himself given the epithet Nazarene as well as Nazoraean. In Acts 24:5 Paul's opponents give him the title 'leader of the sect of the Nazoraeans' and de Blois argues that while this passage could have been understood as giving Biblical sanction to the use of the name Nazoraean to designate the followers of Jesus of Nazareth as a community, this was not so. He states that the epithet Nazoraean in 'extant early writings does not seem ever to be used as a current self-designation of Christians and even in the medieval period Nazoraeans is not the usual word for Christians in any language with the exception only of Arabic'.[20] De Blois explains that from the latter part of the fourth century, Nazoraeans is used by Christian authors to designate one or more of the 'supposedly heretical sects of the type which in modern theological literature are usually called Jewish Christians'.[21] Furthermore, de Blois also contests the view that the Aramaic designation for Christians is *nāsrāyā*, stating that the usual Syriac word for 'Christian' is *kristyān*, plural *kristyānē*. One of the conclusions of his arguments is that the Qur'ān uses *nasārā* to refer to Nazoraean 'Jewish Christians' and not catholic Christians.

Over the years scholars have illustrated a variety of ways to understand the notion of People of the Book, but it seems two particular themes have emerged. In his magisterial work on Mary, Jaroslav Pelikan writes that despite some of the more difficult passages, at its heart the Qur'ān affirms Judaism by honouring the

Jews as 'The People of the Book'. When the Qur'ān refers to the Jews as the Children of Israel, the *Banī Isrā'il*, it basically repeats how they have been addressed by God in the Hebrew Bible, not how the Qur'ān regards them through the unifying claim of Abraham as the common ancestor and father in faith. Pelikan writes, 'A case can be made for the thesis that the Qur'ān was a large-scale effort to redress the balance after six centuries of Christian anti-Judaism'.[22] This type of bridge-building perspective has captured the popular and academic imagination, but it is premised on the acceptance that the idea of book remains conceptually of equal importance. Conversely, the concept of scriptuary implied in the term *ahl al-kitāb* has been brought into question by scholars such as McAuliffe and Sharon who contest which Jews and which Christians are being alluded to in this designation. Sharon says:

> Except for a few cases, *ahl al-kitāb* in the Qur'ān does not necessarily refer to either Jews or Christians. Even if such identification can be made, it is not clear to what kind of Jews and Christians the text refers.... Whether defined as Jews or Christians, *ahl al-kitāb* were defined by the end of the Prophet's lifetime, accused of having forsaken the true monotheistic religion of old prescribed in their book and having adopted polytheistic doctrines that put them in the same camp as the *mushrikūn*, i.e. those who associated with God.[23]

When the Qur'ān refers to an accepted Christianity, it refers to an ideal form of that Christianity. In this ideal form, Mary and Jesus as well as the Bible are all precursors to Muḥammad and the Qur'ān. David Marshall states that this ideal of Christianity 'must find its proper goal in Muḥammad and the Qur'an' but that the failure of the Christians to acknowledge Muḥammad and the Qur'ān 'reveals that such Christians are distortions of what followers of Jesus should be; that they hold a distorted understanding of Jesus and Mary; and that they have distorted the scripture brought by Jesus'.[24]

One of the most intriguing texts that points to the complex consequences of affirming earlier scriptures and using the biblical tradition to assert a new God consciousness is in the Qur'an:

> I shall ordain my mercy for those who are conscious of God and give the prescribed alms; who believe in our revelations; who follow the messenger, the unlettered prophet they find described in the Torah that is with them and in the Gospels, who commands them to do right and forbids them to do wrong (Q7:156–157).

Basit Koshul explains there is a tension about the legitimacy of the common ground which the Qur'ān shares with Judaism and Christianity:

> The Qur'ān is squaring the circle in relation to the Abrahamic/Biblical tradition. The Qur'ānic narrative is simultaneously playing the role of a dissenting prophetic witness from within the Biblical tradition while at the same time affirming its identity on Biblical grounds. In very concrete and direct terms the Qur'ān links its own identity to the Abrahamic/Biblical tradition – which is the very tradition it is criticizing (in its Jewish and Christian variations).[25]

Methodological concerns over abrogation did not begin with Islam. Abrogation was a well-known motif stemming from late antiquity and also appears in polemical writing between Christianity and Judaism. Christians, however, emphasise the fulfilment of Judaism through Christianity, whereas there is in Islam a sense that through the Qur'ān, Judaism and Christianity are being restored to their primordial truths. The Qur'ān does not contain an explicit abrogation of previous scriptures or the annulment of previous scriptures through the emergence of the Prophet's mission and message. Nevertheless, it does contain the sense that some people are hiding the truth in their scriptures, falsifying the truth or refusing to accept the truth, and it poses these issues as questions:

> O People of the Book, why do you clothe the truth with falsehood? Why do you hide the truth when you know? (Q3:71).
>
> O People of the Book, our messenger has come to make clear to you much of what you have kept hidden of the Book and to overlook much [you have done]. A light has now come to you from God and a Book making things clear (Q5:15).

Despite such Qur'ānic verses which are concerned more with making things clear rather than nullifying previous books, classical exegetical literature developed various theological perspectives on the continued divine purpose of the historical chain of revealed religion. Here, the issue of Jewish and Christian scriptures as having been abrogated in their laws or corrupted in other ways became an important theological consideration regarding both the earlier faiths. It was not the Qur'ān but later Muslim polemics which targeted both Jews and Christians with the concept of *naskh* abrogation and more significantly *taḥrīf*, whereby Jews and Christians are accused of having corrupted their original scriptures. There is nevertheless a distinction between the accusation of textual corruption (*taḥrīf al-lafẓ*) by the Jews and Christians of their own scriptures on which there was little unanimity and the misinterpretation of the meaning of their sacred books on which there was far more agreement.[26] According to some, it was a form of corruption which had resulted in the deletion of Muḥammad's name from previous books. However, J. Sweetman rejects the view that the Qur'ān itself can be accused of justifying *taḥrīf*. He quotes Ibn Qayyim al Jawziyya on this issue:

> It is an entirely false idea when it is asserted that Jews and Christians have conspired together to expunge this name (i.e. the name of Muḥammad) from their Scriptures in all the ends of the earth wherever they live. None of the learned Muslims asserts this, and God said nothing about this in the Qur'ān, nor did any of the Companions or Imams or the Qur'ānic scholars after them express themselves thus. It is, of course, possible that the common people think they can help Islam by such an interpretation, but herein is the proverb true which says, 'The clever opponent can wish for nothing better than that an ignorant friend should help the enemy.'[27]

There is very little sustained mention of this concept in the Qur'ān itself, but it developed essentially as Islam's self-legitimisation for a new monotheistic order in the heavily competitive sectarian milieu of seventh-century Arabia. For some this meant separating the salvation history of the Muslim community from other Abrahamic faiths by making supercessionist claims against other forms of monotheism, namely Judaism and Christianity. The issue of *naskh* or abrogation posed a different problem. The jurists had to try to resolve their understanding of the laws of the previous revelations and decide whether Muslims should accept these laws as part of their own heritage or whether these laws had been abrogated by what had appeared in the Qur'ān. In this context, *naskh* assumes the meaning of a repeal of an earlier ruling by a later ruling owing to changed circumstances. However, there was no consistency on this issue among the early or later exegetes, or even among those who argued for the exclusive salvific status of Islam.

Despite this tension, the Qur'ān repeats the theme of salvation for Christians, though the question remains, which Christians is the Qur'ān referring to? If it is only within a particular ideal of Christianity that Muslims can truly embrace Christians as belonging to the 'People of the Book', then how can Muslims understand the Bible and Biblical Christianity as a 'confirmed scripture'? Another way to look at this issue is to ask ourselves whether identifying the Christians namely as the People of the Book is problematic itself in so far as the concept of 'book' is not a particularly Christian focus. In contrast to the Qur'ān, it is not an earthly book connected to a prior heavenly existence which forms the locus of revelation. Contesting the idea that Judaism, Christianity and Islam are all religions of the book, 'branching from a common Abrahamic trunk', Adolfo Montes writes:

> Only a few schools deriving from the Reformation came close to anything like the religion of the book. Strictly speaking, only Islam is a religion of the book in that the worldly and historical shape of revelation is embodied in the Qur'ān as the book that has been revealed in a way that is not comparable with the Bible and the New Testament, which are sacred texts in so far as they bear witness to the incarnation of the Word, but are in no sense identical with the incarnation in their objective material, written or phonetic form.[28]

Nevertheless, the Qur'ān's repeated theme of book means that various books are mentioned by name as being repositories of prior revelations. Its reference to the Gospels is always through the word *Injīl*, which occurs twelve times in the Qur'ān and is a word that has its origins in Evangel, Good News:

> Why do you dispute about Abraham, seeing that the Torah and the Gospel were not sent down till after his time? (Q3:65).
>
> We gave Jesus the Gospel, containing a guidance and light, confirming the Torah which was before it (Q5:46).
>
> O People of the Book, you have nothing to stand upon until you establish the Torah and the Gospel and what has been sent down to you from your Lord (Q5:68).

The Qur'ān emphasises divine revelation in the form of a book when it describes previous revelations, so that the Gospels are the revelation from God, and there seems to be nothing in the Qur'ān which would suggest that the Gospels or 'book' given to Jesus differs from the canonical Gospels of Christian piety. But the Qur'ān gives no information as to how the canonical Gospels came into being or how they were written. It only speaks of the Gospels being given to Jesus, as if there was a Biblical descent similar to a Qur'ānic descent. It states, 'Then we sent following their footsteps our messengers and followed them with Jesus, the son of Mary, and gave him the Gospel' (Q57:27). From the Qur'ānic perspective, a divine book was given to the son of Mary, though there is no elaboration on how this book was given or how Jesus received the *Injīl*. The Qur'ān parts company with Christian doctrine on this very fundamental point, continuing to insist that revelation in Christianity came in the form of a book, not in human form through Christ.

For Muslims, revelation as speech originates in God, as in those verses in which God speaks in the first person, 'I have sent down the Qur'ān' (Q2:41) or 'We have sent down the Qur'ān' (Q44:3). In the case of Muḥammad, prophecy is confirmed when revelation is sent directly from God through the intermediary of Gabriel who brings revelatory speech upon the heart of the Prophet. It is in Q2:97 that Gabriel is introduced as the one who 'by the leave of God brought the Qur'ān down upon' Muḥammad's heart. Revelation in Islam is mediated revelation, where Gabriel is a messenger to the messenger. Josef van Ess writes that 'Gabriel's function is thus ambiguous; he is a mere instrument in the hand of God, but he also serves as a means to separate God from man.'[29] Gabriel is a messenger with a specific vocation.

In Islam the Prophetic role of Muḥammad is the transmission of the Qur'ān, and his words and actions encompassing the *sunna* (custom/Prophetic practice) are understood as part of the revelatory process. The descent of the Qur'ān with Muḥammad as recipient confirms Muḥammad's status as not only prophet but one in whom most Muslims saw the seal of prophecy as meaning the finality of prophecy. Neither message nor mode is a radical break from the past. The word does become book, but the book is guidance only, it is not the descent of God even if it contains God's speech.

Although the word *nuzūl* is not Qur'ānic, it conveys the sense of 'coming down' and 'sending down', both vital for a correct understanding of the Qur'ānic hermeneutics of God's speaking to man.[30] This concept of scripture as originating in God who is in the upper world and descending to humanity in the lower world is in opposition to what we find in the Gospel writers, who talk of the passing on of oral tradition as well as its recording. For example, we find in Luke and John that both books use the notion of account or record to describe their function, for example Luke 1:1–4:

> Many have undertaken to draw up an account of the things that have been fulfilled among us, just as they were handed down to us by those who from the first were eyewitnesses and servants of the word. With this in mind, since I myself have carefully investigated everything from the beginning, I too decided to write an orderly account for you, Theophilus, so that you may know the certainty of the things you have been taught.

Also John 21:24–25:

> This is the disciple who testifies to these things and who wrote them down. We know that his testimony is true. Jesus did many other things as well. If every one of them were written down, I suppose that even the whole world would not have room for the books that would be written.

The Qur'ānic description of the Gospels as a revelation given to Jesus is not how Christians or Biblical scholarship has understood the nature and process of the four written Gospels of Matthew, Mark, Luke and John. Furthermore, the Qur'ān does not point specifically to how many Gospels it confirms. Does it see Christian scripture in the singular form, one scripture or four Gospels, or even indeed the complete canon of the Bible? The Qur'ān is not regarded by Muslims as the 'teachings' of Muḥammad in the way the 'teachings' of Jesus are contained in the Gospels. For Muslims, the traditional approach to the Qur'ān is that it is divine in origin and human in compilation only. Its main purpose is to remind people of God, his prophets and the day of judgement; it is not a biography of Muḥammad. Muḥammad is not the event, it is the Qur'ān which is the event as the gradual coming down of divine speech. We find in the Qur'ān the transition from the pre-Islamic but prophetic 'Thus saith the Lord' to 'Thus speaks your Lord' (*qāla rabbuka*), where the 'your' refers to Muḥammad. It was not the Prophet who spoke in the name of God, but rather God who spoke through the Prophet.[31] The Gospels are not understood as divine in the same way, as speech descending, but they are understood as the words about the Word Incarnate, human speech about God. Van Ess examines the differences of approach:

> Pope Gregory the Great and before him especially St Augustine developed the concept of God having dictated the Gospels (the 'Scripture') to the Evangelists. This theory had some backing in the Scripture itself, but again in the Old Testament rather than the New one; according to Exodus 34:27, the Lord had said to Moses: 'Write down these words!' In Islamic theology, however, the metaphor does not occur, in spite of the fact that dictation was a well-known procedure in academic life.[32]

The Evangelists were scribes and disciples. As F. E. Peters writes, 'Even if it is the very different post-Easter light that bathes the entirety of the New Testament, it is not so much the words of Jesus that were illumined as his deeds.' He continues:

> The Evangelists were not simply recording; they were arguing. The conclusion to that argument was already fixed in their minds when they began their work, a fact they made no effort to disguise, namely, that their subject was no mere man but the Messiah of Israel and the Son of God; that he was embarked on a series of events governed not by the historian's familiar

> secondary causality but by God's provident will; that Jesus was both completing the past – and thus 'the Scriptures were fulfilled' – and breaking forth into a new and only gradually revealed eschatological future.[33]

Sallie McFague summarises the goal of the New Testament writers in their use of metaphors. She writes of their appreciation of Jesus as 'a movement of the human – the human in its totality – beyond itself, in such a way that the totality of human life was itself re-created'. God's word was not tied to some prophetic mission, but to the life and death of Jesus himself:

> They saw the word of God coming to them through the events and sayings and stories of the man Jesus. They *saw* it that way and reported it that way, not stripping the husk from the kernel or translating it into general existentialist terms or systematizing it into statements about God, but following the way it had come to them. What began to come clear to them through the life and death of Jesus, that basic metaphor, became the touchstone for creating hundreds of other metaphors – old and new Adam, bread and wine, lost and found, free and slave, water and Spirit – which also, they hoped, would evoke the remarkable thing they believed had occurred in and through the life of Jesus.[34]

But if both Muḥammad and Jesus are seen as founders of a faith, they have been subjects of different kinds of historical inquiries. In understanding the historical Jesus, the documents included in the New Testament were all written on the hither side of Easter or, as Peters argues, 'their authors viewed their subject across the absolute conviction that Jesus was the Christ and the Son of God, a conviction later rendered explicit in Christian dogma'. In contrast to Jesus, he continues:

> There is, however, no Resurrection in the career of Muḥammad, no Paschal sunrise to cast its divinizing light on the Prophet of Islam. Muḥammad is thus a perfectly appropriate subject of history: a man born of woman (and a man), who lived in a known place in a roughly calculable time, who in the end died the death that is the lot of all mortals, and whose career was reported by authorities who share the contemporary historian's own conviction that the Prophet was nothing more than a man. What is at stake in Islam, then, is not dogma as it is in Christianity, but rather piety.[35]

It has been argued that the Bible as a whole came to be seen as the Word of God only after the Reformation and that prior to the Reformation, Christ alone was the Word of God. Nevertheless, the Bible with its variety of literary genres and numerous human authors is still regarded as 'divinely inspired', albeit without the sense of each word being directly from God. Van Ess explains that 'before the age of Biblical criticism, verbal inspiration was for some time the official doctrine of Lutheran orthodoxy'.[36]

Furthermore, the concept of prophecy also points to two different discourses between Muslims and Christians. Islam does not have Christology central to its doctrine of God, but it does have a Christology of sorts: outside the Gospels, the Qur'ān is the only world scripture where Jesus is really present and has significance in both realms of prophecy and eschaton. Christian doctrine, Christians (*naṣārā*) and Muslim attitudes to them as communities of believers are alluded to over a hundred times in the Qur'ān. Jesus, or ʿĪsā as he is called in the Qur'ān, is mentioned in 15 *sūras* of the Qur'ān and in 93 verses as either 'sign', 'mercy' or 'example'. He is a revered prophet but is also the Prophet, Word and Messenger of God, though there is no one particular Jesus narrative which brings together the Christic, miraculous and prophetic nature of Jesus under his most dramatic epithet, 'spirit of God' (*rūḥ Allah*). Yet for all this, Jesus is defined as a human prophet, who was a precursor to Muḥammad and, according to Muslim theology, never claimed to be anything else but a servant of God. It should be noted that Jesus does not use this title of servant for himself in the New Testament except in Acts 3:13 and 26, and Acts 4:27 and 30, as for example, 'The God of Abraham, Isaac and Jacob, the God of our fathers has glorified his servant Jesus'.

In Islam, there is no divine accolade bigger than the election of prophecy. The prophet/messenger is chosen to be close to God and to receive something from God while remaining responsible to his immediate social context. The elements in the human–divine dialectic come together, but they remain in distinct realms. In Christianity, however, human prophecy is not sufficient to define Jesus in either his being or acts. The Hellenistic development of Christology, the Christological councils of Nicaea and Chalcedon, pointed to a different truth, a truth which stated that Jesus was the Christ, the Word and the revelation of God. Nevertheless, it is not that Jesus' role as prophet was ignored, for there are many Biblical verses which speak of his prophetic role. We find in Luke 7:16, 'And there came a fear on all and they glorified God, saying, "A great prophet has risen up among us and God has visited his people."' In Luke 24:19, '"What things?" he asked. And they said to him, "Concerning Jesus of Nazareth who was a prophet mighty in deed and word before God and all the people."' Also, Matthew 21:46, 'And when they sought to lay hands on him they feared the multitude, for they took him for a prophet.' Again, in Matthew 13:57, 'And they took offence at him, but Jesus said, "A prophet is not without honour except in his hometown and in his house."' This sentiment appears also in John 4:44, 'A prophet has no honour in his own country.' James Dunn points out that the evidence strongly suggests that Jesus saw the negative responses he received as 'of a piece with the tradition of rejected prophets. At the same time, the talk is of "a prophet" and there is no suggestion that Jesus saw himself as "the prophet".'[37] What kind of prophet Jesus thought himself to be is open to question. Whether he saw himself as an eschatological prophet or a prophet commissioned/sent by God, he shared the prophet's rapture and insight in being 'full of joy through the holy spirit' (Luke 10:21). In the speeches in Acts, Jesus is twice alluded to as the 'prophet like Moses' of Deuteronomy 18:15 (Acts 3:23; 7:37). Jesus had a prophetic role as well as a priestly mission, and Luke's Gospel has a number of details suggesting that Jesus was, or at least was regarded as, a prophet. However, in his notable article C. H. Dodd also observes that Jesus said not only 'I was sent', but also 'I came', suggesting that the latter indicated something more than prophetic commission.[38] The significance lies in the 'good news' announcement Jesus makes as proclaimer of the kingdom in Matthew 11:5 and Luke 7:22. As Dunn explains, 'This chimes in with the sense of eschatological newness which comes through in several of Jesus' sayings: something greater was happening than the repetition of prophetic hope.'[39] Johannine evidence has parallels in the Synoptics. But as Vincent Taylor claims, a new element is introduced in John by the use of the term prophet. In John 6:14, after the Feeding of the Five Thousand, people saw this as a sign and exclaimed, 'Surely this is the prophet who is to come into this world'. In John 7:40, when Jesus invites those who are thirsty to go to him, we find, 'Some of the people when they heard these words said, "Truly this is the Prophet", while others said, "this is the Christ"'. Taylor argues that the term prophet in John and Acts must be regarded as a limited attempt at Christological interpretation, but one which proved abortive. He concludes:

> . . . as in the use of the terms 'Rabbi' and 'Teacher', we have in the titles 'Prophet' and 'the Prophet', names which passed out of use because they were felt to be inadequate. Like the prophets of old, Jesus was seen to be filled with the Spirit and to speak the words of God, but unlike them, he left the abiding impression of possessing far more than the prophetic commission. In contrast with the formula, 'Thus saith the Lord', there remained in the memory of the primitive community his majestic 'But I say unto you'.[40]

In his discussion of the prophet's task to engage his community in an alternative consciousness and alternative community, Walter Brueggemann describes the radical break of Moses and Israel from imperial reality. He writes that in showing how the gods had no power and were no-gods, Moses shattered the mythic claims of the empire by the alternative religion of the freedom of God; the politics of oppression was replaced by the politics of justice and compassion. Brueggemann states, 'We will not understand the meaning of prophetic imagination unless we see the connection between the *religion of static triumphalism and the politics of oppression and exploitation*'. He concludes, 'It is the marvel of prophetic faith that both imperial religion and imperial politics could be broken'.[41] It is in the context of changing the consciousness, the present order, that Jesus should be understood. Brueggemann quotes from Luke1:51–53, 'He has scattered the proud in the imagination of their hearts, he has put down the mighty from their thrones, and exalted those of low degree; he has filled the hungry with good tidings and the rich he has sent empty away.' The birth of Jesus ended the 'Herodian reality' by creating a new historical situation for marginal people and this leads to a radical dismantling of the present order. The problem with the promises of the newness of the Gospel is the abrupt order of things as they are – slavery, oppression and the wretched lives of the poor. Brueggemann states that the newness of the Gospel 'never promises without threatening, it never begins without ending something, it never gives gifts without also assessing harsh costs', and he concludes:

> Clearly Jesus cannot be understood simply as a prophet, for that designation, like every other, is inadequate for the historical reality of Jesus. Nevertheless, among his other functions it is clear that Jesus functioned as a prophet. In both his teaching and his very presence Jesus of Nazareth presented the ultimate criticism of the royal consciousness. He has in fact dismantled the dominant culture and nullified its claims. The way of his ultimate criticism is his decisive solidarity with marginal people and the accompanying vulnerability required by that solidarity.[42]

For the early Christian faith, both appearances of Jesus are eschatological. It believes in a fulfilment already present and, as Cullmann argues:

> What distinguishes the Gospel of Jesus from Judaism, even from the highest form of prophetism, is the conviction that 'the kingdom of God has come upon you' (Matt. 12:28); that Satan

> is fallen 'like lightning from heaven' (Luke 10:18); that 'the blind receive their sight and the lame walk, lepers are cleansed and the deaf hear, and the dead are raised up, and the poor have good news preached to them' (Matt.11:5). When the present is seen in this light, the whole eschatological process as taken over from Judaism must be prolonged, for a time of fulfilment is now inserted, which is not yet consummated.[43]

Taylor outlines some fifty-five names and titles of Jesus, over half of which have established themselves in the Christian vocabulary as of either soteriological or Christological significance. The title of Jesus as the suffering Servant of God (*'ebed Yahweh*) is one of the oldest titles used by the first Christians to define their faith, but like that of the Prophet it is a title that soon disappeared. It was the concept of divine sonship that pointed to a vertical relationship and vocation with God whom Jesus called '*Abba*' or father,[44] which shows that Jesus represented something more than human prophecy, however that was understood. In the Hellenistic world of the first century AD the title already had a long history behind it in Babylonian and Egyptian usage. For example, the kings of Egypt were believed to be the descendants of the god Ra and the Ptolemies claimed divine honours described by epithets such as *a diis genitus, filius Isidis et Osiris*.[45] The concept of 'son of God' in Jewish thought had a long history, but it did not describe a divine being, but rather people who stood in a particularly strong relationship with God. In Jewish thought the phrase was attributed to a range of subjects, in particular the chosen people and their king. For example, in Deuteronomy 32:19 the Lord is angered by his 'sons and daughters'. In Isaiah 1 the Lord is angry because 'I reared children and brought them up, but they have rebelled against me'. In Hosea 11:1 God's love for Israel is poignantly expressed, 'When Israel was a child, I loved him, and out of Egypt I called my son'. In 2 Samuel 7:14 God's promise about an everlasting Davidic dynasty mentions Solomon, David's son and successor, as 'I will be his father and he shall be my son'. In Psalm 89:26 God puts a prayer in the mouth of the king in the Davidic line as 'He will call out to me, "You are my Father, my God, the Rock my Saviour"'. Although there are many more instances of son/children used in relation to God, 'son of God' was not used as a messianic title in the Old Testament.

The Synoptic Gospels reveal that Jesus understood his relationship to God as one of divine Sonship, although he does not speak explicitly of the 'Son of God'. The nature of this Sonship is reflected in various ways, indicating intimacy with God and also limitations to knowledge. Sometimes, as in Mark 13:32, only 'the Father' knows, as in relation to the end times. At other times, as in Matthew 11:27, the Son and the Father share a unique, exclusive relationship: 'All things have been committed to me by my Father. No one knows the Son except the Father, and no one knows the Father except the Son and those to whom the Son chooses to reveal him.' There is also a very familial use of the Father as in Mark 14:36, when Jesus calls out in his prayer in Gethsemane. He cries, 'Abba, Father, everything is possible for you; take this cup from me; yet not what I will, but what you will.' Gerald O'Collins, in analysing this language, writes that in the Synoptic Gospels, if one excludes the parallel cases, Jesus uses the word Father fifty-one times:

> Even if '*Abba*' was not a child's address to its male parent, Jesus evidently spoke of, or rather with, God as his Father in a direct familial way that was unique or at least highly unusual, in Palestinian Judaism. In other words, '*Abba*' was a characteristic

> and significantly distinctive feature of Jesus' prayer life. Jesus' example, at least in the early years of Christianity, encouraged his followers to pray to God in that very familial way.[46]

We find evidence of this use in Paul. In Galatians 4:6 we read, 'Because you are his sons, God sent the Spirit of his Son into our hearts, the Spirit who calls out "*Abba*"', and in Romans 8:15, 'The Spirit you received does not make you slaves, so that you live in fear again; rather, the Spirit you received brought about your adoption to sonship. And by him we cry "*Abba*."' In his analysis of the Aramaic address *Abba*, Dunn writes that the *Abba* prayer was so cherished among the first believers precisely because it was Jesus' own prayer form:

> Gentile (Greek-speaking) churches continued to use an Aramaic prayer-form. This must be because it had become such a firmly established form in the earliest (Aramaic-speaking) churches that the first Greek speakers were simply inducted to it as new converts, and thus it became a regular expression and mark of Christian devotion. In both passages the prayer is seen to express the Christians' own sonship which is obviously seen as a reflection of Christ's sonship. The Spirit who cries '*Abba*' is the Spirit of the Son; the cry is the proof that those who so pray share in his sonship and inheritance.

Although there is dispute as to what *abba* precisely meant at that time, James Barr has argued that it did not have the special intimate sense that has generally been attributed to it and that the word simply meant father, whether used by adults or children.[47] Barr states that *abba*, though commonly used in address to one's own father, did not specify 'my' father expressly. Whether the word is Hebrew or Aramaic, Barr insists that *abba* is one of those Semitic words quoted in the New Testament that has often been taken as evidence that Jesus normally spoke Aramaic. Within both languages it was probably possible to use a form that specified 'my' father as distinct from father. Although the use of *abba* in address to God *may* have been first originated by Jesus, it remains difficult to prove how constant and pervasive this element was in his expression of himself; and it is therefore difficult to prove that it is a quite central keystone in our total understanding of him.[48]

It is worth noting here that in recent New Testament scholarship, a point of broad agreement has emerged regarding the development of Christology. Many notable scholars have stated that it is extremely unlikely that the historical Jesus thought of himself as God or God the Son incarnate. In his study of the origins of Christianity James Dunn writes, 'there was no real evidence in the earliest Jesus tradition of what could fairly be called a consciousness of divinity'.[49] Yet despite this assertion, the significance of the whole Christ event led to a more radical understanding of who Jesus was by his followers. Dunn continues:

> We cannot claim that Jesus believed himself to be the incarnate Son of God; but we can claim that the teaching to that effect as it came to expression in later first-century Christian thought was, in the light of the whole Christ event, an appropriate reflection on and elaboration of Jesus's own sense of sonship and eschatological mission.[50]

What Jesus' Sonship meant for his disciples is probably best summarized by Dunn, who contests that this sense of relationship was a secret mystery taught only to an inner group or at a higher stage of initiation, a goal to be achieved along the path of discipleship. The Jesus tradition indicates that Jesus sought to induct his disciples into the same sense of Sonship, not least by teaching them to pray as he did, and that he encouraged them all to live out of their own relationship to God as Father. Jesus saw 'his disciples' relationship to God as Father as in some sense a sharing in his own Sonship to the Father'.[51]

As John Hick has argued, however, there are Catholic and Protestant scholars who are reconfiguring Christological beliefs. John Macqaurrie is one Protestant scholar who claimed that Jesus did not profess his own deity. Macquarrie writes, 'What the disciples came to believe is that Jesus *is* the Christ, and also Lord, Son of God and so on, not that he *said* he was Christ, Lord, etc.' Macquarrie also argued that Son of God must be understood metaphorically, not literally:

> To speak of Jesus as 'Son of God' is to use a metaphor. It is certainly an important metaphor and affirms a close relation to God, but it does not imply deification. . . . The metaphor arises within a long traditional usage, in which a person close to or considered to be an agent of God might be called his son. . . . God's metaphorical sending of his metaphorical son can be understood in ways that do not imply pre-existence, once we accept that the language is metaphorical and not literal.[52]

Despite rejecting the orthodox two-natures dogma of Chalcedon, Macquarrie insists on the theology of the Incarnation. He affirms Jesus as the 'God-man' and says, 'Indeed I do not think, that if we remain Christian, we can ever escape the fundamental paradox, that

Jesus Christ is both human and divine'.[53] While crediting Macquarrie with relatively new thinking on this issue, albeit working within an inherited Christian faith, Hick criticises him for accepting Jesus' deity as a given fact. Hick contests that if Macquarrie does not rely on Gospel stories, he might as well concur with Kierkegaard's famous statement, 'If the contemporary generations had left behind them nothing but the words, "We have believed that in such a such a year God appeared among us in the humble form of a servant, lived and taught among us and then died – this is more than enough."'[54]

The gradual emergence of Christological doctrines which focus on Jesus as Lord, with all the layers of meaning, firmly eclipsed the idea of Jesus as a prophetic figure alone. In his interpretation of the *Apostles' Creed*, Wolfhart Pannenberg writes of the two titles by which Jesus came to be known in the early church. The title Son of God expressly describes Jesus' relationship to God, but only implies his position with regard to the world. Conversely, the title *Kyrios*, Lord, describes Jesus' relationship to the world in the sense of rule. Pannenberg concludes that 'The Apostles' Creed apparently already understands the two titles in this sense when it talks about Jesus as *God's* only begotten Son, but *our* Lord.'[55]

New Testament and Christian scholars generally maintain that the idea of Jesus as a prophetic figure does not feature prominently in the teaching of the early Christians as recorded in Acts. Furthermore, even where Jesus' prophetic role has been mentioned, it is not the most important category to express the deepest truth about Jesus. As Sarah Stroumsa explains in her work on prophetology:

> From an early date in mainstream Christian theology, Jesus was not considered to be a prophet. Those who spoke of Jesus as a 'righteous man' and a prophet were definitely in the minority and

> their views were pushed aside by the predominant Christology. Prophets were thus usually given a secondary role; they are those who announce the coming of Jesus; who are, in some respects, his *figura*; or even those who propagate his gospel.[56]

Although Christians admitted the prophecy of Moses, in many ways this was an outdated issue. Jesus may have been familiarly Jewish, but he was also different from many of his contemporaries in advocating a more internal, conscience-driven morality. Jesus was grounded in the Torah, but spiritually he rose above it. Furthermore, he taught differently from the rabbinic teachers, whose methodological approach was based on the authority of previous teachers and past tradition. His contemporaries knew him as 'the carpenter, the son of Mary' (Mark 6:3), but what surprised them was that Jesus spoke with authority in the call for spiritual change and the revision of the Mosaic Law. In the Qur'ān there is a strong image of Jesus as one who is placed intrinsically within the chain of prophecy as a messenger to the Children of Israel bringing a similar message to Muḥammad. Jesus confirms the past yet still comes with something new within God's plan. Frithjof Schuon gives succinct expression to this by saying that 'Christ shattered ethnic Israel to replace it with a uniquely spiritual Israel, and he gave precedence to the love of God over the prescribed act'.[57] The Qur'ān speaks of Jesus' intentions:

> I have come to confirm the truth of the Torah which preceded me, and to make some things lawful to you which used to be forbidden. I have come to you with a sign from your Lord. Be mindful of God, indeed God is my Lord and your Lord, so worship Him, that is a straight path (Q3:50).

Conversely, Jesus is used to legitimise Muḥammad's own actions by giving the impression that Muḥammad is doing what Jesus had done before him in his mission:

> O you who believe, be God's helpers as when Jesus Son of Mary said to the disciples, 'Who will be my helpers in God's way?' The disciples said, 'We are God's helpers.' A group of the Children of Israel believed and a group disbelieved. We supported those who believed against their enemies and they were the ones who gained victory (Q61: 14).

As Neal Robinson writes, 'The believers are urged to fight at Muḥammad's side on the grounds that in so doing they will be following the example of Jesus' disciples and that like them they will prove victorious.'[58]

Prophecy was never really central to Christian understanding of Jesus, but the issue of prophecy foretold became a fundamental theme in Christian–Muslim apologetics. For many Christians, Muḥammad's prophecy could not be a divine truth because there was no mention of him in the Gospels; this was often contrasted with the mention of Jesus in the Torah. One celebrated incident of such a conversation which reflects a more nuanced view of this issue is that which took place over two consecutive days between the Nestorian Patriarch Timothy I and the 'Abbāsid Caliph al-Mahdī soon after 780. The following extract is part of the response from Timothy I when questioned by the Caliph as to why he does not believe that Muḥammad is the Paraclete:[59]

> If he were mentioned in the Gospel, this mention would have been marked by a distinct portraiture characterising his coming,

his name, his mother, and his people as the true portraiture of the coming of Jesus Christ is found in the Torah and in the prophets. Since nothing resembling this is found in the Gospel concerning Muḥammad, it is evident that there is no mention of him in it at all, and that is the reason why I have not received a single testimony from the Gospel about him.

And the God-loving King said to me: 'As the Jews behaved towards Jesus whom they did not accept, so the Christians behaved towards Muḥammad whom they did not accept.'—And I replied to his Majesty: 'The Jews did not accept Jesus in spite of the fact that the Torah and the prophets were full of testimonies about Him, and this renders them worthy of condemnation. As to us, we have not accepted Muḥammad because we have not a single testimony about him in our Books.'—And our King said: 'There were many testimonies but the Books have been corrupted, and you have removed them.'—And I replied to him thus: 'Where is it known, O King, that the Books have been corrupted by us, and where is that uncorrupted Book from which you have learned that the Books which we use have been corrupted? If there is such a book let it be placed in the middle in order that we may learn from it which is the corrupted Gospel and hold to that which is not corrupted. If there is no such Gospel, how do you know that the Gospel of which we make use is corrupted?

'What possible gain could we have gathered from corrupting the Gospel? Even if there was mention of Muḥammad made in the Gospel, we would not have deleted his name from it; we would have simply said that Muḥammad has not come yet, and that he was not the one whom you follow, and that he was going to come in the future. Take the example of the Jews: they

> cannot delete the name of Jesus from the Torah and the Prophets, they only contend against Him in saying openly that He was going to come in the future, and that He has not come yet into the world. They resemble a blind man without eyes who stands in plain daylight and contends that the sun has not yet risen. We also would have done likewise; we would not have dared to remove the name of Muḥammad from our Book if it were found anywhere in it; we would have simply quibbled concerning his right name and person like the Jews do in the case of Jesus. To tell the truth, if I had found in the Gospel a prophecy concerning the coming of Muḥammad, I would have left the Gospel for the Kur'an, as I have left the Torah and the Prophets for the Gospel.'[60]

The denial of Muḥammad's prophetic status in any scripture or revelatory event became a particular aspect of Christian–Muslim polemics. For Christians there was no parallel to Jesus' coming as being foretold in the Hebrew Bible. Here Timothy condemns the Jews who refused to believe in Jesus despite the written testimony in the Torah. Christians, on the other hand, cannot be condemned for refusing to believe in Muḥammad as there was nothing in the Gospels which alluded to a future prophetic arrival. Indeed, Timothy goes as far as saying that had there been any mention of Muḥammad in the Gospels, he would have left his Christian faith.

Conversely, it is worth noting that the Muslim Hanbali jurist Shams al-Dīn Abū Bakr Muḥammad ibn Abī Bakr al-Zarʿī Ibn Qayyim al-Jawziyya (1292–1350) wrote in his own polemic that if Muḥammad had not come, Biblical prophecies would have remained unfulfilled. He states, 'If Muḥammad son of ʿAbdullah had not appeared and had not been sent, the prophethood of all former prophets would have been reduced to nothing.' He concludes this line of argument by saying, 'We shall demonstrate that they cannot prove any of Christ's virtues, prophecy, sign or miracle, without first acknowledging that Muḥammad is God's apostle. Otherwise, by making him a liar, none of these other things with regard to Christ will be able to stand.'[61]

Nevertheless, on the second day of the conversation we have what may be termed a conciliatory approach to Muḥammad's prophetic status by Timothy:

> And our gracious and wise King said to me: 'What do you say about Muḥammad?'—And I replied to his Majesty: 'Muḥammad is worthy of all praise, by all reasonable people, O my Sovereign. He walked in the path of the prophets, and trod in the track of the lovers of God. All the prophets taught the doctrine of one God, and since Muḥammad taught the doctrine of the unity of God, he walked, therefore, in the path of the prophets. Further, all the prophets drove men away from bad works, and brought them nearer to good works, and since Muḥammad drove his people away from bad works and brought them nearer to the good ones, he walked, therefore, in the path of the prophets. Again, all the prophets separated men from idolatry and polytheism, and attached them to God and to His cult, and since Muḥammad separated his people from idolatry and polytheism, and attached them to the cult and the knowledge of one God, beside whom there is no other God, it is obvious that he walked in the path of the prophets. Finally, Muḥammad taught about God, His Word and His Spirit, and since all the prophets had prophesied about God, His Word and His Spirit, Muḥammad walked, therefore, in the path of all the prophets.

This response depicts none of the usual polemic about Muḥammad's charlatan status, nor is it a confession of his being a good leader but not a prophet. Timothy seems comfortable in acknowledging Muḥammad in the way Muslims understood him, largely in the context of turning people away from polytheism. Muḥammad's teaching was in line with previous prophets and so Muḥammad too had the status of a prophet. Timothy mentions the 'Word' and the 'Spirit' specifically as God's attributes described by previous prophets also. By making an allusion to concepts which Christians emphasised but accepting that Muḥammad is a prophet, Timothy's reply reflects no theological angst that he might have confused or compromised his own Christian faith.

The Muslim polemic against Trinitarian beliefs and the Incarnation was only matched by the Muslim defence of Muḥammad's true prophetic status and his message, which Muslim scholars claimed was the same as the original message of Jesus. This was manifest in many works in the formative and later periods, often in response to Christian treatises against certain Muslim beliefs. One such treatise was Paul of Antioch's *Letter to a Muslim Friend*.[62] Paul belonged to the Melkite – i.e. Chalcedonian or Greek Orthodox – community and became bishop of Sidon. The exact period of his life is unknown, but it is claimed that he was active somewhere between 1027 and 1232. His cultural milieu was the Arabic-speaking community of the Greek Orthodox Patriarchate of Antioch and all his writings are in Arabic. His *Letter* is one of the few polemical writings which brought about significant reaction by many Muslims, and a much extended and reworked form of this *Letter*, composed in Cyprus in the fourteenth century, prompted the celebrated Hanbali jurist and theologian Ibn Taymiyya (1263–1328) to write his own very lengthy reply called *The Correct Reply to Those who have changed the Religion of Christ*. For the purpose of our discussion, it is worth noting that Paul claimed in his *Letter* that the Qur'ān and Muḥammad were only sent to the pagan Arabs and that Islam is not a universal religion. Thus, Muḥammad could be considered a person with a religious message, but only for those Arabs in the pre-Islamic period. In essence, the Qur'ān did not require Christians to become Muslims.[63] In his reply Ibn Taymiyya writes:

> The missionary does not realise that selective preaching of the prophets (to various people) separated over time does not necessitate the exclusivity of the call. As Christ spread the extension of his call, so did Muḥammad.
>
> Before Muḥammad was sent, Christians had already changed the religion of Christ, for they innovated the trinity and divine union [in Christ] and changed the legal prescriptions of the Gospel. These are not things brought by Christ, rather they are opposed to what he brought. Over these matters they split into numerous sects, with each sect declaring the others unbelievers. When Muḥammad was sent, they rejected him and so became unbelievers by changing the interpretations of the first book and its laws and by rejecting the second book.
>
> Those who did not change the religion of Christ were all following the truth. This is like someone who, at the sending of Christ, had been following the law of the Torah and would have been holding fast to the truth like the rest of those who followed Moses. When Christ was sent, all those who did not believe in him became unbelievers, and similarly when Muḥammad was sent, whoever did not believe in him, became an unbeliever.[64]

These kinds of disputes and polemical treatises show that Muslims and Christians approached and understood God's medium and purpose of revelation in distinct ways. Prophecy was valued, but its significance varied in both religions. Muslim scholars argued that prophecy was necessary for the transmission of the divine message and that Muḥammad had come essentially with the same message as Jesus in relation to obedience to the one God. In Christianity the prophetic message was not the most important part of divine revelation. But Muslims saw the concept of prophecy as understood in the Qur'ānic and Islamic sense to be the primary and ideal manner in which God has chosen to convey and reveal in history. Why God reveals through prophecy and through authoritative direction is not directly explained in the Qur'ān, though the Qur'ān states that 'It is not fitting for a man that God should speak to him except by inspiration, or from behind a veil, or by the sending of a Messenger to reveal' (Q42:51). God acts through the words which the prophets speak, and those who hear and accept these words become the new community of believers.

However one understands these types of verses in the Qur'ān, there is a sense that revelation has been a series of acts by God where his will has been expressed by those whom he chose to make his prophets, to confer prophecy or messengerhood. Prophets may have experienced different encounters with God, but their own nearness to God did not transform their human essence; they never became a human image of the divine. Prophets are in God's presence in sacred time, but they do not share in the divine essence either eternally or temporally. This is a fundamental parting from Christian belief in how Jesus was seen, an example of which can be seen in the following from John 14:8–10:

> Philip said, 'Lord, show us the Father and that will be enough for us.'
>
> Jesus answered: 'Don't you know me, Philip, even after I have been among you such a long time? Anyone who has seen me has seen the Father. How can you say, "Show us the Father"? Don't you believe that I am in the Father, and that the Father is in me?'

New Testament writers and early Christians broke away from the way God's revelations had been understood previously. God was now revealing himself directly in the 'living word' of Jesus Christ. Early Christians were less focused on how God had spoken and what he had said to his people and more on how Jesus himself embodied the divine communication. Jesus came with more than prophecy; in him God acted to redeem man. As Rudolf Bultmann wrote:

> The man Jesus came, to be sure, as prophet and teacher. He gave no teaching about his own person, but he said that the fact of his work was the ultimate decisive fact for men. His teaching is not a new teaching because of its conceptual content; for in its content it does not differ from pure Judaism, from the pure prophetic teaching. The unheard of thing is that he is speaking *now*, in the final decisive hour. What is decisive is not *what* he is proclaiming but *that* he is proclaiming it. *Now* is the time.[65]

This is why ultimately the concept of human prophecy, however complete or perfect, cannot be used to define Jesus from the Christian perspective. Jesus is not just a different kind of prophet from Muḥammad, exalted and revered but who essentially came with the same message. If Muḥammad is the recipient of divine words, Jesus is the embodiment of the Word. God acts in the present through the word which he, Jesus, speaks. But he brings the Word 'not as a world view but as a call to repentance before the coming kingdom of God'.[66] In the Prologue to John's Gospel, Jesus is called *the Logos, the Word*, meaning:

> All the activity of Jesus is centred in the Word; his works are his words; his words are his works. When he does his father's will and consummates his work, that work is his speaking the Word, his witnessing to what he has heard and seen with the Father.

Everything depends on hearing this Word and as Bultmann concludes, 'in the hearer's decision, the fate of the hearer is decided':

> For whoever is ashamed of me and of my words in this adulterous and sinful generation, of him will the Son of Man be ashamed when he comes in the glory of the Father with the holy angels (Mark 8:38).[67]

This central Christological issue has been questioned by some Christian theologians in recent times. During the winter of 1899–1900, the German theologian Adolf von Harnack (1851–1930) delivered a series of sixteen lectures at the University of Berlin. In his eleventh lecture he takes issue with the Christian identification of Jesus with the Logos. Harnack considered this linkage illegitimate, stating that this was a fusion of Greek philosophy with original Christian testimonies and hence 'inadmissible because the way in which we conceive the world and ethics does not point to the existence of any Logos at all'.[68]

But for most Christians Jesus is the final Word which God has spoken and is speaking. It is therefore not surprising that there is a struggle to find an adequate response to Muḥammad as the final Prophet when the final Word has already appeared. From the Islamic perspective, the Qur'ān already contains a very reverential Christology, but the Qur'ānic view of Jesus reflects a different Christic phenomenon. By rejecting the dual and divine nature of Jesus even though the Qur'ān calls Jesus the Word and Spirit of God, Islam continues to revere Jesus but sees in him neither the fullness of prophecy nor the fullness of God. In emphasising Jesus' humanity, however elevated, the Islamic concept of prophecy remains true to its own definitions of prophecy, but it limits, even reduces, Jesus in whom God himself reveals and is revealed. In other words, human prophecy is sufficient in Islam but is insufficient in Christianity to show the full grace and sovereignty and purpose of God's love and self-revelation.

The Finnish New Testament scholar Heikki Räisänen considered the Logos Christology of John's Gospel to be the most obvious contrast to the overall Qur'ānic Christology. He writes that it might be tempting to see in the notion 'word' a reflection of the Johannine conception of Jesus as Logos. But in the Qur'ān the word of God is clearly conceived of as created by God and not as an agent in creation.[69] Thus, if Jesus is a revered prophet in the Qur'ān, he is also a controversial prophet:

> He is the only prophet in the Qur'an who is deliberately made to distance himself from the doctrines that his community is said to hold of him. The term the Qur'an employs in this regard is 'cleansing' (Q3:55). Jesus will be cleansed from the perverted beliefs of his followers, and furthermore he himself

> plays an active role in the cleansing process. In answer to God, Jesus explicitly denies any responsibility for advocating tritheism. God meanwhile denies the Crucifixion. With Jesus, as with no other prophetic figure, the problem is not only to retell the story accurately. There are major doctrinal difficulties with the Christian version of his life and teachings to which the Qur'an repeatedly returns. In sum, the Qur'anic Jesus, unlike any other prophet, is embroiled in polemic.[70]

The term 'revelation' is complex in terms of a 'manifestation' of God by God. The Christian term 'revelation' (Latin *revelatio*, Greek *apokalypsis*) is a metaphor meaning something like unveiling and the word epiphany (*epiphaneia*) means becoming visible. God unveils himself, as it were, to become visible and audible to mankind.[71] In the Christian theological context, in the person of Jesus Christ the word became flesh and the incarnation became a more technical term, prompted by the prologue to the Fourth Gospel, 'And the Word became flesh' (John1:14). But however one understands incarnation, revelation refers to God's presence in the message and life of Jesus. Carmelo Dotolo explains this as follows:

> To understand revelation as the word of God means to affirm that listening is a decisive experience, without which existence is incapable of opening itself to the encounter with God and with other human beings: a difficult encounter, certainly, that requires readiness to move and to search, but also a seductive one and rich with promise because it is capable of transforming the way of seeing life in its reality. . . . if God would not settle in history as Lord of history, he could not be seen as the God

> free and provident, tender and love of life, close to man and yet totally other from him.[72]

Muslim teaching similar to Christian teaching on the life and ministry of Jesus is neither monolithic nor consistent. But there is an overriding Muslim emphasis on prophetic message, command and law which does not encapsulate the totality of the Christian Jesus story. As Dan Madigan poignantly argues, some Christians, like some Muslims, will state that the kernel of Jesus' teachings lies in the greatest commandments:

> But are they right? Is that all there is to the Gospel? Does the Word become incarnate simply to remind us of a few important verses from Deuteronomy and Leviticus that some of Jesus' contemporaries among the rabbis would also have recognised as summing up the 'Law and the Prophets'? Is Jesus' mission primarily to remind us of an obligation revealed centuries before? Is all the rest of his living, dying and rising somehow only ancillary to this?[73]

And yet Mahmoud Ayoub has argued that Muslims have thought much about Christ and that the Qur'ān presents at least the basis of an Islamic Christology, a fact that so far has not concerned Christians in a profound way. But Ayoub also writes that the Qur'ān presents a Christology of the human Christ, 'empowered by God and fortified with the Holy Spirit. It is a fully Islamic Christology.'[74] In the context of the dominant Muslim understanding of Jesus, we are left with a dilemma. Jesus is understood in a radically different way from the way Christians have understood his nature and presence, and the Qur'ān itself contains a critique of some kind of

Trinitarian Christology, albeit one that Christians may not recognise. In this context, what is the purpose of a Christology which does not recognize the divine, redemptive role of Christ, where his living is recognized but not his dying and rising? To focus only on his human prophecy within the long chain of prophetic missions creates an immediate obstacle for any kind of new awareness, since prophecy alone is incompatible with the perspective in which Christian devotion to Jesus recognises his unique relationship with God. Yet even though prophecy is not an adequate response to Jesus from a Christian perspective, it remains the dominant Qur'ānic response. As Heikki Räisänen writes, the Qur'ān cannot be explained by the New Testament, but only in the light of the new Qur'ānic context:

> The Qur'ān must be explained by the Qur'ān and not by anything else. This is the lesson to be learnt from the 'redaction-critical' studies of the Old and the New Testament. No matter what the Christians meant, for instance, when they spoke of Jesus as the 'Word' of God, from the point of view of the Qur'ān the only relevant question is: 'What could Muḥammad possibly mean by that expression in the context of *his* total view?' Seen against the background of Muḥammad's theology as a whole, the Qur'ānic portrait of Jesus stands out as coherent and clear.[75]

In the Qur'ān, prophecy is connected to the divine and is sufficient to warn, persuade and offer hope to the community, even though it is God's mercy that ultimately delivers any final success (*falāḥ*). Prophecy, however, can only guide, it cannot save, and Muḥammad is not a saviour for Muslims. But from the Christian perspective, Jesus' life and death save and point to something new, the decisive thing has happened in the Incarnation, though the consummation is yet to come. As Cullmann writes, 'The title Prophet proves to be inadequate as a solution to the Christological problem when we consider that it is precisely the exalted present Christ who stands at the centre of the faith of the early Church.'[76] Yet for all the Muslim insistence on keeping prophecy and divinity separate, the centuries of prophecy being a mediating theme between Christianity and Islam, prophecy is always touched by divinity. As Kenneth Cragg writes, the whole prophetic mission is on behalf of God and 'No authentic prophet sends himself. There is at work a divine-human proxy. We cannot have prophethood and elude this divine recruitment of stake in, and share with, the human means.'[77]

In recent years some Christian theologians have tried to formulate new ways of thinking about Muḥammad within a Christian context. For example, the Catholic theologian Hans Küng writes: 'isn't it . . . simply a dogmatic prejudice for Christians to recognize Amos and Hosea, Isaiah and Jeremiah and the extremely violent Elijah as prophets, but not Muhammad?' He undergirds this theological position by recalling the early Jewish Christian understanding of Jesus in which Jesus was not seen as the Incarnation of the Word of God. While the Christologies of Nicaea and Chalcedon may have eclipsed such views, Küng argues that Islam reconnects Christians to their Jewish Christian past.[78]

But we must ask whether the tension between the human and divine natures in the person of Jesus Christ is a meaningful struggle today in the theological engagement between Christians and Muslims. Evidence may show that Jesus considered himself to be a prophet and was regarded by his contemporaries as such, but what is far more significant is that his closest followers soon came to regard him as much more than a prophet. Prophecy ended with Christ and Muḥammad, but for different reasons. This is a question which should matter to Muslims, where the Christian belief in the divine/human nature of Christ could be explored further and not simply be dismissed as implying the association of another being with God or *shirk*. What is it about the human condition which led to Christianity seeing in Christ God himself? Muslims may not fully agree with what Christians believe about Jesus, but the boundaries of prophecy are open to interpretation, and in the case of Jesus it cannot be denied that alongside Qur'ānic praise and honour of Jesus, albeit mainly as a human prophet, there remains a certain mystery around the events of his life. Christian devotion to Jesus is not limited to what scripture says about him, but as Jürgen Moltmann writes, 'The earthly, the crucified, the raised, the present One: these are the stages of God's eschatological history with Jesus. . . . Confession of Christ leads to the way and along the way and is not yet in itself the goal.'[79] This is what is meant by Christ and provides the framework for Christology. But this should also be a point of Muslim inquiry into how Christians experience Jesus, and the significance of this life for Jesus is not experienced only by Christians. He lives in Muslim scripture, exegesis and poetry as well as Islamic ritual and piety. However understood, the Jesus of the Qur'ān is both a 'Word' and 'Spirit' of God, epithets not used for any other prophets. How these epithets might resonate meaningfully in the lives of Muslims may not sit comfortably in popular Muslim piety, but the exploration of possibilities should be seen as a worthy and necessary exercise in interreligious theology and individual piety.

CHAPTER 2

God as One: Early Debates

In the previous chapter we saw how prophecy as a mode of divine communication and divine presence has been understood and defined in the persons of Muḥammad and Jesus. While prophecy as a conceptual paradigm of God's purpose remained central to Islam, it gradually assumed a lesser relevance in Christianity. Here, in the person of Jesus, God himself was present and thus the status of prophecy was eclipsed by the doctrine of the Incarnation. The divine/human nature of Christ unfolded as a unique event which went far beyond prophetic mission and guidance for Christians. For Muslims, however, this Christic complexity was for the most part refuted as impinging on the very essence and purpose of God. Jesus was to be considered human and a prophet only. Muslims did not question this stance as Islam's radical departure from the existing Christian doctrine and belief, but saw it rather in the context of the Qur'ānic ideal of monotheism. Even though Christians explained Jesus' significance and role in all kinds of doctrinal and devotional terms in which the Trinity and Incarnation were not seen as conflicting with God's oneness, the expression of monotheism became a fundamental point of discussion between the scholars of both religions.

In this chapter I wish to outline how key Muslim and Christian scholars defended their doctrines of God's oneness and transcendence through their own defences, but also in response to one another's accusations. Much of what follows is what the theologians themselves were saying as it is important to understand how certain theological concepts became the defining points of discussion and polemics, irrespective of what was happening in political and social realities between the two faiths.

> The rapid rise of Islam in the seventh and eight centuries placed Christian thinkers in an unaccustomed position. From its earliest days Christianity had defined itself against classical paganism on the one hand and Judaism on the other, but the religion of Muḥammad demanded a different response, for it proclaimed itself the very culmination of Christianity.[1]

In his work on Christian writers of the East and their theological engagement with Islam, John Moorhead writes that the earliest Christian discussion of Islam is that contained in the *History of Heraclius*, the classical Armenian text, attributed to the Armenian bishop Sebeos and probably completed in 661. The text reflects a mixed image of Islam. Sebeos may have called the leader of the Ishmaelites 'the great ally of Antichrist', but he also asserts that Muḥammad taught his people to know God and to turn to the living God.[2] Sebeos also uses the theme of Biblical prophecy and Daniel's vision of the four beasts to identify the fourth beast with Muslims. Daniel's four beasts are associated with four kingdoms in which the fourth is the kingdom of Muslims which 'shall consume the whole earth'.[3] As the authors of this translation explain, not only Daniel but other prophets too had foreseen the appearance of the Muslims. In Genesis, it had been stated that his 'hands would be on all' and Isaiah too had spoken of their invasion when speaking of the tempest coming from the south. The relationship of the Arabs to the Jews as sons of Abraham from different mothers was a theme picked up by various commentators writing on early Islam, but Sebeos was the first Armenian to draw on broader scriptural prophecies to explain the vigorous rise of the Muslims.[4]

A common theme for many Christians of the time was an attempt to understand why Muḥammad had been able to draw people to him with his teachings on God. Pseudo-Dionysius of Tell Mahre, a Monophysite author writing in about 775, explains why the Arabs called Muḥammad 'the prophet':

> He had turned them away from different cults, had taught them the existence of one God, the creator of the Universe, and had given them laws when they had been given over to the cult of demons and the adoration of idols, especially trees. Because he taught them the unity of God, because they triumphed over the Romans under his guidance, and because he gave them laws according to their desires, they called him Prophet and Messenger of God.[5]

Politics and theology affected much of the Christian assessment of Islam. While there were irenic as well as hostile attitudes to Islam among the Christians of the East, much of the doctrinal debate wrestled with the positive aspect of Islam which was the affirmation of one God and its negative doctrine which denied the divinity of Christ. Many of the Christian writers of the East placed Islam in the broad context of a monotheistic belief but critiqued the religion for its misunderstanding or denial of Christ's salvific status.

In the concluding remarks to his book *The Church in the Shadow of the Mosque*, Sidney Griffith laments that 'Western Christian thinkers engaged in interreligious dialogue with Muslims in the modern world, and those who in recent times have been concerned with comparative theology in the study of Christianity and Islam, have seldom if ever taken useful cognizance of the intellectual history of the Christians who lived for centuries in the world of Islam and who wrote Christian philosophy and theology in Syriac and Arabic.'[6] It is true that relatively speaking there are only a few scholars today who have focused on the Greek, Syriac and Arabic writings of eighth- to ninth-century Christians who lived in the Arab world and who saw themselves challenged by the new rise of the Islamic faith and civilisation. Their writings reflect this tension of Christians living under an expanding Islamic empire and witnessing the flourishing of a faith which, for all its doctrinal convergences with Christianity, rejected the essential creed of Christian belief.

One of the first and most significant Christians of the East to address the Muslim faith and its particular doctrines relating to Christianity was John of Damascus, also known as John Damascene. As a major figure of the Eastern Church, John of Damascus (c.675–749), a Christian priest and monk of the eighth century, left two important theological legacies. The first was his defence of iconography in religious worship in conjunction with other monastic circles during the iconoclastic controversies. These began in the early eighth century as a reaction against the growing importance of holy icons in religious worship as developed by the Byzantine Church. When the Byzantine emperor Leo III (717–741) banned the veneration of icons in 726, he shook the very foundations of Greek orthodoxy:

> Scholars have suggested many reasons for the introduction of Iconoclasm (literally, 'the smashing of images') by a series of

> emperors beginning with Leo III in 730, including fear of God's wrath in the face of 'idolatry', Muslim or Jewish influence, or increased political and military disruption in the empire owing to the rise of the Islamic state. It is also possible, however, that the iconoclasts saw themselves as reformers from within, aiming to return Christianity to the pure, aniconic state which they believed had existed in the earliest Church.[7]

The most basic charge of the iconoclasts was that of idolatry, but John of Damascus had argued that an icon is not an idol. The real controversy was whether Christ, the Son of God, could be depicted as an image. John of Damascus argued that although an icon of Christ depicts his human nature and not that which is unseen, 'these two natures are "acknowledged without confusion, change, division or separation" as the Council of Chalcedon confirms'.[8] Church historians mention John's name as the first in the context of the Synod of 754 in which the Iconoclasts in Constantinople accused him of having 'Saracene opinions' and called him a 'worshipper of idols'.[9]

The second of his theological legacies was the masterpiece which he wrote in the later years of his life known as *The Fount of Knowledge* or *Pēgē Gnōseōs*. Although John of Damascus, or Mansūr ibn Sarjūn as he was known in the Arabic-speaking world of Islam, lived all his life amongst Muslims, his surviving works are in Greek, 'the theological and liturgical language of the burgeoning Melkite Christian community, whose chief spokesman he was to become'.[10] Greek had remained the official language of the Umayyad administration in Syria, although Syriac and Arabic were widely spoken. It was not till the caliphate of ʿAbd al Mālik (684–705) that Arabic became the official language of government and administration, thus making it likely that John of Damascus did know Arabic and was acquainted with Muslim sources, though it is difficult to ascertain to what level. John of Damascus wrote *The Fount of Knowledge* in Greek probably in the Mar Sabas monastery, which was a centre of theological learning and liturgical tradition in the Judaean desert.[11] *The Fount of Knowledge* was divided into three parts and compiled with the purpose of providing a compendium of the 'teachings of the fathers' of Christian orthodoxy on the articles of Christian faith. He states in *The Fount of Knowledge* that his aim was not to say anything new, but to display what the 'saintly and wise men have taught at different times'.[12] The three parts consist of a philosophical introduction (*Dialectics*), a refutation of heresies (*Concerning Heresies*), and a scholastic survey of faith (*Exposition of the Orthodox Faith*). If this work came to represent the last of the patristic era in the East, Griffith also contends that the challenge posed by Islam entailed a confirmation and validation of true Christian doctrine:

> One must consider that the full range of the developing Islamic sciences in the first half of the eighth century presented an almost unprecedented, comprehensive challenge both to Christianity's principal articles of faith and to the Christian way of life. In response, the challenge called for a comprehensive, summary exposition of the truths of Christian faith, along with a compendium of definitions of the philosophical terms in which the Christian doctrines were expressed.[13]

Divided into these three parts, it is the section on heresies which concerns us here. *The Fount of Knowledge* contains one section on 100 heresies, *De Haeresibus*. The relatively longer 101st heresy is the

Heresy of the Ishmaelites.[14] While *De Haeresibus* is written principally for a Christian audience to contrast what is heretical with what is orthodox, this tractate is regarded by many as one of the first polemical Christian writings against Islam discussing many of the themes which became the defining issues raised in later Christian–Muslim encounters. In using a Christological criterion, John calls Islam a heresy because he does not distinguish between heresies and other religions, since in his view 'they are equally to be judged as deviations from Christological truth'.[15] However, John also introduces Islam as the prevailing 'superstition of the Ishmaelites' and the 'forerunner of the Antichrist'. As Daniel Sahas explains, the term Antichrist was not just confined as an insult against Islam and Muḥammad, but used against anyone who was understood to lead people astray from the Orthodox faith. John considered an Antichrist not only Satan but any man 'who does not confess that the Son of God came in flesh, is perfect God and He became perfect man while at the same time He was God'.[16]

Jesus' divinity is central to any Christian Christology, and any religion, ideology or any Christology which did not recognise this had to be false, even if attempts were made to understand it. Scholars disagree over whether John had detailed knowledge of Muslim sources and Arabic, but he was fully aware of the idolatrous character of much of pre-Islamic Arabia. Against this knowledge, he also recognised that Islam was a new and powerful threat to the region, albeit a proclaimed monotheistic threat. It was in this pre-Islamic idolatrous society of Mecca that Muḥammad had, according to John of Damascus, appeared as a false prophet. He is accused of knowing a little of the Old and New Testaments and using them to produce his own heresy which finds its origins in the Qur'ān. John also uses the Islamic legend of the Arian Monk Baḥīrā, whom

Muḥammad supposedly encountered as a young boy and who recognised the mark of prophecy on Muḥammad's person. Muḥammad was travelling with his uncle Abū Tālib and the monk told Abū Tālib to take good care of his nephew as he was destined for a great future. John Merrill states that John may have identified the monk as an Arian, because in John's view Islam was largely a Christological heresy with teachings which resembled Arianism.[17] Arius (250/256–336) was a Christian monk in Alexandria who opposed Trinitarian Christology, making himself a controversial figure in the first Council of Nicaea convened by Emperor Constantine in 325. The controversy over the Son's precise relationship to the Father had been around for decades before, but Arius intensified this debate. He claimed that Jesus as the Son of God was not co-eternal with God the Father, that the Logos and the Father were not of the same essence (*ousia*), that the Son was a created being, and that there must have been a time when Christ did not exist.[18] Arius taught that Jesus was created in time by God and was also distinct from God.[19] His main adversary on this issue was St Athanasius (c.296–373), who became the twentieth bishop of Alexandria. In Athanasius's view the Father would not be the Father without the Son and therefore he was never without the Son. The issue was no splitting of theological hairs; salvation itself was at stake. Only one who was fully human could atone for human sin; only one who was fully divine could have the power to save us. To Athanasius, the logic of New Testament doctrine of salvation assumed the dual nature of Christ, and at the Council of Nicaea he said, 'Jesus that I know as my Redeemer cannot be less than God'. Thus, Jesus shares in the divine attribute of eternity, his personal existence is that of an eternal Subject within the oneness of God. As Gerald O'Collins writes, 'Pre-existence means rather that Christ personally belongs to an order of being other than the created, temporal one. His personal, divine existence transcends temporal and spatial categories.'[20]

However this was understood, most Christians engaged with Islam knew that the oneness of God formed the very basis of Muslim monotheism. But if unity in the Trinity seemed confusing to Muslims, the Qur'ānic message of divine unity was derided because Muḥammad's claims were derided. John too scoffed at the Muslim belief in the divine origins of the Qur'ān, accusing Muḥammad of falsely claiming that a 'scripture had been brought down to him from heaven', whereas in fact the Qur'ān's pronouncements are worthy of laughter.[21] But John knew that Muḥammad's message in the Qur'ān, however understood, was one which urged people back to monotheism, to one God. John therefore embarks on an imaginary debate, beginning with the core Qur'ānic doctrine, the unity of God or *tawḥīd*. Keen to speak of the oneness and uniqueness of God in his own Christian theology, John also recognises the centrality of this doctrine in Islam. Nevertheless, he uses the Christian understanding of Christ as Word of God to critique Muslim interpretation of this doctrine in the Qur'ān. He writes of Muḥammad,

> He says that there is one God, Creator of all, who is neither begotten nor has begotten. He says that Christ is the word of God, and his spirit, created and a servant, and that he was born without a seed from Mary, the sister of Moses and Aaron. For, he says, 'the Word of God and the Spirit entered Mary and she gave birth to Jesus who was a prophet and a servant of God. And the Jews, having themselves violated the Law, wanted to crucify him, and after they arrested him, they crucified his shadow, but Christ himself, they say, was not crucified nor did

> he die; for God took him up to himself into heaven because he loved him.' And this is what he says, that when Christ went up to the heavens, God questioned him saying, 'O Jesus, did you say that I am son of God, and God?' And Jesus, they say, answered, 'Be merciful to me, Lord, you know that I did not say so, nor will I boast that I am your servant; but men who have gone astray wrote that I made this statement and they said lies against me and they have been in error.' And God, they say, answered to him, 'I knew that you would not say this thing'.[22]

For John of Damascus, this conversation between God and Jesus is absurd, similar to many of the other Qur'ānic stories. This is partly because it denies all that is fundamental to Christian belief by having Jesus himself deny his divinity, but also because the Qur'ān could not possibly have been a heavenly text, for Muḥammad himself was not a true prophet. Like many Christians, John of Damascus held the view that the truth of Christ as Messiah can be found in the Old Testament, that 'all the prophets, starting from Moses and onward, foretold of the advent of Christ and that Christ is God'.[23] The Old Testament prophets do not, however, foretell the coming of Muḥammad. In fact, John pushes this point to a comparison between Moses and Muḥammad. Whereas Moses received the law at Mount Sinai, witnessed by several people, Muḥammad received his book with no witnesses present. When the issue of witnesses is so significant in ordinary matters in Islam, how can Muslims have a faith and a scripture where there were no witnesses? Furthermore, when Muslims claim that Muḥammad received God's message in his sleep, John's response is that if this is so, it means even Muḥammad could not testify to the circumstances in which the Qur'ān was revealed. Yet as Davids and Valkenberg write,

> At this point John of Damascus seems to forget the theological nature of his point. Not only is the fact that Muḥammad was asleep during the *Layla al-Qadr* used by Muslims to ensure that he could not have contributed anything of his own to this revelation; but the idea that God reveals God-self to people when they are asleep is well documented in both the Old and the New Testament as well.[24]

Perhaps the biggest contention for John is the question of monotheism between Christians and Muslims, for John was well aware that Muslims saw Christian monotheism in a very different light. He was not prepared to accept the Muslim accusation that Christians were themselves actually 'Associators' (*mushrikīn*) because they saw Christ as the 'Son of God'. In a vehement theological attack, he writes:

> The Muslims accuse the Christians of being 'Associators' for ascribing a partner to God, by calling Christ 'son of God', and 'God'. The Christians in turn accuse the Muslims of being 'Mutilators' by having disassociated God from His word and Spirit.[25]

For John, if Christ is a Word and a Spirit coming from God, he must be in God and thus he must be God. When Muslims deny this, they separate and place outside of God what is part of God, thus mutilating God. If one takes Word and Spirit away from God, God becomes an inanimate object like a stone or a piece of wood. Furthermore, if Muslims can accuse Christians of idolatry because they venerate the cross, how do Muslims explain venerating the stone of the Kaʿba? While the Qurʾān does not accuse Christians of being idolators for venerating the cross, it does define them at times as being 'associators', i.e. ascribing partners. However, later Byzantine theologians used the short Qur'ānic *Sūrat al-Ikhlās*, translated as the 'Unity', to discuss or attack Muslim ideas of God's unity:

> Say, 'He, God, is one,
> God the eternal refuge,
> He begetteth not, nor is he begotten,
> And none is like unto Him.'

Sahas and others explain that the notion of 'eternal' in the Arabic word *samad* was distorted in translation as 'spherical' or 'solid and round', corresponding to the concept of *holosphairos* used by Byzantine theologians. This probably began with the Melkite bishop of Harran, Theodore Abū Qurrah (John's pupil, 750–ca.820), who translated *Sūrat al-Ikhlās* in the following way:

> God is single. God is *sphyropectos* (beaten solid to a ball), who has neither given birth nor was he born and no-one has been his counterpart.[26]

Thus, the Muslim God was spherical in shape, just like the stone in the Ka'ba, in other words the Muslim God was lifeless. However, the concept of Muslims having a 'mutilated' God is not a repeated theme in Christian Muslim polemics, but John's response raises the fundamental issue which lies at the core of how Muslims and Christians have theologically defended the oneness of God in their own form of monotheism. It is that Muslims have failed to appreciate that the unity of God is not compromised by Christian Christology; rather, it is only through Christian Christology that one can know God. As Sahas writes:

> For John of Damascus the issue at stake is not whether God is one or many; he simply assumes the former as a *sine qua non*; the issue at stake is how God can be known. The question of the Trinity, therefore, is for John of Damascus an answer to the question of the knowledge of God.[27]

He wrote, 'We know one God', and for John this one God had in him the properties of Father, Son and Spirit. That Muslims shared with Christians some doctrines, but rejected this concept of the triune Godhead, inevitably meant that they failed to understand not only the true nature of Christ, but also the true nature of God.

The spread of Arabic as the language of administration by the end of the first century of Islam influenced the Christians living under Muslim rule. They embraced it as their language of business, and some 'adopted the language of the Qur'ān in the ecclesiastical sphere as well'.[28] Griffith claims that the Melkite community, whose liturgical and patristic tradition remained in Greek, used Arabic as their *lingua franca*. Christians in the Holy Land, and especially those who belonged to a monastic order, were among the first to translate Christianity into Arabic and also compose works of theology in Arabic for an audience which was familiar with the Qur'ān. While many of the works translated were those required by the Church such as Scripture, homilies, canon law and liturgical works, other writings responded to the new challenges which came with the rival claims of Islam. This scholarly defence of Christianity could be construed as theology in dialogue. Even though the language of Arabic was bound over to the religion of Islam, Arabic language provided a new and challenging context for the Christian monks to expand Christian doctrines, as well as to write original works in Arabic during the late eighth and ninth centuries.

According to current scholarship on early Christian writers in Arabic, Theodore Abū Qurrah was one of the first Melkite monks to write in Arabic in his theological defence of Christianity. We know little about his life, but it is speculated that he was probably a native of Edessa born somewhere around the middle of the eighth century and died some time after 829. The monastery of Mar Sabas was an important centre of Melkite theology in the early ʿAbbāsid period in the vicinity of Jerusalem, a base not only for expounding the Melkite creed but also for responding in Arabic to Islamic critiques of Christian doctrine. But there has been some disagreement amongst scholars regarding Theodore Abū Qurrah's affiliation and stay at the monastery of Mar Sabas and whether he was, as Lamoreaux coins it, the 'continuateur arabe' of the monastery's most famous theologian John of Damascus. Lamoreaux himself states that the evidence that Theodore was a monk at this monastery is 'slight at best and non-existent at worst'. However, both Christian and Muslim sources attest that he was for a while the bishop of Ḥarrān in Mesopotamia.

The expansion of Islam and the subjugation of much of the territory that had belonged to the Christian empire of Byzantium meant that Theodore faced two significant challenges. The first challenge was to defend Chalcedonian Christianity as alone possessing the fullness of Christian truth in relation to other Christian sects, and the second was to defend the fundamentals of Christian doctrine against Islam, the new religion of the new empire. The corpus of Theodore's writings is large, including an extensive collection of Arabic works and around forty Greek treatises ascribed to him. Griffith claims, however, that all indications are that the compositions in Greek are translations from the Arabic. Basing his statement on the findings of Reinhold Glei and Adel Khoury, John Lamoreaux further contends that many of what were thought to be Theodore's Greek works against Islam were not written by him but are rather part of a collection of dialogues purporting to be a record of the debates in which he participated.[29] One such debate in which Theodore is participating is illustrated by his 'Refutations of the Saracens'.[30] While various tensions between Muslims and Christians form the substance of these debates, a recurring theme is that of Muḥammad's prophecy in relation to God's oneness. A conversation occurs in which Theodore complains that when the Saracen meets a Christian, he offers no greeting but demands that the Christian proclaim that God is one and Muḥammad is his messenger. Theodore's major contention here is that Muslims are bearing false testimony because no one had testified Muḥammad as a prophet.[31] Theodore argues:

Theodore: My father taught me to accept someone as a messenger only if he was prophesied by an earlier prophet or through signs established himself as worthy of belief. Your Muḥammad, however, could appeal to neither of these conditions. No earlier prophet declared him to be a prophet and he did not engender faith in himself through signs.

Saracen: That's not true. In the Gospel, Christ wrote: I shall send to you a prophet named Muḥammad.

Theodore: The gospel has no such prediction.

Saracen: It used to, it's only that you all deleted it.

Christians saw the Muslim acceptance of Muḥammad as a prophet of God and their understanding of him as a prophet foretold in Christian scripture as a fundamental error. For most, Islam had no credibility as a true religion because Muḥammad had no credibility as a true prophet. This is not because Christians emphasised Jesus' finality as a prophet, rather that it is through Christ that humanity witnessed the fullness of God. In denying this, Muslims were denying the very nature of God. This formed the background to further polemics as to how Muslims and Christians understood divine oneness, but also divine omnipotence. Theodore claims that the Muslim theology of God as one 'who did not beget nor was begotten and has no partner' is the theology 'of one who is insane'.[32] For Theodore, the failure of Muslims to see the light and holiness which proceeded from God was tantamount to denying the true divinity of God. He blames Muḥammad for this erroneous teaching: 'Indeed, it was only because their false prophet was the disciple of an Arian that he gave them this godless and impious teaching.' For Theodore, it was 'impossible that he [God] not have a son', because God rules his son by his nature. The explanation given to the Saracen is this:

> It is because of him that God is known to be an eternal ruler and Father and this because everything that is by nature precedes wilful choice. Before willing to breathe, we breathe. Before willing to hear, we hear. Before willing to see, we see. You who deny the divinity of the Word of God, it has been demonstrated to you that God has a son who shares his essence and like him is without beginning and end.[33]

Thus, Jesus is God's son because God by virtue of his nature must have a son. This particular point in defence of Chalcedonian Christology appears also in a separate work where Theodore explains that although Muslims exalt God, they diminish his power by refusing to acknowledge that he can beget – it is a concept that Muslims hate just because they associate it only with human sexual intercourse and pregnancy and fail to understand how begetting and sonship could occur in God.[34] He argues:

> Tell me how God is alive when life among us is accompanied by necessities of which you are not ignorant, things like eating, drinking, nourishment . . . you are unable to say how God is alive notwithstanding these necessities. Accordingly, you should deny life to God, because you do not understand how it occurs and because it is contrary to the type of life you see with your own eyes, even as you deny the sonship because you do not understand how it occurs and because it is contrary to the type of sonship your own senses can perceive.

The belief in Jesus as Son of God has remained one of the major theological differences between Muslims and Christians. The Gospel of Luke is a primary source on the nativity of Jesus, analogous to the story of the angel and Mary in the Qur'ān. Mary is told of a power that will engulf her, to which the angel answers, '"The Holy Spirit will come on you, and the power of the Most High will overshadow you. So the holy one to be born will be called the Son of God"' (Luke 1:35). Along with Logos, this became a 'high' title of Jesus, pointing to the eternal, divine side of things, but not implying any generation or sexual union. However, as Mahmoud Ayoub comments:

> Abū Qurrah's language would leave no doubt in the mind of a Muslim reader that Jesus is the son of God, engendered by him from eternity. For while Abū Qurrah uses *ibn* for son, he always uses the verb *walada*, to engender or give birth to, when speaking of God the father and Jesus His son. In fact this direct language remains the language of Syro-Arabic liturgy and worship to this day.[35]

Theodore challenges the Muslim by using their own internal debates on the anthropomorphic verses in the Qur'ān. This alludes to the Muʿtazilite denial that God had attributes of seeing and hearing, even though the Qur'ān states that God is the all seeing and all hearing. Theodore argues that just as Muslims say God hears and sees without attributing human qualities or limitations to him, so do Christians talk of divine sonship: 'In the same way, we must think purely of his begetting and exalt him above the defects of our own begetting in a way that befits his noble essence.'[36]

In his Arabic treatise, 'On the Existence of God and the True Religion', Theodore attempts to show through a series of explanations how Christianity is the only true religion. He accuses other religions of not being able to give a true account of God because they describe their God 'according to the imaginings of their human and earthly minds' and 'their descriptions are from the earth, not from God'. Theodore is quite explicit in his condemnation of the way other religions think about the blessings of the next world: 'All they can think about is the earth, food and drink, fornication and the pleasures of the body. They know nothing else. Like beasts, it is for this alone that their souls yearn and it is of this alone that they think.'[37] For Theodore, it is the Gospels which alone are from God and for which Christians can cast aside all other religions. He defends the Gospels as being true to human nature and states, 'We know this because it offers us what our own nature taught us.'[38]

Arabic had become the primary vehicle for the defence of Christianity in the Muslim-dominated lands of the East. By the beginning of the ninth century each of the three major Christian denominations existing in the Arab-dominated land had produced an important apologist in Arabic: the Nestorian ʿAmmār al-Basrī (c.800–850), the Melkite bishop of Ḥarrān, Theodore Abū Qurrah (d.829), and the Jacobite Abū Rā'iṭah (c.775-c.835).[39] These three notable Christians were the first to delineate the basic controversies between Christians and Muslims, but their task was also to convince other Christians who were shaken by the spread of Islam, of the truth of the Christian faith.

Against their Syriac background, writing in Arabic presented these Christian writers with some difficulties inasmuch as they had to translate complex ideas of Christian belief into a language already dominated by Qur'ānic and Islamic images. Scholarly polemical debate between Muslims and Christians evolved into a form resembling the *munāzara*, a way of debating to arrive at the truth rather than displaying mastery of rhetoric alone. Each side aimed to convince the other side of the truth of their religion and it would appear that there were penalties for the person who lost the debate. In most cases the *munāzarāt* were debates which took place between Muslim intellectuals or between Muslims and Christians of various backgrounds. Basing her findings on the works of Sidney Griffith, Sandra Keating explains that 'existent texts claiming to be eyewitness accounts of debates were written much later as theological exercises and were simply effective literary forms for presenting apologetical arguments'. Keating claims that despite having been redacted or softened by later editors as well as other issues of authenticity, it is most likely that these *munāzarāt* conversations did take place.[40]

At the turn of the ninth century, 'Abbāsid rule witnessed the gradual Arabization of culture throughout the empire. It was a period in which the flowering of doctrinal apologetics saw Christians writing vigorously to defend their faith against the Muslims who rejected fundamental Christian doctrines such as the Trinity and Incarnation. It is in this environment that along with Theodore Abū Qurrah, we have the works of Ḥabīb ibn Khidmah Abū Rā'iṭah al-Takrītī, who is also reputed to be one of the first Christians to write in Arabic. Keating explains that although there is no mention in the sources of

Abū Rā'iṭah's status as a bishop in the Jacobite church, he was actively involved in the life of the Syrian Jacobite church. Likely to be a native Syriac speaker who had learned Arabic well, he may have held the ecclesiastical office of *verdapet*, a teacher and exegete, tasked with explaining and defending difficult doctrines of the church. He was writing at a time when the churches in the East were being slowly cut off from those in the West. Furthermore, this was a time when the Eastern churches were still involved in inter-confessional squabbles, even as their own society was becoming gradually Islamicized. However senior his official position was, it is evident that he was someone whose writing had won over the respect of the clergy.[41]

Abū Rā'iṭah's writings can be divided into two groups: refutations of the theological positions of other Christians, namely the Melkites and the Nestorians, and responses to either questions or accusations about Christianity from Muslims. By writing in Arabic, Abū Rā'iṭah was making his ideas accessible to a Muslim audience as well, even though his primary adversaries are Muslims and Melkite Christians. Abū Rā'iṭah's fundamental purpose in his writings is to convince his listeners of the truth of Jacobite Christianity. Keating has provided short introductions to the existing corpus of his writings which she has translated from the original Arabic so that his works can be 'better known and appreciated'. She adds two specific points about Abū Rā'iṭah's work. Firstly, he does not appear to have had an Arabic translation of the Bible available to him and 'was forced to render the necessary passages himself, which he sometimes does rather freely'. Secondly, many of the Muslim listeners would have been 'untutored in the standard philosophical and patristic texts to which Abū Rā'iṭah could have appealed among Christians'.[42] The following is a selection of his writings from across his works that Keating has translated together with the Arabic text in one volume. The translated texts give a flavour of the kind of arguments being made in defence of his Christian faith against his opponents, the *mukhālifūnā*, at a time when for a variety of political and social reasons Christianity was witnessing mass conversions to Islam.[43]

Abū Rā'iṭah's *On the Proof of the Christian Religion and Proof of the Holy Trinity* is the longest and most comprehensive of his writings. The selections below are from his *First Risālah on the Holy Trinity* and *Second Risālah on the Incarnation*. They do not exhaust all his arguments, but they provide another glimpse of how Arab Christians defended their Christology in their discussions about God. A long opening lists the reasons why people belong to certain religions and why Christians accept Christianity for its inherent truths, not because 'of worldly desires or fear or aspiring to a known afterlife'. He continues:

> Our opponents say, 'O Christian people! You describe God as three gods, in that you affirm [God is] three *hypostaseis* and a single one in number.'

Abū Rā'iṭah uses analogical reasoning (*qiyās*) to explain the nature of God. He uses the example of the light which emanates from three lamps, light which is equal to one other, and asks whether this light is one light or three separate lights:

> Now if they say: '[It is] three [lights],' we say: Why is this? There is no difference among them in the light and the illumination, and no separation in the place [of the light]. Rather, what is necessary for light is proper [to them] in all of their states. So they should know that the light described is one and three together [simultaneously] and with regard to the quiddity

> of the light and its *ousia*, and three with regard to the number applicable to the being of the particular lamps necessary for each one of [the lights].
>
> They may say: 'The light which you describe, is it a plurality and a unity together, [so that] one speaks of it generally as "light" and "lights"? [Either] each one of them stands alone without a relationship to another, or they are related, one to the others. What prevents you from describing these *hypostaseis* which you have presented as "God" and "gods"? If each of them is a cause in itself and stands [alone], without being related to the other *hypostaseis*, then this contradicts your statement itself [that they are] Father, Son and Holy Spirit. Is one of these lights related to the other as you have related one of the *hypostaseis* to the other, and which you have named Father, Son and Holy Spirit?'

The hypothetical Muslim critique of the light analogy is whether the light from each lamp is a separate light or united as one light. In similar terms, what is the relationship between the Christian term *hypostaseis* and God's triune nature? Abū Rā'iṭah's response is that the light analogy bears a partial similarity to the relationship between God's essence and *hyspostaseis*. Plurality in the Christian sense does not mean speaking of gods and God, or lords and Lord as Muslims argue.[44]

It is worth noting here that light is a popular symbol for talking about God's oneness and essence in monotheistic traditions. God is the eternal source of light, and earthly light is understood as an image of divine light. In Islam the light verses of the Qur'ān and light imagery have been used extensively to explain the essence of God. The Qur'ān says that God is the 'Light of the heavens and the earth' (Q24:35), but light is unseen, as is God. God remains invisible to human eyes, but without God's radiance there would be neither heaven nor earth. As Uri Rubin states, 'Light serves as a symbol of the prospective expansion of the Islamic faith'.[45] There is God's light, the light of Muḥammad's prophetic emergence, and the light motif used as representative of divine presence amongst the Shīʿa. For the Shīʿa, light is an allegorical symbol of the Prophet, ʿAli, his sons, and the rest of the imams. Amongst all the sects, the Shīʿa have made the most of light in the concept of divine light. 'Light as an element of communication between the imams and the rest of humankind is sometimes described as a cosmic column. It is erected as such on the birth of each imam . . . and it also communicates between the imam and the heavenly world.'[46] The prophets too are created with light, and traditions extol Muḥammad as being created with a primordial light, a substance which places him above other prophets.

In his esoteric treatise *The Mishkat al-Anwar, The Niche for Lights*, Abū Ḥāmid al-Ghazālī explores the Light verse and the veil traditions as a way of explaining God's essence and human attempts to know God:

> Allah is the Light of the heavens and the earth. The similitude of his light is, as it were, a niche wherein there is a lamp: the lamp within a glass, the glass, as it were, a pearly star. From a tree that is blessed it is lit, an olive tree neither of the East nor of the West, the oil whereof were well-nigh luminous though fire did not touch it; light upon light, God guides to his light whom he wills (Q24:35).

For al-Ghazālī, it is not enough to talk of God as veiled, but rather 'Allah has seventy thousand veils of light and darkness. Were he to withdraw their curtain, then would the splendours of

His aspect surely consume everyone who apprehended him with his sight.'

Al-Ghazālī talks about the real light which is God and the significance of using light as a theme in human–divine relations. Heavenly realities all have their symbols on earth and there is a certain ineffable likeness between man and God, but all of us have only a veiled understanding of God. Human intelligence has a capacity for perceiving the divine through the stages of contemplation, the Qur'ān contains the vocabulary which allows humankind to identify with God's goodness, and yet ultimately the divine reality may always elude human understanding. Only for the very few will 'nothing remain except the Real'.[47]

Abū Rā'iṭah continues to explain the relationship between Father, Son and Spirit as being in eternal existence. God's being and existence are from eternity:

> His life proceeds from Him without time: three existent properties (that is, three substantial *hypostaseis*), a Father, Who begets His Word ceaselessly, and a Son, who is begotten without time, and a Spirit, Who proceeds from Him, without interruption, One God, one Lord, one *ousia*.

But he adds that it is the 'Father [who is] the eternal cause of the Son and Spirit, for they are from Him, he is not from them, without being earlier or later [in time], two perfects from a perfect, two eternals from an eternal'.[48] Like many Christians, Abū Rā'iṭah claimed that Muslims and Christians understood God's oneness in very different ways and much of his reasoning is about how to understand oneness and the Christian expression of this oneness. He argued that Christians saw in God one *ousia* (essence) and three *hypostaseis*; it is in his essence that God remains exalted above all his creatures, for his *ousia* 'approaches everything closely without blending or mixing'.[49]

For Abū Rā'iṭah, the three *hypostaseis* are one *ousia* in all aspects. As for Muslims, they say God is one, but they cannot explain what they mean when they say God is one.

Abū Rā'iṭah also explains the Incarnation in similar debating style. To the Muslim question of whether the Incarnation is an act of God or a part of God, Abū Rā'iṭah replies that the Incarnated One is God become human. The incarnation of the Word in the body was not 'done' by anyone, but 'the body was an act of the three [*hypostaseis*],[at the same time] we say, [an act of]one of the three, not of the three'.[50]

Abū Rā'iṭah wishes to stress the eternal aspect of the Word as something which was with God from the beginning, as opposed to the idea of a sonship which was 'begotten' in time and which the Muslim rejected. He states that the eternal Word is incarnated in an eternal body and that the Word has 'taken to itself a body without the Body being a part of [the Word]. The Word dwells in the body, even though it is not contained in or by the body.' He uses varied natural imagery to convey this:

> For the disc of the sun is encompassed by its light, not [the light by the sun], and the coal is encompassed by the fire burning in it, [the fire] is not encompassed by the coal, and the body is encompassed by the soul, not [the soul] by [the body].[51]

The Muslim cannot understand how the human body is associated with the divine in the way that Abū Rā'iṭah explains, for the body is seen to be limiting the Word. In his analysis of Christological defences of the Eastern churches, Mark Beaumont explains this paradox:

> Christians claim that the eternal word was limited to a particular human body, while at the same time they believe that the eternal Word was fulfilling divine control over the entire creation. The Muslim concludes that Incarnation cancels out divine rule.[52]

Abū Rā'iṭah continues to explain that what caused God to be incarnated and become human was to deliver Adam and his descendants from 'the error that had mastered them'. He did have the power to do this without becoming human, but in a rather convoluted argument he explains that unless he became incarnated as a human, human beings would not have participated in the plan for their own salvation.[53] When people saw the divine nature in human flesh, they were able to respond to God's will, and for his part, God could show his goodness directly to people, something which cannot be done through sending human messengers alone. Finally, divine unity is explored through the discussion on death:

> The death of a human being and His disintegration is the separation of his soul and his body, and [the soul's] leaving [the body]. What statement is a greater contradiction between two things than this? You claim that God was united with His body in an eternal union, having no disintegration or no separation, then you describe [Him] as having been killed and died. It must be one of two things: either His union is a lasting and eternal union, then He cannot have been killed or died, or His union with His body is a transitory, separable union, because it is necessary for Him what is necessary for one who is killed and dies concerning a separation of His body from His divinity. Whichever of these two statements you assert, it will contradict your teaching.

> The Messiah, may he be praised, is God become human and he was only killed and died in His body, not in His divinity, and His death in His body was the separation of His created soul from His created body, not the abandoning of His body and His soul by His divinity.[54]

Christian apologists were keen to show the non-contradictory nature of the Incarnation. As Beaumont argues, Abū Rā'iṭah, being sensitive to Muslim rejection of God's 'sonship', is keen to stress that it was not God who took a son but the eternal Word of God who took a human body.[55]

These three examples of Arab Christian apologetics show how theology became the subject of polemics between Muslim and Christian scholars from the very beginning of Muslim theology, crystallising into intense discussions during the first three centuries of Islam. While many verses in the Qur'ān deny Christians the status of singularity in that Christians often fall into one of the many typologies of those who believe in God, Qur'ānic commentaries focus on Jesus as embodying Christianity's particular challenge to monotheism.[56] Christian understandings of Jesus' divinity meant that many Christians understood God's absoluteness in a way markedly different from the way the Muslim understood the transcendent. Thus, whether the focus lay on essence or attributes, refutation of Trinitarian beliefs formed an essential part of Christian–Muslim conversations to determine how God was one and three at the same time. Muslims refused to accept that plurality in a divine being could mean anything other than plural divine beings. The multivalent expressions of God's oneness had both philosophical and theological underpinnings. The Muslim philosopher al-Kindī (c.800–870), a central figure in the translation movement of Greek works into Arabic in ninth-century Baghdad, not only denied the multiplicity of God but emphasised that God is the cause of unity in everything else. God is one and stands outside the set of things which are one and many. It is in virtue of his oneness that he exercises causality over creation, for he is the only true agent:

> Since every one of the sensible things, and what attaches to sensible things, has both unity and multiplicity in it together, and any unity in it is an effect from a cause and is accidental in it and not by nature, and multiplicity is necessarily a collection of unities, therefore it is necessary that if there is no unity, there is no multiplicity at all.[57]

Furthermore, the very idea of how the divine and the human came into contact was constantly challenged in these works. This was within the milieu where the doctrine of God's oneness or *tawḥīd* was being debated with vigour by the Muʿtazilites who were using the style of speculative *kalām* or debate against other Muslims to distinguish between God and his creation.

In his translation and analysis of Abū ʿĪsā al-Warrāq's polemic against Christianity, David Thomas states that disputes around faith and the flourishing of polemical literature between Christians and Muslims contributed to the pluralist landscape of ninth-century Baghdad. In the Christological explanations of these Christian authors who wrote in Arabic, there is ample evidence of the requirement to state their doctrines and teachings in new ways which were sensitive to Muslim criticisms of the Trinity, but despite these discussions he concludes:

> As we examine the Christological explanations of these Christian authors who wrote in the Islamic world around the beginning of the third/ninth century, we can detect elements in the structure of their thought that appear to be sensitive towards the Qur'ānic portrayal of God and criticisms built upon it. They respond by presenting their teachings about the person of Christ in new ways. Alongside the particular Christological formulas and explanations they themselves advocate against other Christian sects, they now seek to defend points of belief that were not previously given prominence. Chief among these are the impossibility of God having a Son, and the illogicality of the divine changing when it became human in the act of uniting. While we cannot go as far as to say that in the Islamic context new Christologies were fashioned, we cannot avoid noticing the new emphases and configurations that were given to traditional explanations, which in consequence assumed distinctive forms. At the same time, Christian sects continued to express their beliefs in the Incarnation, and among themselves actively debated the varying interpretations of exactly how this uniting of divine and human had taken place.[58]

It is to Abū ʿĪsā al-Warrāq that we now turn to give us a sense of how one of the foremost Muslim intellectuals and theologians of the time wrote his refutation against Christian doctrines.[59] Thomas describes him as unsurpassed as a Muslim intellectual of his time, penetrating in his questioning and knowledge of other faiths, including Islam. While there is much controversy over his own Muslim stance and affiliation, many claiming that he was Shīʿa, others also linking him with Manichaeism and dualism, Thomas argues that it is most likely that he was really a religious sceptic. He was active in the second quarter of the ninth century and his writings cover non-Islamic religions, Shīʿī beliefs, and critical works on Islam.

Abū ʿĪsā's *Refutation against the Incarnation* is the second part of the author's ambitious work *Refutation of the Three Christian Sects (Kitāb al-Radd ʿalā al-thalāth firaq min al-Naṣārā)*. The work as a whole is a polemic against the main Christian doctrines of Trinity and Incarnation as held at the time by the major Christian sects, the Melkites, Jacobites and the Nestorians. Indeed, Abū ʿĪsā's style is of one who often addresses each of the sects separately, showing a deep knowledge of their internal divisions on doctrine. The format is 'question and answer' (*masāʾil wa-ajwiba*), a method prevalent in the great majority of Muslim polemical writing on Christianity. Thomas's translation *Against the Incarnation* follows from his earlier translation of the first section of the book, *Against the Trinity*, which was published in 1992. *Against the Incarnation* is the second and last part of the author's work. The following is a selection of writings from this second part which shows the style and nature of arguments by a scholar who, for all the controversies around his own Muslim beliefs, insisted on the oneness of God as traditionally understood in Islam. In the following section, the issue framed from the Muslim perspective is how the Word was united with the human being:

> Say to them all together, 'Tell us something about the uniting of the Word (*ittiḥād al-kalimat*) with the human being with whom it united. Was this an action of the word and not of the Father or the Spirit, or was it an action of the three hypostases? If they claim that the uniting was an action of the three hypostases, we say: Then why was it the uniting of the Word and not of the Father or the Spirit? And why was it the Word that

> united and not either of the others, although it had no part in the action of uniting that they did not have?
>
> And if they claim that the uniting was an action of the Word and not of the Father or the Spirit, they acknowledge an action of the Son which is other than the action of the Father or the Spirit. And they single him out in carrying out an act which the Father and the Spirit did not. But if it is possible for one of them to act alone without the others, this is possible for each of the other two hypostases. And if this is possible, it is possible for each of them alone to control a world without its two companions, and to create a creature without its two companions. This is a departure from their teachings.[60]

Abū ʿĪsā's argument is that if the three hypostases are equal in essence as Christians claim, then it is not possible to single out one as the doctrine of Incarnation requires. Why did only the Son become incarnate and not the other two? He further asks that if it is possible for the 'Word to act alone in uniting without the Father or the Spirit', then is it also possible that the Father and the Son might have effected a uniting for themselves? Furthermore, how can Christians be certain that the 'Father may not have united with a human in time past, or will not unite with one in time to come?'[61]

Staying with how the Word is united in Mary, Abū ʿĪsā questions at what moment the uniting took place. Did it happen at the birth and, if so, did the birth include the Word or did the birth only happen to the human? His argument is that if the birth only happened to the human and the human was not the Messiah, then this invalidates the teaching that Mary gave birth to the Messiah. Furthermore, it nullifies what has been foretold of Mary giving birth to a Divinity.

On the matter of the crucifixion Abū ʿĪsā asks whether the crucifixion and all the suffering happened 'to the body of the Messiah without this divinity, to his divinity without his body, or to his body and divinity together?' He poses an answer:

> If they claim that this happened to the body without the divinity, they move towards the teaching of the Nestorians. We say to them also: According to you the Messiah was other than the body (*ghayr al-jisd*), because according to you the Messiah was the divine and the universal human, or the eternal hypostasis possessing two substances. And this body was individual and was not the eternal hypostasis. So all these things affected someone who was not the Messiah in any respect.[62]

Abū ʿĪsā follows by asking if the divinity was crucified with the body. He says, 'If the Creator made him die, they are claiming that the Creator made the Creator die and that the Divinity made the Divinity die – may our Lord be exalted above this.' However:

> If they say: It was he who made himself die, we say: 'Then is it possible for the Father to make himself die as the Son made himself die; and likewise for the Spirit to make itself die, so that they will all be lifeless? This is complete confusion, although it is inescapable for them as long as they hold onto their principles.[63]

For Abū ʿĪsā, the need to clarify the ontological structure of the Messiah, and the way Divinity remains distinct as opposed to being caught up in the experiences associated with humanity, seem to be central contentions in his refutation against the Incarnation. His questions around the crucifixion aim to tease out exactly what was the nature of the Messiah who died, who caused whom to die, and he does not preoccupy himself with Christian concerns for salvation or atonement in the event of the crucifixion. The conceptual models of how to talk about God reveal that Muslims and Christians did not think that they were talking about a different God, but that they understood this God in very different ways.

The Trinity and the Incarnation were consistent points of debate between Muslims and Christians. Muslims could not accept that God who is eternal could be incarnate in time and that he could have a human birth from Mary. Resorting to metaphors was one way of explaining how the Word and the Spirit were not separable from God. Many of these discussions focus on the ontological approach to Christ, which is primarily concerned with how he relates to God and thereby the eternal, what scholars have called 'high' Christology. This Christology developed from the theme of the pre-existent Logos or Son of God who descends into our world (John1:14). The 'high' Christology acknowledges the divinity of Christ, but the term does not give the total picture of the full humanity of Christ, his human life encapsulated by some in the notion of 'low' Christology.

To end this discussion, the following is a section touching upon these very themes in the much celebrated and theologically rich conversation between the Nestorian Patriarch Timothy I and the Caliph al-Mahdī which dates just after 780. Most scholars of Christian–Muslim relations place this conversation within Christian conciliatory approaches to Islam. The East Syriac Catholicos, Timothy I, was invited by the ʿAbbāsid Caliph al-Mahdī to answer a series of questions about Christianity over two days. The discussion took place at Baghdad, while the Caliph's son, Harūn al-Rashīd, was conducting a campaign against the Byzantines, the very Christians who were persecuting the Nestorians. The following extract relates to the issue of Incarnation and the Trinity–Unity debate:

> And our King said to me: 'How was that Eternal One born in time?'—And I answered: 'It is not in His eternity that He was born of Mary, O our King, but in His temporalness and humanity.'—And our King said to me: 'There are, therefore, two distinct beings: if one is eternal and God from God as you said, and the other temporal, the latter is therefore a pure man from Mary.'—And I retorted: 'Christ is not two beings, O King, nor two Sons, but Son and Christ are one; there are in Him two natures, one of which belongs to the Word and the other one which is from Mary, clothed itself with the Word-God.'—And the King said: 'They are, therefore, two, one of them created and fashioned, and the other uncreated and unfashioned.'—And I said to him: 'We do not deny the duality of natures, O King, nor their mutual relations, but we profess that both of them constitute one Christ and Son.'
>
> And our King said to me: 'Do you believe in Father, Son and Holy Spirit?'—And I answered: 'I worship them and believe in them.'—Then our King said: 'You, therefore, believe in three Gods?'—And I replied to our King: 'The belief in the above three names consists in the belief in three Persons, and the belief in these three Persons consists in the belief in one God. The belief in the above three names consists therefore in the belief in one God. We believe in Father, Son and Holy Spirit as one God. So Jesus Christ taught us, and so we have learnt from the revelation of the books of the prophets. As our God-loving King is one King with his word and his spirit, and not three Kings, and as no one is able to distinguish him, his word and

his spirit from himself and no one calls him King independently of his word and his spirit, so also God is one God with His Word and His Spirit, and not three Gods, because the Word and the Spirit of God are inseparable from Him. And as the sun with its light and its heat is not called three suns but one sun, so also God with His Word and His Spirit is not three Gods but is and is called one God.'

Then our King said to me: 'Are the Word and the Spirit not separable from God?'—And I replied: 'No: never. As light and heat are not separable from the sun, so also (the Word) and the Spirit of God are not separable from Him. If one separates from the sun its light and its heat, it will immediately become neither light-giver nor heat-producer, and consequently it will cease to be sun, so also if one separates from God His Word and His Spirit, He will cease to be a rational and living God, because the one who has no reason is called irrational, and the one who has no spirit is dead. If one, therefore, ventures to say about God that there was a time in which He had no Word and no Spirit, such a one would blaspheme against God, because his saying would be equivalent to asserting that there was a time in which God had no reason and no life. If such adjectives are considered as blasphemy and abomination when said of God, it follows that God begat the Word in a divine and eternal way, as a source of wisdom, and had the Spirit proceeding from Him eternally and without any beginning, as a source of life. God is indeed the eternal source of life and wisdom; as a source of wisdom He imparts by His Word wisdom to all the rational beings, and as a source of life He causes life to flow to all the living beings, celestial and terrestrial alike, because God is the creator of everything by means of His Word and His Spirit.'

> Our King then said to me: 'Did Christ then worship and pray?' And I answered his Majesty: 'He did worship and pray.' And our King retorted saying: 'By the fact that you say that He worshipped and prayed, you deny His divinity, because if He worshipped and prayed, He is not God; if He was God, he would not have worshipped and prayed.' And I replied: 'He did not worship and pray as God, because as such He is the receiver of the worship and prayer of both the celestial and the terrestrial beings, in conjunction with the Father and the Spirit, but He worshipped and prayed as a man, son of our human kind. It has been made manifest by our previous words that the very same Jesus Christ is Word-God and man, as God He is born of the Father, and as man of Mary. He further worshipped and prayed for our sake, because He Himself was in no need of worship and prayer.'[64]

Timothy is at pains to explain that the plurality of natures within God does not mean that God's essence is not one; God's unity is not compromised by the Word and Spirit. The Muslim accusation that Christians 'make three'(*tathlīth*) is based on seeing this doctrine as tantamount to three separate entities in the Godhead. Timothy's response uses the analogy of the sun and its heat and light to show that God's Word and Spirit are not separable from him; just as the sun remains one despite its elements, so does God. Timothy goes further by adding that the Word and Spirit are essential to the nature of God, without which God would cease to be God. Later on, in response to how Christ prayed, Timothy emphasises the human nature of Christ in that he prayed as man for man and not for himself, for he had no need for prayer. This conversation is not just about the mode of relationship between God, his Word and

Spirit, but also shows the kinds of metaphors Christians used in responding to Muslim questioning and bewilderment at the relationship of the divine eternal essence to the human temporal being. But however perplexing Muslims found Christian explanations of divine unity in the Trinity, both Muslims and Christians challenged each other's definition of monotheism. As J. Sweetman summarises:

> An enthusiasm for monotheism and a dread of polytheism led to a doctrine of the unity of God which affected the conception of the divine essence. Men were not content to assert the unity of God as a defence against a plurality of gods, but also sought to extrude from the conception of the divine every vestige of multiplicity.[65]

These early discussions are fundamentally about points of doctrine in which Christians and Muslims explored how best to defend the notion of God's oneness. They did this ingeniously by observing both form and logic in their arguments to the extent that all kinds of apologetics on both sides appear theologically convincing. Interreligious dialogue today very rarely explores doctrines in the same way, often viewing the discussion of creeds and dogma as obstacles to better relations. In my opinion this is understandable but a shame. Such writings can be used today in the area of interreligious dialogue to show how believers can share a passion about their own beliefs but also be passionate about making these beliefs comprehensible to others. For in fact, similar conversations have the potential to enrich the encounter between Muslims and Christians rather than diminish good relations.

CHAPTER 3

Scholastic, Medieval and Poetic Debates

In Chapter 2, we looked at select writings to explore how God's nature was discussed by Christians and Muslims, especially the Christians of the Arabic/Syriac-speaking world. Christian theologians realised that despite some disagreement on the exact expression of the inner character of the doctrines of the Incarnation and the Trinity, both these doctrines were fundamental to an authentic faith in Christ. Even if these doctrines continued to be contentious between Christian groups centuries after the first ecumenical councils, they remained essential to the faith and had to be made intelligible to a Muslim audience which quite simply rejected any idea of an incarnation or trinity in God. Theologians wrestled with images and metaphors to try to convince other Christians and, more importantly, Muslims. In this chapter we shall analyse how certain concepts continued to drive mutual perceptions. This period of history takes us from the eighth/ninth centuries to the sixteenth century, and our focus is primarily on the Christians of the Latin West and Muslims across many parts of the East. This chapter also provides extracts of primary texts in translation to enable the reader to grasp the arguments as they were presented, rather than simply my own paraphrase.

The rise of Muslim writing on Christianity flourished in the intellectual context of speculative theology of *kalām* which began in the late eighth and early ninth centuries. Mustapha Shah offers a definition of the nature of *kalām*:

> Despite the somewhat pervasive background of the term *kalām* in the classical Islamic tradition, it is in the realm of religious dogma that the term, which literally denotes speech, acquired formal significance, serving as a generic name for the Muslim discipline of theology. The theology associated with *kalām* was not simply a catechism of religious creeds as sourced to scriptural dicta, but it also embodied the rational explication of theological doctrines. It was under the aegis of the *kalām* umbrella that a rich and diverse stock of literature was developed. This included treatises that expounded upon creeds; polemical tracts and epistles; historical surveys of religious movements and sects within the Islamic tradition; and even apologetic treatises dealing with Judaism, Christianity and Zoroastrianism.[1]

A leading authority on early Muslim theology, Joseph van Ess was convinced that Christian influences had exercised a key role in the inception of *kalām* and that converts from Christianity had served as conduits for the transmission of dialectical methods. He also remarked that the history of Islamic theology during the second and third centuries (eighth and ninth centuries) is essentially a history of Muʿtazilism.[2] There has been a tendency among researchers to restrict the religious and political ascendancy of the Muʿtazilites to the early years of ʿAbbāsid rule (750–850). More recently, however, Daniel Gimaret has shown that the movement's influence was chronologically more widespread.[3]

The Muʿtazila was a theological school which relied on rational arguments and logic as central principles. Its members engaged with a variety of Muslim and non-Muslim schools, sects and philosophies, and according to Guy Monnot they were 'the pioneers of polemical religious literature'.[4] They distinguished themselves from other Muslim theological schools by the development of their five principles, which can be briefly summarised as follows. The first is the oneness of God, which denied corporeality or anthropomorphism to God. The second principle is God's justice, which means that all of God's acts are good and that human beings have been given free will to choose their acts. The third principle is called 'the intermediate position', referring to the status of the Muslim who has committed grave sins and whether he is to be branded a believer or unbeliever. The fourth principle is referred to as 'the promise and the threat' in that God will reward those who have been obedient and punish those who have been disobedient to him. The fifth principle is commanding the right and forbidding the wrong, whereby Muslims are obliged to advise others to be obedient to God. One defining episode pertaining to Muʿtazilite history is the *mihna* (Inquisition) imposed by the ʿAbbāsid caliph al-Maʾmūn (813–833) on the advice of leading Muʿtazilite theologians, who wanted the doctrine of a created Qur'ān imposed upon the class of learned scholars; in other words, the Qur'ān was God's speech but created in time. This they based on their conviction of the pure unicity of God and thereby 'the necessity of denying that there could be any essential or objective attribute different or separate from the divine essence'.[5] The reason for the imposition of this doctrine has divided academic judgements. The orthodox champion of the *mihna* was the Sunnite scholar Ahmad ibn Hanbal (780–855). He along with a number of scholars refused to subscribe to the doctrine of the Qur'ān's createdness, arguing that there was nothing in the scriptural sources to substantiate this doctrine. For his views he was imprisoned and flogged on the instructions of the caliph al-Maʿmūn. After the death of al-Maʿmūn, the *mihna* continued during the successive caliphates before being rescinded by the caliph al-Mutawakkil in 847.[6]

The Muʿtazila school was divided into various groups, but there were two main schools, the Basra school and the Baghdad school.[7] The Muʿtazila emphasised rational demonstration of truths and for the most part this was reflected in the question–answer style of theological discussion. Scholastic theology was also cultivated by the Ashʿarite school, and the school's eponymous Abūʾl- Ḥasan al-Ashʿarī, had originally been famous for his association with the Muʿtazilites. Yet, at some point in his life, al-Ashʿarī renounced Muʿtazilism, and spent much of his intellectual life in refuting the theological theses of his former school of thought.

In both schools, a defining feature of their theological refutations of Christianity was concerned not so much with Christianity as a unified set of beliefs, but rather with the Trinity and the Incarnation, the uniting of the divine and the human in Christ. In this chapter we shall look at selections from three Muʿtazilite and one Ashʿarite writers. They are ʿAli ibn Rabbān al-Ṭabarī (d.855 or 861), Abū Uthmān ʿAmr b. Baḥr al-Jāḥiz (776–869), Abū Bakr al-Bāqillānī (c.950–1013) and Qāḍī Abū ʾl Hasan ʿAbd al-Jabbār (932–1025). Even a small selection of their writings shows that during this period Muslim theology was strong and flourishing in all dimensions, which included its intellectual engagement with Christian doctrines.

ʿAlī al-Ṭabarī was a Persian physician of Nestorian Christian background who produced one of the first encyclopaedias of medicine. He converted to Islam very late in his life and writes that until that time he was neglectful and unaware of the right direction. He wrote his famous *Kitāb al-din wa-l-dawla, Book of Religion and*

Empire, at the invitation of the caliph al-Mutawakkil (822–861), whom he thanks several times in the book for this honour. The text used here is the translation by A. Mingana published in 1922, *The Book of Religion and Empire*. Al-Ṭabarī explains in his prologue that the reason for writing the book is to show those to whom revelation was previously given how they have denied Muḥammad's prophecy as foretold by previous prophets:

> They have hidden his name and changed his portrait found in the Books of their prophets – peace be with them. I shall demonstrate this, disclose its secret, and withdraw the veil from it, in order that the reader may see it clearly and increase his conviction and his joy in the religion of Islam.[8]

Al-Ṭabarī's major defence is levelled at the Christians, though a small section at the end of the book depicts his arguments against the Jews. He writes that he has 'set forth one hundred and thirty arguments against them [Christians] from the Books of the prophets, apart form rational demonstrations, illustrative examples, and illuminating analogies'. Underlying many of the discussions in this book is the Christian refutation of Muḥammad's prophecy on the basis that it was not prophesied by anyone or in any scripture. Al-Ṭabarī argues at some length that prophets have been acknowledged and accepted throughout history for various reasons and many performed no miracles nor was their prophecy prophesied beforehand:

> If we ask the Christians why they disbelieve in the Prophet – peace be with him – they would say because of three reasons: first, because we do not see that a prophet has prophesied about

him prior to his coming; second, because we do not find in the Kur'ān the mention of a miracle or a prophecy ascribed to the man who produced it; third because the Christ has told us that no prophet will rise after Him. These are their strongest objections and I will refute them by the help of God. If I am able to prove that the contrary of what they assert is true, and that for our belief in prophets there is no such necessary condition as that they mention, they will have no more excuse before God and their conscience, and those who adduce such pleas and cling to them are in the path of unbelief and perdition.

The answer to their saying that no prophet has prophesied about the Prophet, and that the prophetic office of the prophets is not true and acceptable except when it is preceded by other prophecies, because he who believes in a prophet who has no previous prophecy about him would be in error and unbelief, is this: let them tell us who prophesied about the prophet Moses himself – may God bless him – or about David, or about Isaiah, or about Jeremiah, who are considered by them as the greatest of the prophets – peace be with them; and since there is no previous prophecy about them, he who believes in them would, therefore, contradict truth for falsehood, and thus incur the wrath of the Lord of the worlds. The answer to their saying that in the Kur'ān there is no mention of a miracle wrought by the prophet – may God bless and save him – and that he who has no record in his book of a sign or a miracle has no reason to be acknowledged, is this: let them show us the miracle wrought by David and recorded in his Psalter; if they do not find it for us, why and for what reason have they called him a prophet, while no prophet has previously prophesied about him, and there is no record of a miracle in his Book?[9]

Al-Ṭabarī has two tasks. The first is to show through his exegesis of the biblical prophets that Muḥammad's prophecy was already foretold in these books; the second is to argue that people have accepted earlier prophets even though their prophecies were not prophesied nor did many perform miracles. There is no difference therefore between these earlier prophets and Muḥammad. But he also uses biblical verses to refute other familiar polemical points:

> If somebody reprobates the saying of the Prophet – may God bless and save him – that in the world to come there is food and drink, the answer would be that the Christ – peace be with Him – declared also such a thing to His disciples when he drank with them and said to them: 'I will not drink of this fruit of the vine until I drink it another time with you in the kingdom of heaven.' In this He declared that in heaven there is wine and drink; and where drink is found, food and pleasures are not blamed. And Luke declares in his Gospel that the Christ – peace be with Him – said: 'You shall eat and drink at the table of my father.' And John declares that the Christ – peace be with Him – said, 'There are many mansions and dwellings at my Father's.'[10]

The theme of physical pleasures in the afterlife is brought up to show that Christians are accusing Muḥammad of emphasising physical pleasures because they are denying that which Christ has said about the afterlife. He tries to show through his own reverence for the prophets that Islam cannot be blamed for simply confirming past rules, those which had been brought by previous prophets. For al-Ṭabarī this includes issues of sacrifice, inherited from Abraham, and circumcision practised by Christ himself and by those who preceded Christ. In this list Al-Ṭabarī also includes divorce, and swearing by God, stating that the apostle Paul said that 'God made His promises to Abraham, in his seed and swore to him by Himself'.

Furthermore, al-Ṭabarī adds that all prophets, including Jesus, brought new rules for which they cannot be blamed as these were their prescriptions from God:

> If people were permitted to slight and reprobate divine orders and economy of this kind, one would be allowed to say about the Christ that He once believed in the Torah and said: 'I am not come to destroy it but to fulfil it; verily I say unto you, Till heaven and earth pass, one letter shall not pass from it', and then He openly contradicted Moses and flung the Torah aside to such an extent that the learned men of his community have reason to say openly and publicly: 'The Old Testament has gone and the New Testament has come and appeared. As to the pillar of the Torah – the prop of Judaism – its rites, its circumcision, its sacrifices, its feasts, its laws of retaliation, its decision, its priesthood and its altars, the Christ – peace be with Him – has abrogated and annulled all of them. He did not leave the Jews a feast, without abolishing it; a Sabbath, without infringing it; a circumcision without gently rejecting it; a sacrifice, without forbidding it; an altar, without despoiling it; and a priest, without calling him adulterous and profligate.[11]

Abū ʿUthmān ʿAmr b. Baḥr al-Jāḥiz (c.776–868/869), most probably of Ethiopian origin, was born and died in Basra. He was a true polymath, theologian, intellectual, and litterateur, ultimately known for his masterful and incisive Arabic prose. He wrote an enormous number of books on various subject matters. The work used here is from his *Risālah* (*Letter*) he wrote shortly before the caliph Al-Mutawakkil rose to power. Al-Mutawakkil is known in the history of Muslim annals as a ruler who persecuted non-Muslim and non-orthodox groups; this included destroying new churches, forcing Christians to wear distinct yellow markings on their clothing, and expelling many Christians from state service. In this *Risālah*, al-Jāḥiz covers an array of opinions about Christians, sometimes in the context of comparing Jews and Christians, and at other times by condemning Christians and their views as he understood them in his own socio-political context. He saw the Christians as an 'affliction' for the Muslims and accuses them of atheism because of their hypocrisy and wavering. He blames the Muslims for being impressed with the Christians and their bishops because of their wealth, appearance and prestigious professions, and accuses the Christians of 'entering private conversations with our weak-minded'.[12] The following quote is an example of his surprise at the growth of Christianity:

> And when we finally take into account the numerous wars of the Christians, their sterile men and women, their prohibition against divorce, polygamy, and concubinage – [is it not queer] that, in spite of all this, they have filled the earth, and exceeded all others in numbers and fecundity? Alas! This circumstance has increased our misfortunes, and made our trials stupendous! Another cause for the growth and expansion of Christianity is the fact that the Christians draw converts from other religions and give none in return (while the reverse should be true), for it is the younger religion that is expected to profit from conversion.[13]

For al-Jāḥiz, the one issue which remained intellectually incomprehensible was the Trinity. He wrote that 'By my life, any man who would profess a faith like Christianity would of necessity have to offer blind submission as an excuse as ever'.[14]

Al-Jāḥiz saw contradictions in Christian beliefs and the realities around him. Despite his social observations, he ends on the complex issue of Jesus' divinity, commenting that even those within the same sect of Christianity cannot agree on the nature of Jesus' divinity. To believe in this doctrine, one needs unqualified submission, which Al-Jāḥiz argues is probably the only way one can believe in the divinity of Christ. Finkel argues there is a vacillation in his thought because 'Jāḥiz reverts here to his element, to that corner of his restless soul from which he does not see the oneness of truth but the seven colors of its spectrum'.[15] However, David Thomas wonders whether if al-Jāḥiz is to be believed, it may explain the relatively harsh treatment by the caliph al-Mutawakkil towards Christians:

> He makes a telling list of criticisms, which even allowing for exaggeration, points to the Christians as a group on the margin of society who compensated by regarding themselves as socially and intellectually elite and their neighbours as inferior. It is not surprising that Muslim resentment at what would be seen as haughtiness should occasionally boil over into anger.[16]

Next we come to the works of Abū Bakr Muḥammad bin al-Tayyib al-Bāqillānī (d.1013), one of the most important theologians and philosophers of the Ash'arite school. As well as being a prolific writer and teacher, he was also a leading Mālikī jurist and served as a qāḍī for some time in a small jurisdiction near Baghdad. The work cited here is from his 'Refutation of the Christians' in his *Kitāb al-Tamhīd, The Book of Preliminaries*, written around 975 and considered to be one of the most important Sunnī texts of *kalām*.

Like most Ash'arites, al-Bāqillānī rejected any notion of incarnation or indwelling of the divine, or any of the attributes of the divine in the human form or in any created physical form. Thus, the Trinity and the Incarnation in which the divine and the human hypostases (*aqānīm*) meet in Christ remain fundamental points of debate.[17]

In this section al-Bāqillānī asks about the Trinity, where the Son and the Holy Spirit are particularities of the Father. His point is that if all three hypostases are equal, then why could the Father not be a particularity of the Son and Holy Spirit?

> Say to them: If the hypostases are one substance, and the Father's substance is the substance of the Son, and the substance of the Spirit is the substance of both of them, then why are the Son and Spirit, in that they are Son and Spirit, particularities of the Father, rather than each of them being Father and the Father a particularity to them?[18]

Al-Bāqillānī further locates the discussion on the uniting of the Word with the body in the disputes between the Nestorians, Melkites and Jacobites and the analogies they offer to explain how this uniting and indwelling came about. He writes that for some the uniting of the Word with the human nature was like a 'mingling and mixing of water with wine and milk', while for others 'It's in the way the form of a man appears in a mirror and polished, clean objects when he is in front of them, without the man's form inhering in the mirror.' Then there are those who say that the 'Word united with the body of Christ in the sense that it inhered in it without touching, mixing or mingling in the same way that I say God almighty dwells in the heavens and does not touch or mingle with it.' Al-Bāqillānī offers a rejection to each of these analogies with further questions, one of them being specifically to the Jacobites:

> And why should what was in itself temporal before the Uniting of the eternal with it not have become eternal at the Uniting with the eternal with it, so that it ceased to be flesh and blood at its Uniting with what united with it, and hence the two natures became one and what was not flesh and blood became flesh and blood, and what was flesh and blood became what was not flesh and blood? They will not find a way to reject this.[19]

As Thomas writes, al-Bāqillānī's 'approach can be described as bemusement at what for him is a ridiculous and wholly irrational portrayal of God, though his arguments attempt to show from within the logic of the doctrine itself its weaknesses and incoherence'. He adds that al-Bāqillānī 'was not engaged in dialogue or its equivalent, nor even polemic, but in a demonstration of the errors inherent in this alternative vision of the Godhead to the one he was promoting in the *Tamhīd*'.[20]

The issue of prophecy is also raised in terms of miraculous acts:

> Say to them: Why do you say that the Word of God united with the body of Christ but not the body of Moses or Abraham or any of the other prophets? If they say: Because of the signs performed and miracles made through Jesus the like of which humans are not capable of, such as raising the dead, healing the blind and the leper, making what is little a lot, turning water into wine, walking on the water, his ascension into heaven, healing the sick, making the crippled walk, and other miraculous signs. So he must have been divine, and the Word must

> have united with him; say to them: Why do you claim that Jesus was the performer and the originator of the signs you describe? Why do you deny that he was incapable of a small or great part of this, and that God almighty was the one who performed all this that appeared through him, and his position in this was the same as the other prophets when signs appeared through them?
>
> Then say to them: So why do you deny that Moses, peace be upon him, was divine, and that the Word united with him when he performed marvellous signs, such as changing the staff into a serpent with mouth, two eyes and orifices – it had not been a serpent before and there was no trace of eyes or mouth in it; and such as parting of the sea, drawing out this hand white and other things, and his causing locusts, lice, frogs, blood and so on, which humans cannot do? If they say: Moses was never the originator of any of this, but rather he used to pray and beseech God to show it through him; say to them: Then why do you deny that this was the case with Jesus, and that he used to beseech his Creator, Lord and Owner to show the signs through him?[21]

For al-Bāqillānī, Jesus performed miracles similar to the manner in which Moses also performed phenomenal miracles. Christians, however, claim that Moses prayed to God for signs, whereas Jesus' miracles lay in his divinity. Al-Bāqillānī states that the Christians deny that Jesus too prayed to God for signs and that if Jesus is divine in performing miracles, the same should be claimed for Moses. If the Word united with the body of Christ, why did it not unite with the body of Moses or any of the other prophets? These kinds of questions by Muslims reflect a rationalist style of argument taking the Christian defence seriously. However, they also reveal a complete reluctance to understand the Christian view of Jesus as Christ and the associated doctrines from a Christian logic and devotion.

The final extract comes from the medieval rationalist Muslim scholar Qāḍī Abū 'l-Ḥasan ʿAbd al-Jabbār al-Hamadhānī al-Asadābādī (932–1025), who was born in Hamadhān in Iran. He is considered to be the leading and the last of the great Muʿtazilite thinkers of his time, and wrote on a variety of Islamic sciences. Like al-Jāḥiz, he too was a follower of the Shāfiʿī school of law. He studied in Basra, which had become a seat of Muʿtazilite learning, and he later became a teacher of this theological school as well as becoming a chief judge or *qāḍī* in 970 in Rayy. ʿAbd al Jabbār lived under the dynasty of the Būyids and during this time there was a great interest in philosophy and rational thought, with Jews and Christians also engaged in the intellectual and political life of the empire. In inviting all kinds of poets, scholars, theologians and philosophers to their courts, Margaretha Heemskerk writes, 'The Būyids made their courts into centres of learning just as the ʿAbbāsid caliphs had done before them.'[22]

Before his appointment as chief judge, ʿAbd al-Jabbār began to dictate to his students a serious work on Muʿtazilite doctrine. This eventually became his biggest theological work, stretching over some twenty volumes and completed around 990. Its title is *Al-Mughnī fī Abwāb al-Tawḥīd wa – 'l-'Adl, Summa on the Topics of Unity and Justice*. 'Abd al-Jabbār included in this book a refutation of Christian doctrines, but did so in accordance with the traditional methods of the Muʿtazilite *mutakallimūn*.[23] David Thomas writes of this work:

> This was an ambitious undertaking by any account, a systematic presentation of Muʿtazili theology framed according to their two

main principles of divine oneness and justice, taking in the current issues in religious discourse of the time, all structured into a coherent description of the being of God in himself, the nature of his relationship with the world, and the appropriate forms of human conduct in the moral context in which they are set.[24]

For our purposes we will look at his other polemical work against Christianity, the *Critique of Christian Origins*. This is to be found in his larger work, *Tathbīt dalā'il al-nubuwwa* or *Confirmation of the Proofs of Prophethood*, which according to the author's own indication was written around 995. The quotes below are only a selection of the huge diversity of themes covered, but they still provide an insight into how 'Abd al-Jabbār's arguments were both different from and similar to those of his colleagues.[25] He explains towards the end of his book his reasons for writing the book:

> I have already mentioned that we do not intend to demonstrate the error of Christianity. We simply intend to demonstrate that the Christians deviated from the religion of Christ and opposed it in both doctrine and practice despite their determined testimony.[26]

The discussion around the nature of Christ through the Trinity continues to be a major point of accusation, although 'Abd al-Jabbār says that the Christians made up this innovation after Christ, thereby committing pure *shirk* and anthropomorphism of God:

> Do you see that you are saying: a god who is the Father, Begetter, Living, Omnipotent, Without Beginning, Knowing, Creator and Provider; and a god is the Son, Begotten, Word, Living, Without Beginning, Creator, Provider, neither the

> Father nor the Begetter, and that it is not possible that he be the Begetter or the Father; and god who is the Holy Spirit, Living, Knowing, Without beginning, Creator and Provider? Then you say these are three hypostases. You say that each one of them is a god and a Lord, Without Beginning. You refrained from a general affirmation [of three gods] but you gave the details. The only thing that prevents the Christians from putting forth the statement that there are three, separate, different gods (which they have given in meaning) is that they affirm the Books of God, Mighty and Exalted, which Jesus affirmed. They are filled with monotheism, they declare that He alone is Without Beginning and that he does not resemble [created] things.[27]

He writes that the real purpose of confession is to raise money for the churches and that in any case Christians have no fear of hell. This is because 'They believe that Christ killed himself to safeguard them from sins and punishment.' Furthermore, it is Christ who forgives them and asks his father to forgive them.[28] In ʿAbd al-Jabbār's view, Christians are also very ignorant of Christ because of the conflicting accounts of his life in the Gospels and the length of time that exists between the writers of the Gospels and Christ himself. But one of his greatest criticisms of Christians is in their claim to attribute miracles to their religious leaders be they monks or priests. This adoration of saints meant that they ask for God's mercy on these leaders and treat the graves as a shrine.[29]

ʿAbd al-Jabbār is keen to demonstrate, through a variety of arguments against Christians as a people, their various sects, the Gospels and Christian beliefs and rituals, that the Christians have misunderstood what Christ taught and have wrongfully rejected Christ, whose true role was that of a servant and prophet of God.[30] Furthermore,

Christians make saints out of any who claim to be able to perform wonders without needing any logical evidence. For ʿAbd al-Jabbār, Christians misunderstood Jesus because they also misunderstood the purpose of religious leaders. This kind of polemic addressed to the Christians contests what I call the basic dogmas of Christianity by pulling apart the logic of its doctrines in ways which made sense to Muslims. What the Muslims did not do was to address what faith in Christ actually meant to Christians. They did not speak of the drama of the passion, the relationship between Jesus and Christians who spoke of the realm of the Holy Spirit which breathes new life for those who are 'in Christ' so that he may be 'in' them. Unity between Christ and God means unity between Christ and humankind. The particular Christian concept of love which permeates this relationship, its consequences in all aspects of faith and society, did not form the basis of most of Muslim polemics against Christianity.

Our venture into Latin Christianity and its attitude to Islam begins with Thomas Aquinas. In his analysis of Thomas Aquinas's views on Islam, James Waltz questions the sources Thomas may have used which informed his knowledge of Islam and subsequently influenced his line of argument against Muslims.[31] He posits the view that what Thomas needed was a concise summary of Muslim beliefs and ideas with some Christian interaction. This summary he found in the *Summa totius haeresis Saracenorum* or *The Summary of the Entire Heresy of the Saracens*, prepared by Peter the Venerable, abbot of Cluny, in the mid-twelfth century (1092–1156).[32] This may well be true to some extent, and for this and other reasons a short note on Peter the Venerable merits mention before we turn to Thomas and others of the medieval era.

The twelfth century was a time of warfare between Christians and Muslims. The First Crusade ended when Jerusalem was seized on behalf of the Pope in 1099. Less than fifty years later, Turkish Muslim forces regrouped, and the Turks took Edessa, in 1144. There then followed the Second Crusade (1147–49), and the Third Crusade (1189–92). All had papal approval. Christian support was marshalled against a Muslim adversary. Throughout the twelfth and into the thirteenth century, European Christendom had a double mission: to kill Muslims and to retake Christian lands occupied by infidel Moors. Peter was also of the opinion that winning access to the Holy Places was a legitimate cause, but that what was not legitimate was the manner in which Christians were attempting to achieve it. It was not the 'sword' but the 'Word' which was needed to convert people to Christ. By the time of Peter's translation project, 'literate Muslim scholars in Baghdad and the Islamic West had seen Arabic versions of the Christian Scriptures for over two centuries'.[33] Similarly, Christian scholars were by no means ignorant of the scholarship emerging at that time, particularly from the Islamic world. Many Christian authorities were alarmed that the best and brightest minds were not Christian, but rather heretical Muslims.[34] The medieval Christian ego may also have accounted for the widespread acceptance of Peter's version of Islam:

> In support of this suggestion about [the image of Islam that was created] as a response to a superior culture it is to be noted that, where the Muslim perception of Christianity emphasized its intellectual weaknesses, the Christian perception of Islam, without neglecting the intellectual side, gave rather more weight to moral weaknesses. This meant that Christians could feel that, even if the Muslims were superior to them in various cultural matters, yet they, besides having a true and thus better religion, were in many ways morally superior to the Muslims.[35]

In his seminal work on Peter and Islam, James Kritzeck writes that Peter was shocked that such a large heresy as Islam had not been addressed as other heresies throughout Christian history, but concluded that no-one had yet encountered Islam because no-one knew about it.[36] With this in mind, in 1142 Peter set about commissioning the first Arabic to Latin translations of several primary Muslim texts which included a translation of the entire Qur'ān into Latin by Robert of Ketton. The manuscripts probably came from Toledo in Spain, but the translators were based in the northern Spanish city of Nájera. Along with this *corpus toledanum*, Peter included his own *Summa totius haeresis Saracenorum*, or *Summary of all the Heresies of the Saracens*. The translations of Muslim texts produced by Peter the Venerable, as well as his own responsive texts, collectively became known as the Cluniac Collection. While much in this collection was inaccurate, it still presented an improvement on what had existed before and in reality meant that for the first time the West had an instrument for the serious study of Islam.[37]

Peter tries to dispel the commonly held twelfth-century perception that Muslims were polytheists by emphasising Muslim monotheism, but not in the way Muslims themselves understood revelation. For Peter, the Qur'ān was not revealed by Gabriel to Muḥammad but formed by a combination of Christian heresies and Jewish myths.[38] He called Islam a heresy which had sprung up from 'the diabolical spirit' and the 'greatest error of all errors'.[39] So while Muslims did believe in one God, their denial of the Trinity, incarnation, crucifixion and resurrection meant that they had completely distorted the Christian truth. The position of Islam as a Christian heresy was pervasive in some of the early medieval views of Islam as reflected in Peter's own questioning:

> I cannot clearly decide whether the Mohammedan error must be called a heresy and its followers heretics, or whether they are to be called pagans. For I see them, now in the manner of heretics, take certain things from the Christian faith and reject other things.... For in company with certain heretics (Mohammad writes so in his wicked Koran), they preach that Christ was indeed born of a virgin, and they say that he is greater than every other man, not excluding Mohammad.... They acknowledge that he was the Spirit of God, the Word – but not the Spirit or the Word as we either know or expound. They insanely hold that the passion and death of Christ were not mere fantasies, but did not actually happen.... They hold these and similar things, indeed, in company with heretics.[40]

In his survey of heresies in the medieval period, Norman Daniel, a leading authority on the medieval Christian 'image' of Islam, states that 'Islam was reckoned the greatest enemy of the Christian Church'. But in calling Islam a heresy, 'There is almost a family of Christian error in which Islam may be found a place. The great proportion of Christian truth contained in Islamic belief made this possible although as a heresy, Islam would always remain peculiarly formidable and, in fact, unique.'[41] Many discovered that Muslims shared much with Christian thought but differed on the meaning of certain doctrines and concepts. Peter is vehement in his accusation that Muḥammad is part of a satanic scheme to damage the Christian Church. What Muḥammad advanced were the teachings of Arius, who had been condemned at the First Council of Nicaea in 325 for denying the idea that the Father, Son and Holy Spirit are of the same exact substance and are co-equally God. For Peter, Muḥammad was the mean between Arius and the Antichrist.

In Muslim deviation from spiritual truth, Peter also stressed the physical pleasures, a paradise of eating and drinking which Muḥammad had used to entice 'the carnal minds of men'. This was a theme which Thomas was to follow up in some detail in his own polemics.

Thomas Aquinas (1225–74) was an Italian Dominican priest of the Roman Catholic Church who ranks among the most influential philosophers and theologians in the West. He was raised in the Benedictine monastery of Monte Cassino and completed his initial studies at the University in Naples recently established by the famous emperor Frederick II. It was here that Thomas first came across Aristotle's philosophy with which he developed an enduring fascination. As Henk Schoot writes:

> Aquinas would employ and reinterpret Aristotle in undertaking his most important task: explaining the Bible, disputing theological questions, and preaching. One can hardly pinpoint any area of theology where Aristotle is not employed: whether it is the doctrine of God, the question of the eternity of the world, the discussion of human moral life, natural law, politics, anthropology. His influence is everywhere. One could call this 'Greek' influence, but because of the way Aristotle was transmitted to the West, it is Islamic as well. For it is through a number of Islamic scholars that the West received most of the teaching of Aristotle: their Arabic translations as well as their commentaries were translated into Latin and studied in the West. In fact, whenever one tries to describe Aquinas's relation to Islam, one should make a distinction between Islam as a religion and Islam as the religion of a number of very great philosophers.[42]

Within the course of two decades he wrote and dictated a huge number of works most of which are still read today. His two largest theological treatises are *Summa contra Gentiles* and the *Summa Theologiae*. He is also considered the foremost thinker of the medieval period to bridge the divide between Christian thought and Muslim philosophy. Thomas saw the philosophical contributions from other faiths and the faith interlocutors as a spur to understanding his own tradition. He gave intellectual attention to the inherited philosophies of the Jew Moses Maimonides (1135–1204) and the Muslim Ibn Sīna or Avicenna (980–1037) to articulate his own understanding of certain theological concepts. Norman Daniel writes that Thomas 'can scarcely be counted among writers on the religion of Islam', but others have tried to dispel this by their focus on the nature of Thomas's engagement with Islam rather than the quantity of writings. In this chapter we will look primarily at his arguments in the *Summa contra Gentiles*, which is said to have been written at the request of Raymundus of Peñaforte, Thomas Aquinas's former general master, who was the driving force behind the Dominican effort to preach the Gospel to Jews, Muslims and 'heretics'.[43]

Thomas begins with a kind of preamble to the purpose of this work which is to speak of God in the pursuit of wisdom. For Thomas, the pursuit of wisdom was the most noble of all human endeavours because it is through this pursuit that 'man is joined to God in friendship'. Thomas was well aware of the gravity of his task:

> And so, in the name of the divine Mercy, I have the confidence to embark upon the work of a wise man, even though this may surpass my powers, and I have set myself the task of making known, as far as my limited powers will allow, the truth that the Catholic faith professes, and of setting aside the errors that are

> opposed to it. To use the words of Hilary: 'I am aware that I owe this to God as the chief duty of my life, that my every word and sense may speak of Him' [*De Trinitate* I, 37].

He then almost immediately places the pagans and the Muslims in one group, a group requiring a different kind of convincing about the truth of the Catholic faith as neither pagans nor Muslims accept the scriptural authority of the Old or the New Testament:

> It is difficult because some of them, such as the Mohammedans and the pagans, do not agree with us in accepting the authority of any Scripture, by which they may be convinced of their error. Thus, against the Jews we are able to argue by means of the Old Testament, while against heretics we are able to argue by means of the New Testament. But the Muslims and the pagans accept neither the one nor the other. We must, therefore, have recourse to the natural reason, to which all men are forced to give their assent. However, it is true, in divine matters the natural reason has its failings.[44]

For Thomas, the Christian truth is the supreme truth and the conversion of the world to this faith is the clearest witness of the signs given in the past. In Thomas's view, the Christian faith possessed truths 'that surpass every human intellect; the pleasures of the flesh are curbed; it is taught that the things of the world should be spurned'. The fact that human beings have embraced these truths was the greatest of miracles, a 'manifest work of divine inspiration'. God had foretold this would happen through ancient books and prophets 'held in veneration among us Christians, since they give witness to our faith'.[45] However, he contrasts the uniqueness of the

Christian faith with the approach of Muḥammad and the spread of Islam:

> On the other hand, those who founded sects committed to erroneous doctrines proceeded in a way that is opposite to this. The point is clear in the case of Muhammad. He seduced the people by promises of carnal pleasure to which the concupiscence of the flesh goads us. His teaching also contained precepts that were in conformity with his promises, and he gave free rein to carnal pleasure. In all this, as is not unexpected, he was obeyed by carnal men. As for proofs of the truth of his doctrine, he brought forward only such as could be grasped by the natural ability of anyone with a very modest wisdom. Indeed, the truths that he taught he mingled with many fables and with doctrines of the greatest falsity. He did not bring forth any signs produced in a supernatural way, which alone fittingly gives witness to divine inspiration; for a visible action that can be only divine reveals an invisibly inspired teacher of truth. On the contrary, Muhammad said that he was sent in the power of his arms – which are signs not lacking even to robbers and tyrants. What is more, no wise men, men trained in things divine and human, believed in him from the beginning. Those who believed in him were brutal men and desert wanderers, utterly ignorant of all divine teaching, through whose numbers Muhammad forced others to become his followers by the violence of his arms. Nor do divine pronouncements on the part of preceding prophets offer him any witness. On the contrary, he perverts almost all the testimonies of the Old and New Testaments by making them into fabrications of his own, as can be seen by anyone who examines his law. It was,

> therefore, a shrewd decision on his part to forbid his followers to read the Old and New Testaments, lest these books convict him of falsity. It is thus clear that those who place any faith in his words believe foolishly.[46]

Here Thomas touches on several themes which provide a basis for Christian polemics against Islam, but he also adds his own specific critique. Thomas is keen to stress that the 'truths' Muḥammad brought were fundamentally doctrines mixed with falsehoods with no divine supernatural quality to his teachings. Such teachings appealed to desert wanderers. Furthermore, the charge of concupiscence and carnal pleasure as a means of enticing people to Islam featured often in Christian–Muslim polemics and a fundamental accusation of how Muḥammad 'seduced' people to the faith. This is a theme taken up by Thomas in Book 4 in more detail when he discusses life after resurrection. Islam (and Judaism), unlike Christianity, promised people sexual and other pleasures as a reward for virtue whereas Christianity offered eternal bliss. Thomas devotes much time to his claim that human happiness does not lie in bodily pleasures, chiefly in food and sex:

> By this, of course, one avoids the error of the Jews and of the Saracens, who hold that in the resurrection men will have use for food and sexual pleasure as they do now. And even certain Christian heretics have followed them; they hold that there will be on earth for a thousand years an earthly kingdom of Christ, and in that space of time 'they assert that those who rise again shall enjoy the leisure of immoderate carnal banquets, furnished with an amount of meat and drink such as not only to shock the feeling of the temperate, but even to surpass the measure of

> credulity itself; such assertions can be believed only by the carnal. Those who do believe them are called by the spiritual Chiliasts, a Greek word, which we may literally reproduce by the name Millenarians'; so Augustine says in the *City of God* [XX, 7, 1].[47]

To put this into some context, it is worth briefly noting traditional Muslim perspectives on death and resurrection Once resurrection has taken place at the appointed hour (*sa'a*), it is said that bodies will be reunited with their souls or spirits. After passing through several stages, people will ultimately know their fate. The descriptions of damnation in hell are terrifyingly graphic. Blasts of smoke, boiling and unquenchable thirst await those who have rejected God. But despite the theme of unending torment in hell, it is the delights of a future life of which people are in denial. Sensual images of rivers of milk and honey, pure, non-intoxicating wines in the form of *tasnīm* and *rahīq*, silken couches, jewel-encrusted thrones, black-eyed houris and youths described as 'pearls well-guarded' dominate the popular imagination of heavenly delights. Whether such images are to be understood literally or allegorically, Islamic thought is not apologetic about the heavenly fulfillment of human physical desires. This has been the case even when Christian polemicists have accused Muslims of being obsessed with the flesh and for not understanding that in the next life we are all children of God in eternal life for whom such physical pleasures do not matter. As Frithjof Schuon writes in his classic work *Islam and the Perennial Philosophy*:

> Christianity distinguishes between the carnal in itself and the spiritual in itself, and is logical in maintaining this alternative in the hereafter; Paradise is by definition spiritual, therefore it excludes the carnal. Islam, which distinguishes between the

> carnal that is gross and the carnal that is sanctified, is just as logical in admitting the latter into its Paradise. To reproach the Garden of the Houris for being too sensual, according to the down to earth meaning of the word, is quite as unjust as to reproach the Christian paradise for being too abstract.[48]

Yet for Thomas, seduction to Islam was relatively easy also because the truth of Islam did not require any supernatural manifestation but could be understood by anyone with 'modest wisdom'. Underlying much of Thomas's teaching is that although the truth of the Christian faith surpasses the capacity of reason, nevertheless 'that truth that the human reason is naturally endowed to know cannot be opposed to the truth of the Christian faith'. For Thomas the Christian faith 'promises spiritual and eternal goods' and that is why there are many things proposed which transcend human sense. He writes that we are ordained towards a higher good than human fragility can experience in the present life and 'That is why it was necessary for the human mind to be called to something higher than the human reason here and now can reach.'[49] Muḥammad's message, however, did not contain this kind of spiritualism and that is why no wise men believed him but only those who were brutal and 'utterly ignorant of all divine teaching'. Even these people Muḥammad forced to become his followers through violence. But the theme which resonates most with earlier refutations is the theme of Muḥammad's prophecy. Thomas states that previous prophets had not foretold his prophecy and that Muḥammad had not only used the Old and New Testaments by 'making them into fabrications of his own' but had forbidden his followers to read these scriptures for fear that his followers would find out the truth. What is interesting here is the emphasis on the spiritual dimension of Christianity, the irreducible otherness of a faith in which doctrines went beyond human reason. This is contrasted not so much with Islam but with Muḥammad, a person whose appeal lay not in his reasoned or transcendent faith but in the promise of sensual pleasures.

The second of Thomas's works in which he addresses Muslim beliefs, *De Rationibus Fidei* or *On the Reasons for the Faith Against Muslim Objections,* was written in 1264 and addressed to the Cantor of Antioch. Joseph Kenny writes that this work by Thomas follows right on the heels of his longer *Summa contra Gentiles*, completed that same year. We do not know who the Cantor of Antioch was, except that he must have been in charge of music in the cathedral. Perhaps his bishop, the Dominican Christian Elias, referred him to Thomas. The questions the Cantor asks must have been the subject of lively discussions in a city where Latin Christians mixed with Eastern Christians and Muslims.[50]

In the opening chapter Thomas is clear on what the Christian faith is essentially about:

> The Christian faith principally consists in acknowledging the holy Trinity, and it specially glories in the cross of our Lord Jesus Christ. For 'the message of the cross', says Paul (1 Corinthians 1:18), is 'folly for those who are on the way to ruin, but for those of us who are on the road to salvation it is the power of God'.
>
> Our hope is directed to two things: (1) what we look forward to after death, and (2) the help of God which carries us through this life to future happiness merited by works done by free will.
>
> The following are the things you say the Muslims attack and ridicule: They ridicule the fact that we say Christ is the Son of God, when God has no wife (Qur'ân 6:110; 72:3); and they

> think we are insane for professing three persons in God, even though we do not mean by this three gods.
>
> They also ridicule our saying that Christ the Son of God was crucified for the salvation of the human race (Qur'ân 4:157–8), for if almighty God could save the human race without the Son's suffering, he could also make man so that he could not sin.
>
> They also hold against Christians their claim to eat God on the altar, and that if the body of Christ were even as big as a mountain, by now it should have been eaten up.[51]

Precisely what is the actual reality and tone of Muslim questioning remains unclear from Thomas's arguments. Furthermore, it is difficult to ascertain from this work how much knowledge Thomas had of Muslim dogma, although it is well established that he was hugely influenced by his knowledge of Muslim philosophy largely through the works of al-Farābī and Ibn Rushd (Averroës).[52] Whether Thomas had read the Qur'ān, to which he gives no references, also remains uncertain. But if this was primarily addressing a Christian audience, he does show some knowledge of those particular issues which historically baffled Muslim understanding of Christian doctrine. These are the Trinity, the nature of Sonship, and Christ's crucifixion for human salvation.

Thomas displays some knowledge of Muslim beliefs about Jesus and rejects these on the grounds that Muslims can only think of relationships in carnal terms:

> First of all we must observe that Muslims are silly in ridiculing us for holding that Christ is the Son of the living God, as if God had a wife. Since they are carnal, they can think only of what is

> flesh and blood. For any wise man can observe that the mode of generation is not the same for everything, but generation applies to each thing according to the special manner of its nature. In animals it is by copulation of male and female; in plants it is by pollination or generation; and in other things in other ways.
>
> God, however, is not of a fleshly nature, requiring a woman to copulate with to generate offspring, but he is of a spiritual or intellectual nature, much higher than every intellectual nature. So generation should be understood of God as it applies to an intellectual nature. Even though our own intellect falls far short of the divine intellect, we still have to speak of the divine intellect by comparing it with what we find in our own intellect.
>
> In the divine persons there are not three numerically different divine natures, but necessarily only one simple divine nature, since the essence of God's word and of his love is not different from the essence of God. So we profess not three gods, but one God, because of the one simple divine nature in three persons.[53]

In Thomas's view, it is because of the Muslim approach to generation that Muslims are unable to think of Sonship in any way other than in sexual terms. Thomas emphasises that the concept of generation differs according to the nature of things and God's nature is not that of flesh. It is important to think of God's divine nature in intellectual terms, even though the human intellect is unable fully to comprehend divine intellect.

Thomas accuses Muslims of their inability to understand the concept of varying natures. He then calls Muslims blind for not understanding the mystery of the son of God dying. It was not the divine nature but the human nature of the son which died.

> A similar blindness makes Muslims ridicule the Christian Faith by which we profess that the Son of God died, since they do not understand the depth of such a great mystery. First of all, lest the death of the Son of God be misinterpreted, we must first say something about the incarnation of the Son of God. For we do not say that the Son of God underwent death according to his divine nature, in which he is equal to the Father who is the foundational life of everything, but according to our own nature which he adopted into the unity of his person.[54]

The discussion of Jesus' death continues in chapter 7, where Thomas states:

> First of all, we must observe that Christ assumed a human nature to repair the fall of man, as we have said. Therefore, according to his human nature, Christ should have suffered and done whatever would serve as a remedy for sin. The sin of man consists in cleaving to bodily things and neglecting spiritual goods. Therefore the Son of God in his human nature fittingly showed by what he did and suffered that men should consider temporal goods or evils as nothing, lest a disordered love for them impede them from being dedicated to spiritual things. Thus Christ chose poor parents, although perfect in virtue, lest anyone glory in mere nobility of flesh and in the wealth of his parents. He led a poor life to teach us to despise riches. He lived without titles or office so as to withdraw men from a disordered desire for these things. He underwent labour, thirst, hunger and bodily afflictions so that men would not be fixed on pleasure and delights and be drawn away from the good of virtue because of the hardships of this life. In the end he underwent

> death, so that no one would desert the truth because of fear of death. And lest anyone fear a shameful death for the sake of the truth, he chose the most horrible kind of death, that of the cross. Thus it was fitting that the Son of God made man should suffer and by his example provoke men to virtue, so as to verify what Peter said (1 Peter 2:21): 'Christ suffered for you, and left an example for you to follow in his steps.'

In this view of Christ, Thomas is keen to emphasise the assumed lowliness and poverty of Christ to show people that temporal goods mean nothing against the spiritual life. He speaks of Christ 'choosing' his horrible death on the cross for the sake of human virtue and redemption.[55] Despite Christian descriptions of Christ's life being one of poverty, chastity and ultimately suffering and sacrifice for others, it would appear that Muslim questions and responses chose not to focus on what his life and death meant for Christians. Rather, they were more interested in challenging Christian understanding of the Incarnation and the Trinity, i.e. what did Christ's relationship to God say about the very structure of Christian monotheism. For their part, Christians for several centuries challenged Muslims about their own understanding of God's oneness. On the other hand, however, Christians were particularly critical of Muḥammad's life and baffled as to how Muslims saw in such a life prophecy and divine guidance.

The above shows how prominent Christian scholars recognised monotheistic beliefs in Islam, albeit they considered them to be an incomplete kind of monotheism. This is partly because Muslim views on Jesus did not agree with many of the fundamentals of Christian doctrines, and partly because of the Christian contempt for Muḥammad's teachings. There is a strong sense that people were lured into Islam with its promises of carnal pleasures and that

Muḥammad may have taught some good things but was essentially an imposter. That Islam recognised some aspects of Christian teaching on Jesus but rejected the fundamentals of Sonship and Incarnation resulted in seeing Islam not as a separate faith but rather as a Christian heresy and therefore a teaching which was as threatening as it was deceiving. Muḥammad and the Qur'ān dwelled on God but they rejected the human manifestation of God, the very nature of reciprocity between God and man. Muslims believed in Jesus but not in a life which participated in Christ. In denying the crucifixion, Muslims denied not just an event but the ontological necessity of the ultimate expression of God's love.

In the realm of Latin Christianity the period 1378–1418 is identified as an era in which Europe was at risk of serious fracture with the experience of the Great Western Schism. At its worst, there were three popes, three curias and three college of cardinals, all of whom had different countries lining up to offer support for one or the other.[56] The debate was essentially one of power – does power reside with the Papacy or the Councils? During the 1500s, the concentration on local issues combined with the ending of the crusades, and the erosion of the crusading spirit resulted in European interest in Islam going into a state of suspension. But during the first half of the fifteenth century, European Christians looked towards Constantinople, which, as Nicholas Rescher writes, was a city besieged:

> That great city had slipped by gradual stages into the state of an isolated enclave existing as a beleaguered Christian island within the hostile surrounding sea of the Ottoman Turks. This situation led, on the one hand to an interest in a possible reconciliation between the Church of Rome and that of the East. On

> the other hand, the Turkish threat to Constantinople re-aroused the European interest in Islam which had become dormant since the fervour of the Crusades. The fall of the city in 1453 saw a revival in the Christian polemic against Islam.[57]

Inigo Bocken, however, paints a far more dramatic picture of what the loss of Constantinople to the troops of Mehmet II actually meant to many Christians:

> Until 1453, Islam was seen more as an exterior reflection, a reminder of the unfinished character of the earthly realisation of the City of God. In the traditional notion of a teleologically oriented order (*ordo*) the otherness of Islam had its place as a kind of obstinate obstacle, which sharpened the intellectual weapons for the realisation of a Christian life to be overcome at the end of history (or earlier, if possible). The year 1453 marks a turning point of this model and it is in fact the symbolic end of the reign of metaphysics or order as an interpretative framework of culture and society.[58]

It was in this climate that the philosopher, theologian and cardinal Nicholas of Cusa (1401–64) rose to prominence. Nicholas studied Latin, Greek, Hebrew and later Arabic, and began his public life in 1421 at the Council of Basel. Here he became a passionate advocate for the religious and political unity of Christendom and in 1437 travelled to Constantinople to meet the patriarch of the Greek Orthodox Church in order to negotiate the reunification of the two branches of Christianity. Though his efforts were not successful, this was an important step in the history of ecumenical dialogue. He was created a cardinal by Nicholas V in 1448.

Nicholas wrote his famous dialogue *De pace fidei, On the Peace of Faith* and later his commentary on the Qur'ān, the *Cribratio Alkorani, Sifting of the Qur'ān* (1461). The latter was written under the aegis of his friend Pope Pius II and while it is not a blanket rejection of the Qur'ān, it is still a work of Christian polemics against Islam. For Nicholas, the Qur'ān is of genuine religious merit, but heavily influenced by the Old and New Testaments. Muḥammad hid the secrets of the Gospels from the Arabs and he also went against God's commands in trying to impose Islam on the Arabs.[59] The Qur'ān is 'a mixture in which the sound grains of truth are intermingled with the chaff of falsity'. Muḥammad's basic impulse was good, but he went astray (because of heretical Christians and corrupting Jews) despite having caught glimpses of Christian truth. Nicholas covers a variety of material in the Qur'ān and places them in his own Christian understanding. Below are two extracts in which the first one explains that Abraham's true faith was Christianity because he knew that through Christ he would obtain immortal life.

> But if you rightly understand, O Arab: it is not the case that Abraham existed before Christ – as the Koran alleges in a certain place and consequently denies that Abraham was a Christian. Instead, Christ, who is the Son of God and is co-eternal with God His Father, existed before Abraham. Thus, we read in the Gospel that Christ said: 'Before Abraham was, I am.' Therefore, [Abraham] saw through a prophetic spirit that at some time the Messiah would come into the world as mediator and saviour. And Abraham believed that without the Messiah neither he himself nor anyone [else] would have access to God the Father. And so, Abraham was a Christian, and he hoped that by means of Christ he would certainly obtain immortal life.[60]

This passage contrasts with the Qur'ānic stance on Abraham as a *ḥanīf*, a person who had surrendered himself to one God and rejected idolatry. But from the Islamic perspective Abraham is pre-Christian and pre-Jewish. In the second passage Nicholas juxtaposes what he sees as good in the Qur'ān with what shocks him. It is the paradox of the sexual and the sacral, and the manner in which the afterlife in the Qur'ān through Muḥammad promises sensual pleasures. For medieval Christianity, nothing seemed more sinful about Islam than its promises and descriptions of sensual reward as described in the Qur'ān, even without the exaggerated tone often inserted by the Christian polemicists. Nicholas expresses his bafflement at the Qur'ān which praises chastity, encourages cleanliness and tells the believers how much God loves the good and that 'the unqualifiedly greatest [gift] is nothing but everlasting, incorporeal joy'. Yet at the same time:

> But subsequently I was taken aback by [the Koran's] so often having made mention of maidens and their breasts and of lustful physical copulation in Paradise – saying, [for example,] in Chapter 87 that such copulation is God's best reward for believers. And I was ashamed to read these vile things. And I said to myself: 'If Muhammad ascribes to God this book full of vileness, or if he himself wrote [it] and attributes its authority to God, then I am amazed that those wise and chaste and virtuous Arabs, Moors, Egyptians, Persians, Africans, and Turks who are said to be of this law esteem Muhammad as a prophet. [For] his life cannot be emulated by anyone who aspires unto the Kingdom of Heaven, where [people] do not marry but are like the angels, as Christ has taught. For no one speaks so vilely of such vile things unless he is full of all such vileness; for out of the abundance of the heart the mouth speaks. And that this was true.[61]

In his other notable work *De pace fidei*, Nicholas engages in an imaginary conference on doctrinal matters with people from all cultures and faiths which takes place in the heavenly Jerusalem. The dialogue is situated in the context of a vision of a man who begs God to stop the persecution between people of different religions in the conflicts in Constantinople. In this dialogue everyone is searching for the *una religio in rituum varietate* (the one religion in the variety of rites) so that they can reflect on the deeper meaning of their own religion. For Nicholas as with so many of the Christians defending their doctrines, the Trinity was central in explaining the truth of the Christian faith. This was often done with both the Muslim and the Jew in mind:

> Although Jews shun the [doctrine of] the Trinity because they have considered the Trinity to be a plurality, nonetheless once it is understood that [the Trinity] is most simple fecundity, [the Jews] will very gladly give assent. The Arabs, too, and all the wise will easily understand from the foregoing [considerations] (1) that to deny the Trinity is to deny the divine fecundity and creative power and (2) that to confess the Trinity is to deny a plurality, and an association, of gods. For the [divine] fecundity, which is also Trinity, does not make it necessary that there be a plurality of gods who work together to create all things; for one infinite fecundity suffices to create everything that is creatable. The Arabs will be much better able to grasp the truth [of the Trinity] in this manner than in the manner in which they speak of God as having an essence and a soul – adding that God has a word and a spirit. For if it is said that God has a soul, then that soul cannot be understood to be [anything] except Reason-that-is-God (or Word-that-is-God; for reason is nothing other than

> word). And what, then, is God's Holy Spirit except Love-that-is-God? For whatever is predicated truly of the most simple God is God Himself. If it is true that God has a Word, then it is true that the Word is God. If it is true that God has a Spirit, then it is true that the Spirit is God. For *having* does not properly befit God, because He *is* all things, so that in Him having is being.[62]

This question–answer style relating to the Trinity puts forward the non-Christian perspective followed by a Christian response. The basic reasoning against the Jews is that they conceive of the Trinity as a plurality, whereas the Trinity is about divine fecundity and the creative power of God, thereby relating to the lack of sterility in God. God's creativity lies in his being 'one infinite fecundity'. In his *Cribratio Alkorani* Nicholas had also argued that without fecundity, offspring and love, the world would cease to exist and that the 'three comprise one world'.[63] This does not, however, mean there is any plurality in God or any association. Nicholas argues that this is a much better way to understand the Trinity than what the Arabs hold in speaking of God having a soul and an essence. He states that God does not 'have', rather God 'is' all the attributes like Word, Spirit or Wisdom. What God has, God is. Such debates and defences reveal how differently Christians understood the Trinitarian nature of God from their Jewish and Muslim neighbours who were the main interlocutors in this conversation. The Muslim view cannot appreciate that this Trinitarian nature is about divine love and fecundity, not a sterile oneness in which God jealously guards his own unicity.

Around a century later, the Ottoman Empire reached the height of its military power in the reign of Suleiman the Magnificent (1520–66). The Ottoman advance was especially disturbing to people in Germany. This was partially due to Habsburg propaganda which exaggerated the Turkish threat in an effort to gain support for imperial ambitions in Eastern Europe. However, when the military power of Hungary (the 'bulwark of Christendom') was destroyed at the battle of Mohacs in 1526, even opponents of the Habsburgs were convinced that central Europe was in grave danger. A Turkish presence in neighbouring Hungary was simply too close for comfort.[64] By the time of Martin Luther's rise to prominence, European leaders were accustomed to thinking of Muslims as their main military enemies. Turks, wars and the Ottoman shaped the political background to Luther's time. However, as Robert Smith writes, 'Luther moved beyond constructions of the Turk as a mere military threat to a consideration of Islam itself'.[65] He adds that 'Given their place in the center of European consciousness, it is unsurprising to find references to the "Turks" in writings from almost all of the major Reformers. Among them, however, only Luther substantively engaged the matter, producing theological perspectives both on the possibility of Christian war against the Turk and on the religion of the Turk, Islam.'[66] Struggles between Turkish Muslims and European Christians in the late medieval period were often assumed to bear cosmic significance. Gregory Miller observes:

> To a large degree the Turkish threat was so terrifying because many Germans understood the conflict between the Habsburg and Ottoman Empires to be a struggle not between two political powers but between the forces of Christendom and that of its archenemy, Islam. In the most severe terms used, it was a struggle between Christ and Anti-Christ, between God and the devil. The Turkish advance into south-eastern and central Europe was understood not simply as a military threat, but also

> as a spiritual one. The salvation of individual Christians and the survival of Christianity itself were at stake. A mere military response was therefore insufficient; this spiritual enemy must also be fought with spiritual weapons.[67]

It was against this background in the sixteenth century that Martin Luther, who saw both the challenge and the lure of the Turks and Islam for his fellow Christians, wrote a critique of Muslim doctrine. The principal texts which formed the basis for Luther's knowledge of Islam were the *Confutatio Alcorani* by Riccoldo da Monte di Croce (1243–1320),[68] often described as a 'summary' of the Qur'ān, and the *Cribratio Alkorani* by Nicholas of Cusa. While Luther was amazed at Muslim belief in the 'shameful' things in the Qur'ān, he had an ambiguous attitude towards Islam, reflected largely in his conviction that the function of Islam and the expansion of the Muslim world was to act as both a poison and a cure for Christians: Islam was fundamentally a divine punishment for Christians for their transgressions. On the one hand Luther admired the piety of Muslims and praised much in Islamic culture, but he was also aware of the possibility that Christians as potential subjects of the Turks would eventually convert for whatever reason to the religion of their authorities. Luther defined Islam and the Turks as instruments of Satan. The only person who was seen through a similar prism was the Pope himself as Luther had spent years trying to expose the lies of the papacy. Islam, like the papacy, was just another guise of the Devil. He wrote:

> The Pope has certainly initiated so many wars, murder, bloodshed amongst the kings, has robbed, stolen, plundered, and unrelentingly trashed so much land and so many people, and

> has also conducted himself with such arrogance over all the kings, and most blasphemously [it is all done] under the name of Christ. Muhammad appears before the world as a pure saint in comparison with him.[69]

Islam and the Turks were the external enemy, whereas the papacy was the internal enemy. Luther's identification of the Pope as the Anti-Christ is well known, for he wrote, 'He who sits in the church is the Anti-Christ',[70] but his statements against the papacy force him to liken the Pope to the Turk as neither pays heed to the Christian faith. He questions what is to be done about waging war on the Pope and the Turk, but although he wants them both to receive punishment because both have sinned, Luther maintained that Christians should avoid war and rather oppose both with repentance and trust in Christ.[71]

Fundamentally Luther's critique of Muslim doctrine was based on the bedrock of his theology – the incarnation of God in Christ. Luther wrote in *Heerpredigt* that it was Christological doctrines which distinguished Christianity 'from all other faiths on earth'. As Muslims did not recognise the divine personage of Christ, his Sonship and co-equality with God the Father and the Holy Spirit in the one divine *ousia*, Muḥammad, claimed Luther, 'is a destroyer of our Lord Christ and his kingdom'.[72] Indeed, the religion of Muḥammad rejecting the divinity and redemptive work of Christ means that 'all Christian doctrine and life are gone'. For Luther, faith meant faith in Christ crucified, died and risen. The Christian for Luther lives in Christ through faith and in his neighbour through love. He follows Paul in his claim that being receptive to the spirit in Christ was radically transformative of the human person.

Thus for Luther, the Muslim rejection of the Incarnation and the Trinity was tantamount to idolatry and he accuses the Muslims of inventing 'a god such as they wish to have, not as God has revealed himself'.[73] He knew about the Muslim doctrine of *tawḥīd* and the insistence on God's oneness, thereby excluding any form of division in God. Luther ridiculed the allegation against Christians of *shirk* or association in God by their doctrine of the Trinity, and was also convinced that the most effective defence against the allure of Islam was to remain convinced in the person and works of Christ:

> The Qur'ān lies about Christians when it says that they give partner to God. That is an open lie, for Christians in the entire world say that God is one and is indivisible. Certainly nothing is more united than the Godhead or Divine Essence.[74]
>
> These defences are the articles about Christ, namely that Christ is the son of God, that he died for our sins, that he was raised for our life, that justified by faith in him our sins are forgiven and we are saved, etc. These are the thunder that destroys not only Muḥammad but even the gates of hell. For Muḥammad denies that Christ is the son of God, denies that he died for our sins, denies that he arose for our life, denies that by faith in him our sins are forgiven and we are justified, denies that he will come as judge of the living and the dead (though he does believe in the resurrection of the dead and the day of judgement), denies the Holy Spirit, and denies the gift of the Spirit. By these and similar articles of faith consciences must be fortified against the enemies of Muḥammad.[75]

Luther's accusations against Muslim belief are not simply related to doctrinal matters of Trinity and Incarnation. His fundamental problem with Muḥammad's teachings is not so much that Muḥammad rejects Christ's nature but that he rejects what Christ means in the life of the Christian. The power of Jesus' creative Spirit, the intimate Sonship, the saving power of the life, death and resurrection of Christ, mean nothing in Muslim theology, but these are exactly the beliefs which the Christian must hold on to.

In his *Verlegung*, Luther's purpose is apologetical in that he wishes to attack the foundation of Islam by claiming that Muḥammad was a false prophet. Luther rejected comparisons between Muḥammad and Christ in which both were seen as old and new lawgivers. He stressed that Christ's role was not about the law but about redemption; in that context he came to his people in a radically different way from Muḥammad. Luther understood Muslim concern for God's oneness, but he also derided the Islamic preoccupation with the flesh in their understanding of Sonship and wrote that Christians know full well how God can have a son and that it was not necessary that Muḥammad teach Christians how God must first become a man and have a woman to produce a son or a bull must have a cow to produce a calf. He wrote:

> Oh how overpowered in the flesh of women Muḥammad is. In all his thoughts, words and deeds, he cannot speak nor do anything apart from this lust. It must always be flesh, flesh, flesh.[76]

Muḥammad's sexual life was intertwined with the general reproach towards Islam as a religion where the sexual lay in both the sacred and the profane, a religion where carnal pleasures were extolled as earthly and heavenly blessings. For medieval Christianity, Islam was a religion of sexual laxity, lasciviousness, a religion of flesh and falsity.[77] In Luther's view, doctrine and life were distinct because doctrine is heaven and life is earth where there is sin and error. Furthermore, Islam focused on works which taught that man could achieve righteousness before God through good works, whereas in Luther's view, salvation is not earned through good deeds but received only as a free gift of God's grace through faith in Christ.

In the end, however, Luther looked to the failure of the Christians themselves for the successes of Islam at the time. He wondered that if the Turks were the tool of the devil, and if they were threatening to destroy both the material and spiritual life in Christendom, why does God not stop them? But as Miller explains:

> It was clear to Luther that the seemingly unstoppable Ottoman advance was not due to any innate Turkish advantages or even Satan's assistance. Rather, God was permitting the continued Ottoman victories because of the internal failings of Christendom. Turkish success was permitted by God both to punish a corrupt Christendom and to drive it to repentance.[78]

While the Incarnation and divinity of Jesus continued to be a contested topic between Sunnī orthodox Muslims and Christians, not all Muslims saw the Trinity as a doctrine which divided God's unity. In the world of poetry and Ṣūfī spirituality, it is important to note that Jesus was given a particularly important place. The great Andalusian mystic, poet and philosopher Ibn al-ʿArabī (1165–1240) and other Persian Ṣūfī poets saw the Trinity and the Incarnation as symbolic ways of speaking about the Absolute. For Ibn al-ʿArabī, number did not beget multiplicity in the Divine substance. He wrote in his famous poem, *Tarjumān al-ʿAshwāq (The Translator of Desires)*:

My beloved is three although he is One
Even as the three persons are made one Person in essence.[79]

The Ultimate for Ibn al-ʿArabī is the Essence, God in himself, and thus unrelated to any created thing. The Essence remains unknowable, but God's relationship to created entities can be articulated. Toshihiko Isutzu states that Ibn al-ʿArabī distinguishes between the Essence in itself and its relationship by means of *al-Aḥad* and *al-Wāḥid*:

> The *Aḥad* is the pure and absolute One – the reality of existence in a state of absolute underdetermination, the prephenomenal in its ultimate and unconditional prephenomenality – whereas the *Wāḥid* is the same reality of existence at a stage where it begins to turn toward phenomenality.[80]

Whatever language Ibn al-ʿArabī uses to make this distinction between the Absolute in itself and its relationship to created entities, Royster states 'the distinction itself – even though it lies in the dualistic nature of the human mind and not in the essential nature of the Ultimate – remains consistent'.[81] Ibn al-ʿArabī's metaphysical position on this issue is similar to Meister Eckhart's assertion 'Existence is God' (*esse est Deus*). In identifying existence with God, Eckhart affirms the unity of God's being in which there is no division.

Jesus' wisdom, asceticism and the association of his name with divine breath and love became prominent images in Ṣūfī poetry. Ibn al-ʿArabī concerns himself with the role of the Spirit in the creation of Jesus:

A Spirit from none other than God,
So that he might raise the dead and bring forth birds from clay.

And become worthy to be associated with his Lord
By which he exerted great influence, both high and low.
God purified him in body and made him transcendent
In the spirit, making him like Himself in creating.

Ibn al-ʿArabī refers to the sectarian disagreements over the nature of Jesus, but it was the image of Jesus as divine spirit which is emphasised in his poetry:

> Considered in his [particular] mortal form, one might say that he is the son of Mary. Considered in his form of humanity, one might say that he is of Gabriel, while considered with respect to the revival of the dead one might say that he is of God as Spirit. Thus one might call him the spirit of God, which is to say that life is manifest into whomsoever he blows.[82]

But even mystical poetry did not reflect the full significance of Jesus' life. Sorour Soroudi writes that 'Jesus' image as a persecuted man who bore his burden with love and who did not give up his belief even at the cost of his life which he sacrificed to save others does not receive attention in classical Persian poetry nor, indeed, in Muslim writing in general. There are examples in classical poetry in which slanderous talk against Jesus, his intended crucifixion, and his ascent to heaven, are mentioned. But classical poets, even the persecuted ones, rarely heeded the social aspects so essential to Jesus' personality as depicted in the New Testament.[83]

In the poetry of the thirteenth-century Turkish Persian mystic and poet-theologian Jalāl al-din Rūmī we find a variety of themes which dominated mystical poetry in its expressions about Jesus. Rūmī, also known as *Maulana* (Our Master), is considered the greatest of the Persian poets and is certainly one of the most popular. Rūmī's poetry gives different images for Jesus and Christianity. While Jesus is viewed less as saviour and Son of God and more as the Muslim prophet, Rūmī sees in Jesus much more than a miracle worker. As a prophet, Jesus is identified by Rūmī as representing 'the perfection of humanity', a concept elaborated in Nicholson's commentary on the *Mathnawi* where he explores Rūmī's concept of this perfection. Nicholson explains that the 'Perfect Man displays to mankind the attributes of God; he heals and purifies souls. He is a manifestation or organ of the Logos; he achieves cosmic consciousness; and he is a microcosm of the universe. He is also a receptor of divine grace and a "pure mirror in which all colors are reflected". He reflects the "universality of God" and at the same time he is united to all other perfect men.'[84]

While abstinence and asceticism are dominant aspects of Jesus' life, Annemarie Schimmel states that Rūmī emphasised Jesus' smiling nature in contrast to his cousin John and that 'The smiling was from confidence, and the frowning was from fear'. The linking of Jesus with spirit also features in Rūmī's verse. Rūmī saw that logic and intellect were limited in their ability to inspire humanity to any great endeavour. It was the prophets and seers, people of no formal knowledge, who captured the hearts of those they encountered:

> The myriad of Pharaoh's lances were shattered by Moses with a single staff. Myriads were the therapeutic arts of Galen; before Jesus and his life-giving breath they were a laughing stock. Myriads were the books of pre-Islamic poems; at the word of an illiterate prophet they were put to shame.

Thus there are categories of understanding other than words:

> Our speech and action is the exterior journey: the interior journey is above the sky. The physical sense saw only dryness because it was born of earth: the Jesus of the spirit set foot on the sea.[85]

For Rūmī, if there was no love, there would be no existence as love is the motive force of all creation. Annemarie Schimmel elaborates on Rūmī's reference to Q 5:110:

> [The Day] when God will say, 'O Jesus, Son of Mary, remember my favor upon you and upon your mother when I supported you with the Pure Spirit and you spoke to the people in the cradle and in maturity; and [remember] when I taught you writing and wisdom and the Torah and the Gospel; and when you designed from clay [what was] like the form of a bird with my permission, then you breathed into it, and it became a bird with my permission; and you healed the blind and the leper with my permission; and when you brought forth the dead with My permission; and when I restrained the Children of Israel from [killing] you when you came to them with clear proofs and those who disbelieved among them said, 'This is not but obvious magic.'

Jesus' quality of breathing life into the dead is for Rūmī the equivalent of a kiss:

> When someone asks you 'How did Christ quicken the dead?'
> Then give me a kiss in his presence. 'Thus!'[86]

This life-giving breath (*dam-i 'Īsā*) became the quality most associated with Jesus, so that Jesus' breath brings life when it brings new concepts or possibilities to human imagination. Rūmī compares man's spirit to Jesus and his body to Mary, so that one must endure the pains of the body to develop the spirit of Jesus. But Rūmī also saw the differences between the Muslim and Christian Jesus: 'That idea the Christian carried abroad, the Muslim has not that idea, that He is slaying this Messiah upon the cross.'[87]

In his summation of where the poet places Jesus in his religious poetics, James King writes:

> So we can say that for Rūmī, Jesus stood at the center of the human creative process and became part of his most extravagant, most poetic, most meaningful store of images. Rūmī carries the meaning of Jesus well beyond what we would normally identify as Islamic norms, well beyond what might be required of a prophet, identifying him as one of a very rare body of individuals qualitatively different from normal human beings and endowed with a special capacity to renew and transform human lives, to render them whole and complete, but without ever going beyond the Islamic insistence that there is no god but God.[88]

In contemporary works on Jesus there has been a renewed interest in how Jesus has been a presence in different kinds of Islamic literature. Away from traditional doctrinal polemics, there is the figure of Jesus who has been incorporated into the Islamic Christology of the Ṣūfīs and whose piety and wisdom speaks to Muslims in a more practical manner. In his introduction to *The Muslim Jesus*, Tarif Khalidi calls the collective sayings attributed to Jesus by various Muslim scholars and mystics the 'Muslim gospel'. While the Islamic Jesus of the Gospel may be a fabrication, Khalidi writes:

> Here is a Jesus who on the one hand is shorn of Christology, but who on the other is endowed with attributes which render him meta-historical and even, so to speak, meta-religious. In his Muslim habitat, Jesus becomes an object of intense devotion, reverence and love. He bears the stamp of Qur'ānic *nubuwwah*, or prophecy, but as he advances inside the Islamic tradition he ceases to be an argument and becomes a living and vital moral voice, demanding to be heard by all who seek a unity of profession and witness.[89]

Below is a selection of these sayings which point to the themes covered by the Muslim poets, largely asceticism and renunciation of this world:

> Jesus said the heart of the believer cannot really support the love of both this world and the next, just as a single vessel cannot really support both water and fire.[90]

The moral model of Jesus is reflected in his struggle with Satan, who wants to accuse Jesus of seeking comfort in this world:

> Satan passed by while Jesus was reclining his head upon a stone. 'So then, Jesus, you have been satisfied with a stone in this world!' Jesus removed the stone from beneath his head, threw it at him, and said, 'Take this stone, and the world with it! I have no need of either.'[91]

Jesus reflects on how his possessions may be construed as a love for this world:

> Jesus owned nothing but a comb and a cup. He once saw a man combing his beard with his fingers, so Jesus threw away the comb. He saw another drinking from a river with his hand cupped, so Jesus threw away the cup.[92]
>
> If you wish, you may repeat what the Possessor of the Word and the Spirit [of God], Jesus the son of Mary, used to say: Hunger is my seasoning, fear is my garment, wool is my clothing, the light of dawn is my heat in winter, the moon is my lantern, my legs are my beast of burden, and the produce of the earth is my food and fruit. I retire for the night with nothing to my name and awake in the morning with nothing to my name. And there is no one on earth richer than me.[93]

The moral imperative of the giving of one's self to alleviate another's suffering; an obligation which has consequences in the heavens:

> Jesus said when someone turns a beggar away empty-handed, the angels will not visit his house for seven days.[94]

Such sayings illustrate how the Jesus of the Gospels was over time embraced by the Muslim Ṣūfīs to become the Jesus of Islamic Ṣūfism. Here is a Jesus who leads by example, who takes on suffering and who utters eternal truths.

Despite the various kinds of accusations and apologetics between Christians and Muslims regarding Jesus, there are certain topics which remained contested throughout this historical dialogue. The fundamental issue, however, remained that for the purpose of Islamic prophecy, revelation appears but divine distance is maintained. For Christians, in the Incarnation, God is revealed and the distance is overcome. Muslims may not agree with this belief, but if Jesus is the full expression of the triune God of Israel for Christians, then there has to be some attempt made by Muslims to understand what this belief and devotion means in Christian life and worship. This is not simply a numbers game. Christianity boasts its own monotheism and Islam understands Christianity to be a monotheistic faith. Yet much of the polemic for over a thousand years has focused not on the commitment to serve God within these monotheisms, but how each has understood the nature of God through Jesus Christ and Muḥammad.

CHAPTER 4

Reflections on Mary

While Jesus remained at the centre of most of the polemical as well as irenic conversations between Christians and Muslims, Mary often featured as a more conciliatory figure between the two religions. As the virginal mother of Jesus in Christianity and Islam, Mary's womanhood and femininity, along with her pious devotion, became the subject of much theological speculation in both religions.

When I was expecting my first child, I started reading the Qur'ān for longer periods of time and more frequently. Very early on my mother encouraged me to read *sūra* Maryam at least once a day throughout my whole pregnancy. It is a *sūra* recommended for women in times of need and vulnerability, a *sūra* which brings solace and comfort and in pregnancy is said to bless the mother and the unborn child. I set aside time and read the *sūra* every day. Yet did Mary/Maryam as a figure speak to me as I read the *sūra* day after day? I was aware of her elevated status in the Qur'ān, the miracle of her own pregnancy, and I tried to read the *sūra* in that spirit. But did she as a woman, 'chosen by God' above so many other women, speak to me in a way which was unique, which I could hold on to as special or symbolic? I don't think that happened. All the figures and characters of the Qur'ān have their unique stories, but they are united by being bearers of a bigger, eternal message of the ultimate story – God's infinite presence and mercy. As I read *sūra* Maryam, I am not sure that I felt anything different from the reading of another *sūra* from the Qur'ān. But maybe I was unaware of the transforming power of the verses, unaware that by reading this *sūra*, I was indeed being blessed.

Mary is revered by many in popular Islamic piety, but she is not the mother of God, she is not in Islam what she is in Roman Catholic Christianity or indeed the Theotokos, 'the one who gave birth to the one who is God', one of her titles in Eastern Christianity. This was her title in theology since the time of Origen (d.254) and the Church confirmed this title at the Council of Ephesus in 431. If Marian theology has exalted her for herself, in Islam her story is an example of virtue, obedience and purity, 'an example of the righteous' (Q66:12). All of this comes to the fore when she is told she will be carrying a child who will be a 'mercy from God', Jesus who is known as the Spirit of God in the Qur'ān.

Mary lives in daily piety within Muslim and Christian communities. Indeed, one could argue that her presence haunts those who desire to see her. 'She appeared on several nights, in different forms – sometimes in full body, at other times only half, surrounded by a halo of bright light. Sometimes she would appear in the domes of the church or above.' This was the description of the appearance of the Virgin Mary published in Cairo's *al-Ahram* paper in May 1968. Muslims and Christians flocked to see this vision because Mary or Maryam in Arabic[1] is a figure with a lasting appeal to the people of both these faiths; many see her as an inspiring and reconciling figure between Islam and Christianity, between the past and the present, between the feminine and the feminine ideal.

Mary is often regarded as a meeting point, a bridge between Islam and Christianity. R. J. McArthy wrote of Mary in the two faiths that though Mary may not be a touchstone, she may well be a stepping stone. He wrote that the phrase 'chosen by God' meant that she was chosen in the same way the prophets were chosen.[2] And in 1988, Cardinal Arinze of the Vatican's secretariat for non-Christians addressed a greeting to Muslims whom he called brothers and sisters in God. He quoted Mary, 'the mother of Jesus whom both Christians and Muslims – without according her the same role and title – honour as a model for believers'. The portrait of Mary was a surprising feature for even the earliest Christian respondents to Islam. The twelfth-century monk Bartholomew of Edessa declared, 'In the entire Qur'ān there do not occur any praises of Muḥammad or of his mother Aminah such as are found about our Lord Jesus Christ and about the holy Virgin Mary, the Theotokos.'[3]

Mary's story is significant on a number of levels. There are prophets in the Qur'ān, God's chosen few, God's messengers to humanity, the bearers of God's word who act as the link between God and humanity. They are the noblest of the noblest. There are women in the Qur'ān. The Qur'ān is full of their stories, stories of the good, the rebellious, the virtuous, the seducers. And then there is *sūra* 19 of the Qur'ān, dedicated to Mary – Mary, the mother of Jesus, Mary the most chaste and virtuous woman, Mary who receives an angelic annunciation of a pure son from God's Spirit, a Word from God cast unto Mary whose name is the Christ Jesus, son of Mary. In the Qur'ān only Moses, Abraham and Noah are mentioned by name more frequently than Mary, but Mary herself is mentioned more times in the Qur'ān than in the entire New Testament. There are seventy verses in the Qur'ān which refer to her and she is mentioned specifically in thirty-four of these.[4] She is in the Qur'ān as an example for the believers. The New Testament says:

> Greetings, O favoured one. The Lord is with you. Do not be afraid, Mary, for you have found favour with God (Luke 1:28–30).

The Qur'ān says:

> Allah has chosen you and purified you and chosen you above women of all peoples (Q3:42).

Mary's story is mysterious and is found within the few references to her in the Qur'ān. Her mother is not mentioned by name in the Qur'ān but referred to as the 'wife of Imrān'. Islamic tradition has given her the name Hanna and she is considered to be a sister to Elizabeth (Zakariah's wife and the mother of John the Baptist). Before Mary's birth, her mother pledges to consecrate her unborn child to God's service. As many commentators have noted, in her Jewish context this pledge would not have been appropriate for women as they were not considered appropriate for servanthood in a house of worship. The combination of menstrual impurity and concepts of shame through mixing of the sexes in a place of worship would not have allowed this.

After Mary is born, Hanna invokes God's protection for her and her progeny from Iblīs (Satan). The result of this wish is confirmed in a well-known *ḥadīth* (in various versions) by which Mary and Jesus escaped the 'pricking of the devil' at birth. Haddad and Smith give two examples from the classical commentators:

'Every descendant of Adam experiences the touch of Satan except Mary, the daughter of Imran and her son', and 'Not a descendant is born but he is touched by Satan and he comes out crying, except Mary and her son.'[5] When Mary is born, she serves in the *mihrāb*, the sanctuary of the temple which emphasises a separate physical location where she could devote herself to worship, a place where men had no access. She stays there under the care of Zakariah, who is surprised to find Mary receiving food miraculously from God:

> Every time Zakariah entered upon her in the prayer chamber, he found with her provision. He said, 'O Mary, from where is this [coming] to you?' She said, 'It is from God. Indeed, God provides for whom He wills without account.' (Q3:37).

There are two annunciation stories in the Qur'ān. The following section is the longer narration and relates the sequence of events:

> Mary withdrew from her family to an eastern place. She took a curtain to screen herself from them. And we sent Our Spirit to appear before her in the form of a perfected man. She cried, 'I take refuge with the Compassionate from you. Go away if you fear God.' He said, 'I am only your Lord's messenger come to announce to you the gift of a pure son.' She said, 'How can I have a son when no man has touched me and I am not unchaste?' He said, 'This is what your Lord said: "It is easy for me – we shall make him a sign to all people, a mercy from Us."' And so it was ordained and she conceived him. She withdrew with him to a distant place. And when the pains of childbirth drove her to [cling to] the trunk of a palm tree, she exclaimed, 'If only I had been dead and forgotten long before all this.' But

> a voice cried out to her from below, 'Do not grieve, for your Lord has provided a stream at your feet and if you shake the trunk of the palm tree toward you, so it will drop juicy fresh dates upon you. So eat and drink and be joyful. And when you see a human being, say I have vowed a fast to the Lord of Mercy to abstain from conversation and I will not speak to anyone today.' Then she went back to her people carrying the child and they said, 'O Mary, you have done something terrible; your father was not a bad man, your mother was not unchaste.' Then she pointed towards him. They said, 'How can we speak to someone who is still an infant?' But he said, 'I am God's servant. He has given me the Book and has made me a prophet. He has made me blessed wherever I may be and commanded me to pray and give alms as long as I live, to cherish my mother. He did not make me domineering or graceless. Peace was on me the day I was born and will be on me the day I die and the day I am raised to life again.' Such was Jesus, son of Mary (Q19: 16–34).[6]

In this narration, the reference is to God's Spirit, taking on the form of a perfect man and one who reassures her that he is only a messenger sent by God. In Q3:35–51, we have the second annunciation story, though this time reference is made to the angels who announce, 'O Mary, God gives you glad tidings of a word from Him whose name is Christ Jesus, son of Mary.' When Mary asks how she will have a son when 'no human has touched me', the reply is that it is easy for God who only has to say 'Be!' These are extraordinary images of female vulnerability and power in the Qur'ān. Although classical commentaries debate exactly how the virginal conception took place, suffice it say here that the Shīʿites, like the Sunnites, suppose that the Spirit who presented himself to her was Gabriel.

Angels can appear in human form, but that does not mean they have become human. On the other hand, there seems to be much less consensus over how an angel appeared to a woman when only men could be prophets. The Qur'ān proclaims Mary as amongst the 'devoutly obedient' (*qanitīn*) of God's servants. However, some Muslim theologians argued that Mary could be considered a prophet because God spoke to prophets – prophecy is different from messengerhood, which is defined as a male role. The Qur'ān calls her a 'woman of truth' (Q5:75), just as it speaks of the prophet Joseph as a 'man of truth' (Q12:46).

As quoted above, Q19:16–34 describes the birth pangs Mary endures when Jesus is born, thus emphasising the natural and human birth of Jesus, and the fact that Mary, like all women, had to suffer pain. The date palm tree which Mary shakes is a dried up tree, but when it is shaken, it showers fresh dates upon her. Annemarie Schimmel writes that this image was taken up by the mystical poets as another sign of divine interjection. For Rūmī, had Mary not felt the pangs of labour, she would not have received such a gift in Jesus. He writes:

> The body is like Mary. Every one of us has a Jesus within him, but until the pangs manifest in us, our Jesus is not born. If the pangs never come, then Jesus rejoins his origin by the same secret path by which he came, leaving us bereft and without portion of him

As far as the miracle of the dates is concerned, the poet Shirvani wrote, 'The word is a witness to the virgin, that is, my thought, as the date palm is for Mary's miracle.'[7]

The birth of Jesus is also held to have had a remarkable consequence in terms of spiritual warfare on Iblīs, the Devil, with events resembling the fall of Dagon before the Ark of the Covenant and the purported collapse of the idols in the Ka'ba before Muḥammad after the conquest of Mecca. In his analysis of Christ in Shīʿa Islam, Anthony McRoy cites from the *Bihār al-Anwār* or *Oceans of Lights* by the Shīʿite scholar Allama Majlisi (d.1698). He writes that the night Jesus was born, 'Iblīs came that night and it was said to him that a child had been born that night, and that there was no idol on the earth that did not fall on its face. Iblīs went to the East and West in search of him. Then he found him in a room of a convent. The angels surrounded him. He tried to get close to him. The angels shouted, "Get away!" He said to them, "Who is his father?" They said, "His case is like that of Adam." '[8]

In the Gospels, the conception and birth of Jesus is described in Luke 1:26–38:

> In the sixth month of Elizabeth's pregnancy, God sent the angel Gabriel to Nazareth, a town in Galilee, to a virgin pledged to be married to a man named Joseph, a descendant of David. The virgin's name was Mary. The angel went to her and said, 'Greetings, you who are highly favored! The Lord is with you.'
>
> Mary was greatly troubled at his words and wondered what kind of greeting this might be. But the angel said to her, 'Do not be afraid, Mary; you have found favour with God. You will conceive and give birth to a son, and you are to call him Jesus. He will be great and will be called the Son of the Most High. The Lord God will give him the throne of his father David, and he will reign over Jacob's descendants forever; his kingdom will never end.'
>
> 'How will this be,' Mary asked the angel, 'since I am a virgin?'

> The angel answered, 'The Holy Spirit will come on you, and the power of the Most High will overshadow you. So the holy one to be born will be called the Son of God. Even Elizabeth your relative is going to have a child in her old age, and she who was said to be unable to conceive is in her sixth month. For no word from God will ever fail.'
>
> 'I am the Lord's servant,' Mary answered. 'May your word to me be fulfilled.' Then the angel left her.

Joseph Ratzinger writes that 'Luke allows the Trinitarian mystery to shine through the angel's words. . . . The child to be born will be called the Son of God, the Son of the Most High. Moreover, the Holy Spirit, personally embodying the power of the Most High, will mysteriously effect this conception. The Gospel thus speaks of the Son and, indirectly, of the Father and the Holy Spirit.' But Ratzinger also points out that in Luke's Annunciation narrative, God waits for the freedom of his creature to say yes and that without this free consent on Mary's part, 'God cannot become man.' Bernard of Clairvaux's homily demonstrates this waiting: 'The angel awaits your answer, for it is time to return to the one who sent him. . . . O lady, give the answer that earth, that hell, that heaven awaits.'[9]

Following this theme, Hans Urs von Balthasar argues for the veneration and imitation of Mary who had acted selflessly in allowing herself to be impregnated:

> If everything in Mary rests upon her Yes to God, this Yes is nothing other than the perfect human echo of Jesus' divine-human response to the Father: 'Behold, I have come to do your will, O God' (Hebrews 10:7); I have come down from heaven,

> not to do my own will, but the will of him who sent me' (John 6:38). The center of Mary's Yes lies in the very center of the Son, but it does not disappear into it. For Mary was the first to utter it, and she did this to make the incarnation possible in the first place and her Yes remains for the members of the Church the central and fully valid answer to the Lord's demands. Christ's Yes and Mary's Yes are fully intertwined. This relationship is such that Mary always declares her faith-filled readiness thanks to a grace that is ultimately Christological, while the Son for his part never denies what he owes to his Mother.[10]

Mary's 'unrestricted readiness' has been described in new ways over time. The Christian Fathers called it 'passionlessness' (*apatheia*); the Middle Ages, 'not remaining attached to worldly things' (*Gelassenheit*). Balthasar writes that if the role of the Church is to serve the ransom and the retrieval of the sinful world, 'In Mary, the Church is embodied even after being organized in Peter. In Mary, the Church is first, and this first is permanent, is feminine before she receives a complementary male counterpart in the form of ecclesial office.'[11]

In the Gospels the title 'Son of Mary' has been exceedingly rare. The only instance in the whole of the New Testament is in Mark 6:3, 'Is not this the carpenter, the son of Mary?' As for Joseph, who was not, we are assured, Jesus' father, he effectively disappears after the Infancy Narratives.

While Mary is hardly mentioned in the New Testament, during the early centuries of the Christian era various Marian legends developed; these stories were recorded in various apocryphal gospels. As Mary Thurkill writes, 'Christian hagiographers fashioned their idealized virgin by transmuting Mary's mundane form into an extraordinary body. Mary's virginal flesh defied common laws of physicality and sexuality; Mary remained a virgin even after childbirth. Christian authors constructed this Marian icon as part of a complex ascetic theology that promoted the virgin's body as one symbolically transformed into the image of the resurrected Christ.'[12] The Church fathers included Marian traditions in the larger rhetorical framework of feminine compliance. The fourth-century bishop of Milan, St Ambrose, championed Mary as the 'discipline of life'.

The Qur'ān and Muslim theology virtually dissolve the complexities of a virginal birth into a simple recognition of divine omnipotence and will:

> O people of the book, do not go too far in your religion and do not assert against God except the truth. Christ Jesus son of Mary is only God's messenger and his word which he conveyed to Mary and a spirit from him. Therefore believe in God and his messengers and do not say 'three'. Cease, it is better for you, God is only God (Q4:171).
>
> Unbelieving are those who say that God is Christ Son of Mary. And Christ said: O Children of Israel, worship God, my Lord and your Lord. He who ascribes partners to God, God has forbidden him paradise (Q5:75).

It is this humanity along with this revered prophecy which is then emphasised in the Qur'ān. She did not ask God for the honour of giving birth to a prophet, and especially one as miraculously conceived as Jesus, but she was given this honour by God. She implored God to protect her chastity and virtue, which were cast into doubt with the birth of Jesus, but God continued to protect her because she continued to have faith in him. Mary's story is dramatic.

By bringing Jesus into this world, she brings forth for Christians God's presence in this finite world, and for Muslims, God's will in prophetic form. She endures a pregnancy and birth which do not reflect mortal sin or desire. Such virtue and chastity are for the special few, because for most ordinary beings, virtue and chastity demand different trials. We are required to be chaste in our own relationships, virtuous in the face of constant desire, and faithful when our loyalties are tested. As Haddad and Smith reflect:

> With the exception of some mystical writings and practice, Mary is not and by definition cannot be a model for human aspiration in Islam because she is clearly recognised and treated as unlike anyone else. Whether or not one acknowledges that she had miraculous abilities or even was in a state of perpetual purity, Mary was virginal and thus in fact categorically opposed to the ideal of a Muslim woman whose virginity is prized but ultimately sacrificed to allow her to play the role for which she was created, i.e. wife and mother.[13]

In her analysis of Rachel, Mary and Fatima as 'female saints whose cults are located within monotheistic, male-dominated religious traditions', Rachel Sered writes:

> Mary, as the Virgin Mother of God, is essentially inimitable, whereas Rachel and Fatima are more realistic models. While women can strive to be faithful, modest, generous, or wise, to be a virgin mother is an impossible goal for mortal women. In a different sense, though, Mary is the most positive model of the three. Fatima and Rachel suffered in life, died young, and weep in eternity; Mary is rarely portrayed as a victim. Especially

> during the past two decades, Mary has been described not only 'as a mother exclusively concerned with her own Divine son, but rather as a woman whose action helped to strengthen the apostolic community's faith in Christ'.[14]

Mary's virginal conception is announced to Joseph in Matthew 1:20 as that which happened 'through the Holy spirit'. But Montgomery Watt places the Virgin Birth story as a story of changing significance. He writes:

> For many Christians, the Virgin Birth, together with the whole Christian story, has probably come to seem more central than it was. It is clear from the New Testament that the virginal conception played no part at all in the earliest Christian teaching. It is described in the infancy narratives in the First and Third Gospels, but is not referred to in the sermons in the Acts of the Apostles nor in the epistles of Saint Paul nor elsewhere in the New Testament. It is a story which came to be meaningful for Christians *after* they had come to believe in the divinity of Jesus on other grounds. Especially for the simple-minded people, the assertion that Jesus had no human father made it easier to think of him as son of a divine father.[15]

Thurkill states that 'Mary's greatest contribution to Christian theology is that she literally conferred flesh upon Jesus the Christ'. But this was a point of dispute amongst early Christians who questioned whether Divinity could be encapsulated in flesh. She writes of the Council of Ephesus in 431 in which the position of Cyril, bishop of Alexandria, was sanctioned over Nestorius, patriarch of Constantinople:

> The Council of Ephesus generated Marian devotion almost as a by-product of Christological explanation. Popular piety had already revealed a vibrant Marian devotion evidenced in prolific tales of her infancy and childhood, yet theologians also harnessed the image and popularity of Mary in their emerging orthodoxy regarding both Christ and his church. Mary functioned as a proof text for Christ's unique nature as well as a metaphor for the church itself. Both Mary and the ecclesia evoke the image of a spotless, pure virgin and fecund mother producing Christian offspring.[16]

Although the issue of Christ's dual nature was largely settled by the fifth century, modern theology continues to examine the ways in which Mary can be understood in terms of her own sexual status and what this means for Jesus' divinity. Jürgen Moltmann outlines the two basic 'mythical forms' of this story. The first is that God brought about the miracle of Mary's pregnancy through the Holy Spirit, so that Jesus is 'conceived by the Holy Spirit and born of the Virgin Mary'. This means that God alone is the father of Jesus Christ in his whole personhood from the very beginning. Here, Joseph is excluded in any concept of earthly fatherhood, the Holy Spirit is the male seed, and Mary, who remains a virgin in the human sense, is Jesus' mother. In the second 'form' the stress lies on the motherhood of the Holy Spirit. The Mary who in human and temporal terms is a virgin must be seen as a symbolic embodiment and as 'the human form of the Holy Spirit, who is the eternally virginal and divine mother of Christ'. In this way Mary should not be thought of as the human woman who becomes pregnant by the Holy Spirit. Rather, the Holy Spirit is the great life-engendering mother of all the living.[17] The theological intention behind both these positions is to emphasise that God is the Father of Jesus from the very beginning, 'that his fatherhood does not merely extend to Christ's consciousness and his ministry. It embraces his whole persona and his very existence.' Jesus is from the very beginning the messianic Son and his beginning is to be found in his birth from the Holy Spirit. But Moltmann also argues that there is a danger of narrowing Jesus' humanity if the virgin birth is taken to mean more of a supernatural–human process. He concludes that 'Christ's birth from the Spirit is a statement about Christ's relationship to God and to God's relationship to Christ. It does not have to be linked with a genealogical assertion.'[18]

Joseph Ratzinger explains in a slightly different manner how the status of motherhood is Mary's first relationship to Christ:

> Mariology underscores the *nexus mysteriorum* – the intrinsic interwovenness of the mysteries in their irreducible mutual otherness and their unity. While the conceptual pairs, bride–bridegroom and head–body allow us to perceive the connection between Christ and the Church, Mary represents a further step, inasmuch as she is first related to Christ, not as bride, but as mother.[19]

Mary's status and the nature of Jesus' birth proved to be a source of heated polemics for those Muslims engaged in doctrinal debate with their Christian counterparts. In his *Critique of the Christian Faith*, 'Abd al-Jabbār questions the exact nature of Jesus in relation to Mary. He asks whether Mary truly became pregnant with Christ, gave birth to him, raised him and fed him like a mother:

> If they say, 'She begot the human nature of Christ' or 'She became pregnant with the human nature of Christ', we reply,

> 'We did not ask you about this, for according to you the human nature of Christ is not Christ, for Christ is also the divine nature. According to you the divine nature of Christ is not Christ. Only the combination of the two is Christ. Now the answer is: If Mary truly gave birth to Christ and truly became pregnant with him, then she became pregnant with God and man, gave birth to God and man. She is the mother of God and man. God and man were killed and God and man suffered. God and man died. It is shown that your statement and the statement of the Melkites and the Jacobites on this is the same.'
>
> If they say 'We say she is the mother of Christ metaphorically and that Christ died metaphorically', we reply to them: 'We did not ask you metaphorically. We asked you truly. For by this supposition Mary's conceiving without a man was metaphorical. Christ's bringing the dead to life, metaphorical, and all of what they claim about him, metaphorical. This is nonsense. For if they divide [Christ's] acts between his divine nature and human nature, this must be done for everything [about Christ]. If he brought the dead to life and made signs appear, that was the action of the divine nature alone. Yet the divine nature alone is not Christ. People did not see the divine nature. Thus, it is not possible to say that they saw Christ. If he ate, drank, slept and woke, these were the acts of the human nature. Yet the human nature alone is not Christ.[20]

ʿAbd al-Jabbār is asking not only about the divine–human nature of Christ born to a fully human mother, but the Christian use of metaphor in explaining Christ's conception and his acts. The emphasis here is on a rejection of the logic of the Christian statements around Mary and the Incarnation rather than the meaning of Mary's life and devotion in Christian piety. The complexity of the divine/human nature of Christ begins with the unique conception and birth in Mary, but this relationship cannot be a metaphor. Mary's virginal character has other consequences. While the Qur'ān emphasizes Mary's chastity and purity, Islam affirming Mary's immaculate conception and the virginal birth, Muslim theology has not regarded sexual purity as a desired aspect of righteous femininity. Chastity before marital relations became morally and legally significant, but it did not equate to a preoccupation with sexual purity as a divine ideal – lawful sex is never sinful. Furthermore, Mary's pure and virginal motherhood has not impacted on lessening the status of ordinary motherhood as being stained or unclean. Rather, motherhood has continued to remain probably the most virtuous and socially desirable role for Muslim women. Some Catholic liberation theologians have also questioned the link between human sex and divine redemption as leading to an obsession with sexual sin and defilement and forgetfulness of major sins such as social injustice or male exploitation. The Sri Lankan theologian Tissa Balasuriya is considered to be the first Asian liberation theologian who called for a new kind of Mariology in which Mary is a model for human and political liberation in the way Jesus promoted social liberation. In his book *Mary and Human Liberation*, he denounced traditional dogmatic theology in the West for its pessimistic anthropology found in the doctrine of original sin. This doctrine of a fallen humanity had evolved in the Latin West but had been forced upon the East as normative theology. Balasuriya claimed that for Mary to be a model for human and especially female aspiration, 'The Mary of real life, and even in the scriptures, cannot be encountered without a deep questioning of this original sin of Mariology. This is an important challenge for the liberation of Mary to be Mary, mother of Jesus, and hence one concerned with all our concerns.'[21]

Mariology in the Roman Catholic Church retains a complex life, especially in regard to the issue of ecumenism. Von Balthasar speaks of a particular tension:

> The place of Mary in the Church's doctrine, in particular Marian veneration and the mariological saturation of Catholic devotion, has long given rise to tensions within the Church, but never more so than in the last decades. Some adhere to the principle 'Of Mary never enough'. Others suspect a twofold danger. Mariology, they say, threatens the hierarchy of Christian truths, at whose center are Christ and the triune God (whereas Mary belongs on the side of the graced creature), and jeopardizes ecumenical dialogue with the ecclesial communities stemming from the Reformation most of which (with some important exceptions) regard the veneration of Mary as perilous excrescence on the organism of Christian devotion.[22]

Perhaps in the West there is no real cult of Mary in Islam, no Marian tradition which could act as a point of common discussion between Christians and Muslims. There are no shrines set up for the worship of Mary, nor do Christians and Muslims come together to celebrate Mary in their respective ways. But does this matter for mutual but distinct attitudes of reverence? The Qur'ān is full of stories which point to some kind of converging narrative between Christian and Muslims scriptures, only for the two scriptures to part on the fundamentals of so many figures. Moses, Abraham and Adam were all involved in the drama of a divine conversation, but their stories overlap and differ. For the Qur'ān, the moral of almost every story points to divine justice and mercy, a God who communicates through humanity by sending messengers who came with the same primordial message, that of the unicity of God and the sovereignty of God. Mary too carried such a person. His birth and vocation could have meant more than human prophecy, but in Islam, Jesus, the son of Mary, remains the human prophet in the long line of human prophets. His virgin mother Mary and his miraculous birth invite the Christic element, yet the Christic element is not tied into the divine-human matrix but is simply a reflection of God's will and power.

Today, if Mary is to be a model for Muslims, what meaning can we derive from her life, as it does not seem to me that she has played a hugely significant role in the history of Islamic thought and piety? As a Muslim I cannot dwell on Mary without dwelling on Jesus; he remains the star of the story, but in a very different way from the Christian story. Mary has no aspirations to be the heroine of this prophetic tale, but longs to remain a true servant of God. Whether or not she too had attained prophethood in her own right, she is almost unique in the Qur'ān as a woman who remains an 'example for the believers' through her obedience and willingness.

The doctrinal density associated with Mary in Christian thought has no equivalence in Islam. Mary is given a special status in the Qur'ān, but one could argue that in the Islamic tradition it is Fatima, the Prophet's daughter and the mother of the tragic heroes Hassan and Hussain, the Prophet's grandsons, who in popular piety is venerated above Mary. As Thurkill says, 'The Christian theologians' Mother Mary extolled a more sublime maternal model wherein the bride wed a heavenly Bridegroom and often (but not always) adopted a life of chastity. Fatima in the Shī'ī tradition is the archetypal mother, and motherhood in its fullest understanding is still the highest accolade for women in Islam.' But Fatima is also a political symbol whose patience and suffering transformed a family at feud into a spiritual family. Sered writes of the ordinary experiences of the saintly female figures in the monotheistic traditions:

> The experiences in the lives of the female saints that have earned cultic attention are not connected to extraordinary spiritual pursuits or powers; Rachel, Mary, and Fatima are not considered holy because of asceticism, contemplation, miracle-working (while alive), or vast learning. On the contrary, the striking features in the biographies of the three saints are the common human situations confronted by each: death of parents and children, marital love and discord, difficulty conceiving and bearing children, conflict with siblings and parents. These are situations that both resonate with the actual life experiences of most human beings, and touch upon grave theological and existential issues.[23]

In Islam, Marian piety is not Advent piety. The Islamic tradition regards Mary's position as unique, but her piety has a limited role and no continuing role in eschatology. Mary's work was complete with Jesus' birth, and the mission of doing God's new work lies with Jesus and not Mary. Jesus, however, has a role in both Christianity and Islam, so that if for Christians he is the primary source of the eschatological hope, for Muslims his return marks the beginning of the end times. The Qur'ānic Jesus along with the Mahdi are the two actors in Muslim eschatology. But Jesus' return to fight against evil and restore justice is not good news in the Christian sense. The gathering around Jesus Christ is not a fulfilment of the Christian church but a fulfilment of divinely ordained prophetic mission that will pave the way for the day of judgement.

Many years ago I remember being on holiday in Malta over the Christmas period. In almost every window there was a Madonna figurine, a porcelain or plastic figure of Mary adoringly holding the baby Jesus. I later realised that the Maltese were devoted to the assumption of the Virgin, locally known as the Santa Marija. Mary is the co-patroness of the islands. Seeing a small or large statue in almost every window seemed strange, almost disturbing to me. It was also the first timc I really noticed how pictures and images of Mary adorn Catholic churches all over the world. Veneration through icons is virtually a thing of the past in much of Islamic piety. Yet at the same time, I wondered how much comfort many of the devotees were getting through their possession of a Mary statue, a feeling that their homes were protected by the watchful gaze of such a holy figure, a universal symbol of God.

Since the Reformation, Mary has been far more significant for Roman Catholicism than for Protestant Christianity. Recognising that the virginal conception is problematic for many Christians, Wolfhart Pannenberg asks how the phrase 'Conceived by the Holy Spirit, born of the Virgin Mary' can still be relevant to Christians in their profession of faith. He responds:

> Probably most Christians today would personally look for a different way of expressing this intention from the one offered by the story of the virgin birth. But that is not of decisive importance when we come into the faith of others. For that, it is enough to agree with the intention, even if the expression of that intention which we take over at the same time cannot be

> our own. This is what justifies us in adopting the creed as an expression of the faith of the church, not only today but from its very beginning. For the alternative would be, not to alter this particular formulation alone, but the whole creed in general. But it is only in the classic form it has acquired that the creed is the sign of the unity of Christianity throughout history; and that is the reason for its irreplaceable function in the services of the church today.[24]

If the creed in its classic form is a sign of the unity of Christianity, then maybe Mary too, as mother of Jesus in all the various understandings of this relationship, can remain a hope for a continuing conversation between Christians and Muslims. For that to happen with any theological as well as devotional relevance, there needs to be a 'resurrection' of Mary in Muslim theology beyond debates around gender, virtue and female piety. This has already happened among some Christian theologians who have wished to promote Mary as an image of the liberation of women from poverty and injustice. But in Islam, Mary has no such role, for the Jesus story pales her own significance. Yet further reflection on her unique nature may well open up new questions and lead to new engagement in the virtual impasse that is the divine/human nature of Jesus for many Christians and Muslims. Mary is the bearer of the Word, but it is the nature of this Word and the significance of his life in the whole eschatological hope of human existence which remains the most decisive and the most contested area for Christian Muslim reflection.

CHAPTER 5

Monotheism and the Dialectics of Love and Law

> Islam may be called a religion that has almost no questions and no answers. In a certain respect its greatness lies there, because this question-less and answer-less condition is a consistent exemplification of its deepest spirit, expressed in its name: Islam, that is, absolute surrender, to God the Almighty Lord.[1]

The early part of the twentieth century saw Christian missionaries travel to Muslim lands where they formulated their own rather ambivalent opinions on the Muslim faith and Muslim life; there was both contempt and admiration for Islam and Muslim piety. In the above quote Hendrik Kraemer (1888–1965) identifies a common perception among many Christians (and also extolled by some Muslims) that Islam is a simple religion in which submission to God' s will and majesty encapsulates the very heart of the faith. But whereas Muslims, rightly or wrongly, see virtue in this 'simplicity', Kraemer saw in it superficiality. Kraemer identified two significant reasons behind this superficiality. Firstly, there is the 'mechanical idea of revelation' in Islam, a rigid form which has become 'externalized and fossilized'. This is in opposition to Biblical realism and 'God constantly acting in holy sovereign freedom, conclusively embodied in the man Jesus Christ'. As Kraemer writes:

> In Islam it is a set of immutable divine words that take the place of God's moveable acts and His speaking and doing through the living man Christ.[2]

Kraemer's second point is that the superficiality of Islam lies in its 'clumsy, external conception of sin and salvation'. Denying that there is any anthropology in Islam, he is amazed that despite Islam having its historical roots in the Bible, there is nothing of the 'stirring problems of God and man that are involved in the terms sin and salvation'.[3]

For Samuel Zwemer (1867–1952), the American missionary and Princeton Theological Seminary professor, the need to evangelise amongst Muslims was paramount. He viewed 'the dead weight of formality called tradition' as 'Islam's intolerable burden'.[4] It was what had led to the decline of Islam, but as Islam lost political power, this became 'a divine preparation for the evangelization of Moslem lands and the winning of Moslem hearts to a new allegiance. Jesus Christ is sufficient for them as He is for us.'[5] Yet Zwemer lamented the fact that Jesus' life had been eclipsed by the life of Muḥammad for Muslims and that whatever differences there were between the various schools and sects in Islam, their position towards Jesus is essentially the same. Zwemer asserted that the central concern for Christians was not western civilization but the anti-Christian character of this 'greatest of all the non-Christian religions'. He could not understand how Muslims saw Jesus only as a prophet in the long history of God's prophets:

> The Muslim doctrine of God and their denial of Jesus Christ, His Incarnation, His atonement, His deity, are the very issue of the conflict. The Koran denies all that which is the supreme

> glory of the Saviour and that which makes Him a Saviour at all.[6]

Lamenting the absence of any real colloquy between Christian missionaries and secular Islamicists, Kenneth Cragg talks of the 'unexamined hostility' in which both faiths lived and writes:

> Much Islamic scholarship has in fact been generated by Christian missionary concern. Some of the greatest names are those of men whose interest in Islam arose from a desire to communicate Christ and dissipate religious misconception. Muslims, however, for their part have almost invariably understood such interest as a menace and have rejected and denounced even the sound scholarship which served it. The longstanding and persistent Muslim inhospitality to genuine Christian contacts has been one of the great spiritual calamities of our time.[7]

In the later part of the twentieth century, the Swiss Reformed theologian Karl Barth (1886–1968) along with Rudolf Bultmann reshaped the questions which informed Protestant theological inquiry. Barth may be considered as the chief exponent of an exclusive Christology on the Protestant side. Barth's theology upholds the unique salvific mediatorship of Jesus Christ to the exclusion of any other mediation of salvation. Although Barth knew and wrote very little about Islam, he criticised Islamic monotheism where the uniqueness of God had been confused with the singularity of numerical unity. He found it inconceivable to worship God apart from Jesus because Jesus is part of the essence of the one God. In his analysis of the unity of God, Barth wrote:

> God is completely individual. He is absolutely simple. In regard to His uniqueness and equally in regard to His simplicity God is therefore the only being who is really one. His unity is His freedom, His aseity, His deity. It is with His deity alone that our concern must be when we ascribe to Him unity, uniqueness and simplicity. Necessarily, then we must say that God's majesty is the absolutely One, but we cannot say that the absolutely one is God. This concept of the 'absolutely one' is the reflection of creaturely unities.[8]

For Barth, monotheism 'is the esoteric mystery behind nearly all the religions with which we are familiar, as well as most of the primitive religions'.[9] He criticised Islam for being 'incurably entangled' in the 'absolutising of the idea of uniqueness' and its 'noisy fanaticism regarding the one God, alongside whom, it is humorous to observe, only the baroque figure of His Prophet is entitled to a place of honour'.[10] But he found Islamic monotheism no different from paganism, a paganism with an 'esoteric essence' with which 'it proclaims the unique as God instead of God as the One who is unique'.[11] For Barth, God's uniqueness is based on his simplicity and although Christ is the unique way that God has chosen to reveal himself, Barth writes, 'The fact that Jesus Christ is very God and very man means that in this oneness of His with the creature God does not cease for a moment or in any regard to be the one, true God.'[12] He explains that divine immanence has its origin and unity in Christ and:

> The religion of heathendom comes about because man simply does not know or refuses to know the ground of divine immanence in Jesus Christ.

If humanity looks for the freedom of divine immanence apart from Jesus Christ, 'it can signify in practice only our enslavement to a false god'.[13] Barth makes a sharp distinction between revelation and religion. Religion is understood as the human attempt to reach God, but this is simply impossible inasmuch as only God can make God known. Revelation is God's outreach to humanity which takes place uniquely in Jesus Christ, the Incarnation of the eternal Word. Not only are human beings unable to know God, they cannot do anything to help themselves.[14]

The above reflections show how much of the doctrinal polemics and apologetics in Christian–Muslim debates has continued to focus on how God is understood *as* revelation and also *through* revelation. Both religions recognise that there can be no adequate account of human experience without reference to God, but they see God's omniscience and freedom to act in different ways. From the perspective of Christian theologians and missionaries, the fundamental ill of Islam is that it continues to revere Jesus only within the realm of human prophecy rather than recognising in him the very presence of God. Muslims have failed to accept or be convinced that the Incarnation 'is the pivot on which the whole tradition of a communion between man and God in Christianity has been based, both intellectually and devotionally'.[15] In fact even modern theologians who may be intellectually distant from Anselm's *Cur Deus homo* and need to search for other routes for their Christological convictions, arrive at similar conclusions. The theologian and philosopher Paul Tillich (1886–1965) wrote that despite historical uncertainties, 'participation, not historical argument guarantees the reality of the event upon which Christianity is based. It guarantees a personal life in which the New Being has conquered the old being.'[16]

From the Islamic perspective, Jesus' special humanity as recognised in the Qur'ān is never translated into any kind of divinity or self-revelation of God. In other words, there was no need for God to reveal himself in any form or body, though God does reveal. Thus the Incarnation and the Trinity continue to challenge Muslims in their understanding of how God remains one and transcendent in both religions. The issue which Muslims focused on, however, was not why God chose self-revelation but how God's self-revelation was ultimately defined. Frithjof Schuon saw absoluteness in the number one and relativity in the number three and he writes:

> The theology of the Trinity does not constitute an explicit and homogeneous revelation; it results on the one hand, like the concept of transubstantiation, from a literalistic and quasi mathematical interpretation of certain words in the Scriptures, and on the other hand from a summation of different points of view, deriving from different dimensions of the Real. The first paradox of the Trinitarian concept is the affirmation that God is at the same time absolutely one and absolutely three.[17]

Traditional theistic interpretations of God's omnipotence do not place any obligations on either God's essence or his attributes, but God chooses to 'reveal'. But why is there revelation in the first place? For Ṣūfīs such as Ibn al-ʿArabī, the central ontological question, why there is anything rather than nothing, was made explicit in the famous *ḥadīth qudsī*, 'I was a hidden treasure, then I desired to be known, so I created a creation to which I made myself known; then they knew me.'[18] The very purpose of creation is for God to reveal himself. For Ibn al-ʿArabī and Hallāj this is not because God needs creation in any way to realise his fullness, but because God's creative love is so strong that it triggers the whole process of creation. God's self-identity is timeless, he does not become less God or more God in the act of creation, but something within God inspires a movement of creative freedom. The Qur'ān, however, focuses largely on human worship of God as the reason for creation:

> I created jinn and mankind only to worship me. I want no sustenance from them nor do I want them to feed me (Q51:56–57).

The tension between self-revelation and complete transcendence has exercised the minds of Christian and Muslim scholars for centuries – reconciling a God who is radically one and transcendent and a God who reveals for a purpose. In both religions, God is not an abstract concept, rather he reveals in diverse ways in history so that we can re-centre ourselves towards him. As Rowan Williams says, 'God is the "presence" to which all reality is present.'[19] In developing the relationship between the divine and the human, Muslims focused on God's modes and purpose in revelation, the human obligation to submit to reading God's presence in the Qur'ān, and understanding and obeying God's will in response to a revealed text. Christianity saw in revelation an aspect of God's self-giving and the centrality of love in Christ. To this Barth said, 'God is he who in His revelation seeks and creates fellowship with us. . . . He does not will to be God for himself nor as God to be alone with Himself.'[20] In both faiths revelation is essentially about divine disclosure of a creative desire or love, but these phenomena are located and expressed in different ways. In harmonising the presence of God with the love of God, Wolfhart Pannenberg writes:

> For the sake of the identity of his name God will not let his elect [Israel] or his whole creation sink into nothingness. He overcomes the turning of his creatures away from himself by sending his Son to reconcile the world. By the unity of reconciliation by love, which embraces the world and bridges the gulf between God and the world, the unity of God himself is realised in relation to the world. This takes us beyond the initially abstract idea of God's unity as a separate reality which is in mere opposition to the plurality of other gods and the world.[21]

In Christianity, the Absolute is reflected in the contingent, the 'ontological foundation of the mysteries of Incarnation and Redemption'. Schuon rightly asserts:

> If we start from the incontestable idea that the essence of all religions is the truth of the Absolute with its human consequences, mystical as well as social, the question may be asked how the Christian religion satisfies this definition; for its central content seems to be not God as such, but Christ – that is, not so much the nature of the divine being as its human manifestation. Thus a Patristic voice aptly proclaimed: 'God became man that man might become God.'[22]

Muslim theology and Christian theology both tried to guard God's unity and transcendence as well as insisting on the gratuity of creation. Scholars gave intellectual explanations as to how the oneness of God had to be recognised alongside the goodness of God where God is neither constrained nor completely arbitrary in his will. In doing so they showed that divine immanence and transcendence were fluid concepts. This struggle is captured in these lines from *The Bezels of Wisdom*:

> If you insist only on His transcendence you limit Him
> And if you insist only on His immanence, you limit Him
> If you maintain both aspects, you are right.[23]

In the historical focus on how God and man are related, doctrinal debates have centred largely on prophecy, Incarnation, Trinity, and to a lesser extent Redemption as the big questions. However, there are also other theological themes which became the 'intended or unintended consequences' of this history. What each faith has seemingly emphasised in its internal theology as well as in inter-religious polemics does not always tell the full story but it does tell a story. Schuon explains that Christianity has opted for an 'inwardness as against the outwardness of legal prescriptions' and as against the 'letter that killeth'. Furthermore, he defines its profoundest sacrament the Eucharist as 'God does not limit himself to promulgating a Law; he descends to earth and makes himself Bread of Life and Drink of immortality'.[24]

The law narrative has often played out against the love narrative as encapsulating the way believers have made and make sense of God and their relationship to God. The two should not be perceived as opposing paradigms, but love and law are often used to conceptualise both faiths, and often in rather simplistic terms, namely that Christianity is a religion of love whereas Islam is a religion of law. In his own deliberation on dialogue with Islam, Hans Küng writes that 'The portrait of Jesus in the Qur'ān is all too one-sided, too monotone, and for the most part lacking in content, apart from monotheism, the call to repentance, and various accounts of miracles. At any rate it is very different from the portrait of Jesus in history, who not only confirms the law, as the Qur'ān records, but rather counters all legalism with radical love which even extends to his enemies. That is why he was executed, though the Qur'ān fails to recognize this.'

But the necessity of the love and law dialectic has a prior story, namely the overlapping concepts of how evil and sin entered the world. Gustave E. von Grunebaum expresses this succinctly:

> Evil is the point where the perpetual contradictions of our existence intersect: our knowledge that we are free, our knowledge that we are not; our knowledge that we are masters and creators, and our knowledge that we are frail and transitory beings, feeble, multiply conditioned, and that our works along with ourselves are condemned to bear the stigma of futility.[25]

One of the major challenges for Christian theologians has been to understand evil not just in terms of the Augustinian notion of the fall and redemptive salvation, but in the earthly and metaphysical dilemma posed by the relationship between an all-knowing, benevolent God, with conditioned or unconditioned omnipotence and human freedom to resist God's goodness. For Augustine (354–430) the curses of sin and death were the consequences of sex and sexual desire. Adam and Eve's fall resulted in a basic disorder between the flesh and spirit, but Augustine tried to exonerate God from any blame by attributing evil to the choices of human will. For Augustine the moral life finds its meaning in the interpretive representation of God as love.[26] In the Irenaean type of theodicy, humankind did not emerge as a finitely perfect but as an immature being who needed to develop and mature within the challenges of this world. In the two-stage process of human development, mankind is not born perfect but rather perfection lies in the future. To grow into that perfect being while exercising genuine freedom requires a certain 'distance' from God in a world where God is not overwhelmingly evident but where humankind has the freedom to grow to know and love God.

Islamic theology, both classical and modern, has been less occupied with this subject as it could be argued that for the most part Sunnī theologians generally denied that humans have the freedom to act. Furthermore, while free will was understood as a necessary corollary to the power to choose good, and for some, reflected ultimately on a God who is good, it is very difficult to be exact about any ontological definition of a word like 'evil' in Islam. The variety of words in the Qur'ān and later Islamic traditions to encompass the sense of human wrongdoing and human erring do not in themselves contain anything similar to the depth of differing but related views of terrible human actions and terrible human suffering which have occupied the minds of Christian and western theologians and philosophers. With the exception of a few medieval thinkers, the issue of evil was not approached directly but rather subsumed within the larger discussions around the unity of God and the goodness of God. Faith in God is not an antidote to evil, but faith kept alive can counteract all the passion and tragedy of evil. Evil in Islam did not appear in some original drama with its own force and beginnings. It is not illusory but lies in real acts. Evil is not some objective malign force or as Jean Baudrillard says, 'a deliberate perversion of the order of the world'.[27] The Qur'ān itself does not give any abstract analysis of tragic evil and human loss, but repeats the theme of human propensity to do wrong and the divine essence to forgive.

The Qur'ānic story is essentially a story of struggle but not alienation from a transcendent God. Firstly, evil is not absolute, for only God is absolute, and therefore evil, appearing in time, can only be transitory and temporary, limited to this world. Secondly, Adam outranks Iblīs in creation's hierarchy and therefore, despite the power of evil as personified through Satan and his passions, all humankind has the potential to be victorious over Satan, that is, over their own passions which lead them astray. Al-Ghazālī also uses the personification of Satan to talk of the dual nature of human beings where human nature is aligned to both angels and the devil. In doing evil (*sharr*), human beings are connected to the devil, and in doing good, human beings are connected to the angels.[28] Iblīs showed Adam and his descendants the consequences of disobeying God so that they now know their real struggle is a struggle against denial of the divine command.

Why evil, moral and natural, exists alongside an infinitely good God and whether some evil is necessary, were not questions which occupied the world view of the majority of Muslim thinkers. Why humans have to suffer natural disasters or be subject to unbearable pain are issues neither dissolved nor resolved within the arguments for an omnipotent and just God. While much of Islamic thought tried to absolve God of actively creating evil deeds and leading people astray, it recognised that human wrongdoing is part of the divine plan and that God has a stake in both the good that we do and the wrong that we do. There is no romanticising of evil in Islam as something which is conquered by a divine or human act. Evil accompanies us along life's journey and human beings who are part of the natural order live with the struggle of choosing right over wrong throughout their lives. Evil is not a contradiction but a challenge to human life. In this pursuit of the good life, God's revelation guides against all forms of wrong, but human conscience has always been vulnerable from the time of Adam. Thus, human suffering and sin are not meant to be wiped out or dissolved through any divine act but are intrinsic to the human condition. As Ayoub writes, 'Redemption in Islam begins with Adam who was made for the earth. He descends to earth, and the battle between good and evil begins on its true stage, the earth. Redemption is when this battle is finally concluded with the divine victory, with the victory of the good.'[29]

However, those Muslim thinkers who did consider human wrongdoing did not look at evil or sin as the ultimate tragedy of creation and human suffering as an abstract entity in the world; they did not speak of evil in some pure state, because it seems, if not impossible, extremely difficult to define pure evil. Rather, they tried to reconcile the inevitability of human wrongdoing and the necessity of divine forgiveness in the face of a merciful (*raḥīm*) and benign creator. Evil is problematic, but wrongdoing exists and wrongdoing is relational as it harms others and ourselves. Yet wrongdoing is closely associated with a God who forgives and wants to forgive, for an unforgiving God is not God. The rationale for their thinking was not so much pointed at individual suffering, rather that human society would suffer if it was not based on the observance of divine laws and ethical directives. Human propensity to sin or 'go against the law' is always met with the promise of divine forgiveness. The Qur'ān and Prophetic sayings are replete with the definition of God as compassionate:

> Say, 'O my servants who have transgressed against themselves, despair not of the mercy of God (*raḥma Allah*), for God forgives all sins: for He is oft-forgiving, most merciful (*ghafūr al-raḥīm*) (Q39:53).

> O son of Adam, so long as you call upon me and ask of me, I shall forgive you for what you have done, and I shall not mind. O son of Adam, were your sins to reach the clouds of the sky and were you then to ask forgiveness of me, I would forgive you. O son of Adam, were you to come to me with sins nearly as great as the earth and were you then to face me, ascribing no partner to me, I would bring you forgiveness nearly as great as it (i.e. the earth).[30]

Evil (*sūʾ* or *sharr*) is the opposite of good (*khayr*). But the nature of evil is fundamentally the wrong which we do to ourselves as well as to others. It can be manifest in a single act or a chain of acts. But human nature is not tainted or defined by evil, for if evil has a beginning, it also has an end. Either way, we act knowingly and freely. Evil is seen largely through the prism of human choice rather than divine damnation. Thus evil is not a state but acts. Minus the tragic element of sin as evident in much of Christian theological reflection, evil loses its transcendental dimension and can appear to be reduced to the more prosaic, even the banality of human wrongdoing. But in Islamic thought, wrongdoing is corrosive, futile for the individual and society, and leads ultimately to an evasion of moral responsibility. It is through the possibility of wrongdoing, repentance and subsequent discernment, that humankind hopes to attain moral growth. Once committed, wrongdoing, wilful or inflicted, has the capacity to transform us into something better and we ourselves are responsible for our redemption. Good deeds create a benign earthly order, but good deeds are also tied to the salvation of the soul. Iblīs is a symbolic but necessary player in the human quest for salvation since without him there is nothing for intelligence to master. Unlike Adam, ordinary mortals have not experienced creation without evil, creation without suffering, but nor have humans experienced creation without love and joy and beauty.

God's revelation as guiding revelation is not the central theme of sin/evil and salvation in Christian doctrine. Maurice Wiles writes that 'The Christian tradition has never believed that men needed only to be shown the truth about God and about human life. Sin has usually been regarded as more fundamental than ignorance. Men need not only to be enlightened; they need to be changed. The forgiveness and transformation of man are at least as basic to Christ's mission as the impartation of knowledge and illumination.'[31] Gerald O'Collins lists the kinds of evils that human beings suffer which include alienation from oneself or from God, death, war, bondage, meaninglessness and ruptured relationships. But he writes that the 'basic evil from which Christ delivers human beings is, of course, sin which has often been defined as a personal and intentional transgression of the divine will'.[32] Sin constitutes the most critical alienation from God, self and others; it creates a profound rupture in one's relationship with God. Human beings want autonomy from God, so they refuse to subject themselves to God's moral demands. An eloquent discussion of original sin is given in Reinhold Niebuhr's *The Nature and Destiny of Man*:

> Man is a sinner. His sin is defined as rebellion against God. The Christian estimate of evil is so serious precisely because it places evil at the very centre of human personality: in the will. This evil cannot be regarded complacently as the inevitable consequence of his finiteness or the fruit of his involvement in the contingencies and necessities of nature. Sin is occasioned precisely by the fact that man refuses to admit his 'creatureliness' and to acknowledge himself as merely a member of total unity

> of life. He pretends to be more than he is . . . his sin is the wrong use of his freedom and its consequent destruction.[33]

Niebuhr believed that ultimate salvation is not a moral possibility, that 'the sinful self-contradiction in the human spirit cannot be overcome by moral action'. As Ng Kam Weng says, 'Original sin is a complex package of unbelief (lack of trust), rebellion, and idolatry; it ends up with human beings replacing God with the self – in effect replacing the Creator with the creature. The Christian tradition associates original sin with Adam's historical act of defiance, but the doctrine of original sin also accurately describes the fundamental relation of every human being to God. Every person is as immediately involved with original sin as Adam and Eve were.'[34] It should be pointed out that Catholic theologians have softened this view by adding that traces of the *semen religionis* (seed of religion) survive the fall and therefore all people, unless they 'are congenitally or invincibly ignorant of God's existence, retain the *sensus divinitatis* (sense of divinity) which is their birthright'.[35] Although this view of human nature has been somewhat diluted today, the concept of sin as the alienating presence between humanity and the divine still remains.

Niebuhr goes deeper into the relationship between Christian sin and hope when he talks of the 'foolishness of God which is wiser than the wisdom of men' in which modern man rejects the Christian drama of salvation. This is because man's modern conception of human nature does not regard life as tragic and does not recognise the inherent contradiction of human existence:

> He thinks that history is the record of the progressive triumph of good over evil. He does not recognise the simple but profound truth that man's life remains self-contradictory in its sin, no

> matter how high human culture rises; that the highest form of spirituality, therefore, contains also the subtlest form of human sin. The failure to recognise this fact gives modern culture a non-tragic conception of human history. To recognise this fact, and nothing more, is to reduce human history to simple tragedy. But the basic message of Christian faith is a message of hope in tragedy. . . . The God of Christian faith is not only creator but redeemer. He does not allow human existence to end tragically. He snatches victory from defeat. He himself is defeated in history but he is also victorious in that defeat.[36]

It is precisely because moral evil disrupts personal and social harmony that it cannot be ignored. But escape from sin is not through observance of the law. Wiles explains the necessity but limitations of the law in this respect:

> In human society, the control of the social effects of evil requires the operation of the law. At times that law has to operate in terms of fixed penalties which must be met before any further more constructive steps can be undertaken. This is necessary and sometimes beneficial. But we recognise it as a blunt instrument, unavoidable for us because of our lack of insight into human motivation and our need for short term deterrence. But it is an aspect of our experience of law which makes little sense when applied analogically to God's dealings with the world. In that context the concept of the fixed penalty which must be met is crude to the point of absurdity.[37]

If Adam's sin was the single historical occasion entailing universal sin, then Jesus' death is the single historical occasion entailing universal redemption. But it is difficult to see how this doctrine is worked out. From an Islamic perspective it is Jesus' humanity, the new consciousness he brought with his re-ordering of the social order, which continues to redeem us, not his death. In this way the emphasis on prophetic 'reminding' through both words and deeds continues its purpose in Jesus. But Sandra Keating makes the valuable point that in the Christian context, God is not content with alienation from his creation. She writes:

> In the *Letter to the Hebrews*, God says of the House of Israel within the context of affirming the prophecy of Jeremiah concerning the New Covenant (Jeremiah 31:31–34): 'For I will forgive their evildoing and remember their sins no more' (8:12) and 'This is the covenant I will establish with them after those days', says the Lord; 'I will put my laws in their hearts, and I will write them upon their minds', ... [and] 'their sins and their evildoing I will remember no more' (10:16–17).

Keating explains, however, that although God leaves past sins aside in perfect remembrance of the new Covenant, 'God's non-remembrance of the past does not obliterate the sin; rather it reduces its significance in the relationship between God and his people'.[38]

The overlapping concepts of sin and evil have continued to preoccupy modern thinking and it would be true to say that within the Christian and western philosophical tradition, there has developed a variety of interpretations on the relationship between death and redemption. Recently Jovan Babić rightly commented that while 'natural evil exists independently of moral evil, yet it serves to produce conditions conducive to much of the moral evil we experience'. While scholars on the subject have often tried to create a typology of evil, there remains one fundamental demarcation:

> The evil that is most intimate to our experience is the evil that we ourselves do, active evil, not the passive evil we suffer. Of passive evils we know many. We undergo them in sickness, suffering and death, in being the victim of the active evil of others, as when we are deceived, cheated, dealt with cruelty in body and spirit, or tyrannised over by the powerful.[39]

The cultural theorist and philosopher Slavoj Žižek contests the traditional account of good and evil, the relationship between mortality and immortality where immortality is linked to the good and mortality to evil. He wrote that what makes us good is awareness of our immortality, God, our soul, 'while the root of evil is the resignation to our mortality'.[40] He presents an alternative:

> What if one wages the hypothesis that the primordial immortality is that of evil: evil is something which threatens to return forever, a spectral dimension which magically survives its physical annihilation and continues to haunt us. This is why the victory of good over evil is the ability to die, to regain the innocence of nature, to find peace in getting rid of the obscene infinity of evil. . . . This is why Christ had to die – pagan gods who cannot die are embodiments of obscene evil.[41]

In his criticism of the fundamental Christian story, the French social theorist Jean Baudrillard imputes blame on God for human wrongdoing and humiliation where God himself is the manipulator, 'in league with the principle of evil'. He writes that the entire history of mankind is one of wrongdoing because God took upon himself an infinite debt and has been constantly passing that debt on to mankind. This is enforced guilt to which has been added humiliation and humankind has no way of wiping out this debt:

> Being unable to take up the challenge it has to humble itself and give thanks. It is at this point that God chose to cancel the debt himself by sending his beloved son to sacrifice himself on the cross. He pretends to humble himself, and in so doing, inflicts an even greater humiliation on humanity by making it conscious of its impotence.[42]

Baudrillard laments that instead of taking advantage of the death of God to be free of this debt, human beings have deepened this debt.[43]

Discussions on evil and suffering have assumed a more complex nature also because of the different kinds of evil and suffering which many see as the product of the modern age. But Peter Dews rightly questions why in a post-theological intellectual universe, there should be philosophical difficulty in coming to terms with the concept and phenomenon of evil:

> It would seem that the problem of theodicy, of justifying the ways of God to a suffering world, should have disappeared for us who live after Nietzsche's proclamation of the death of God. And yet as the recent burgeoning of philosophical literature on the topic of evil suggests, the problem of theodicy seems in some sense to have outlived the explicit belief in a divine creator that first gave rise to it.[44]

Whether or not the use of the concept of evil can be disconnected from theological language to a more secular, moral discourse is debateable. Modern theories of the specific contextuality of knowledge can be considered against the metaphysical speculation about the essence of human beings and the world in which we live and create, but any account of moral evil in the modern age requires 'recognition of the connection between evil and individual moral identity as a whole'.[45]

Whatever way we understand sin and evil, they provide the basic premise to the development of the love and law narratives in Christianity and Islam. If we go first to Biblical and post-Biblical Judaism, we see that love is the principle axis in the relationship between God and Israel. Describing Judaism's relationship to God, Slavoj Žižek writes that Judaism is the religion of desire, 'it desires for God who precisely as the Sublime Beyond remains inaccessible'.[46] But Judaism's desire for God is reflected in its attitude to the law. For some the core commandment of Judaism is Leviticus, 'Love your neighbour as yourself' (Leviticus 19:18). Others have stressed various passages in Deuteronomy which served as the most significant sources for many later authorities. Franz Rosensweig argues that this commandment to love the neighbour arises out of the unique love God has for the children of Israel and the centrality of this love is reflected most poignantly in:

> Hear, O Israel, the lord is our God. The Lord is one, you shall love the Lord our God with all your heart, with all your soul and with all your strength (Deuteronomy 6:4–5).

However, Rosensweig also finds it remarkable that throughout the Tora, God demands that Israel love him but never professes love for Israel except in a future sense, i.e. if Israel loves God, he will bless them in return. Love for God is expressed through carrying out the commandments. This kind of love, *nomos*, sees the cause of Israel's love for God appearing as God's request:

> And now, Israel, what does the Lord your God require of you but to fear the Lord your God, to walk in all his ways and to love him (Deuteronomy 10:12).
>
> If you shall keep all these commandments to do them, which I command you this day, to love the lord your God and walk ever in his ways . . . (Deuteronomy 19:9).
>
> But take great care to do the commandment and the Tora to love the Lord your God (Joshua 22:5).[47]

Abraham is the best example of such love, yet here again observing the law is not seen as a way of acquiring God's love but of showing love for the divine. The believer loves that which comes from God and that is why he studies the Tora. It is said that if the gentiles were able to understand the profound meaning of the Tora, they would love God, that it was due to their love for God that Israel was ready to accept the burden of keeping the commandments.[48]

In terms of God's love for Israel, it is based largely on his love for the Fathers and the oath he swore, 'And because he loved your Fathers, he chose their seed after them' (Deuteronomy 4:37). Again, God loves those who love him, 'I love those who love me and those who seek me early shall find me' (Proverbs 8:17). God's choosing of Israel is an expression of his love and thus God's love is also manifest through the sufferings he brings on those whom he chooses – it is a father–son relationship of education and punishment:

> My son, do not despise the Lord's instruction, nor be weary of his chastisement, for the Lord reproves him whom he loves, and he resembles a father who loves his son (Proverbs 3:11–12).

The problematics of love and law lie primarily in the fact that in both Islam and Judaism the outsider sees law largely through a prism of ritualism in opposition to the ethical. Law is the external, the public and the ceremonial, whereas true spiritualism or true morality is to be found in the internal, the unstructured, the emotional and the personal. In comparing Muslim and Christian views on scripture and law, David Zeidan writes, 'The Christian view of scripture as law is more complex than the Islamic one, as it is tempered by the doctrine of salvation by faith rather than by obedience to a written law.' Amongst Christian fundamentalists 'Most would describe the Bible as God's law, dividing its legal passages into the ceremonial ones fulfilled by Christ and therefore not binding today, and the moral which is eternal.'[49] In his explanation of the legalistic Jewish religion at the time of Jesus, L. E. Browne writes:

> Then came the Gospel, which is represented in the New Testament as fulfilling the Law and the Prophets. It fulfilled them because, by making the Law internal in the heart instead of external and written in codes, it enabled the Law to catch up with prophetic revelation and to make the prophetic ideals practicable in human life. The Christian Law in the heart is not general, but particular. A Law that is written, and intended for all men generally, cannot foresee the exact circumstances of every conceivable case. The Christian Law is the working of the Holy Spirit in the heart, showing the individual how he, under his particular circumstances and at

> that particular moment, can carry out the revealed duty of love to God and man.[50]

But in his recent book *Jesus, A Marginal Jew: Law and Love*, John Meier explores the very nature of this 'law' in the Synoptic Gospels, the Greek phrase *ho nomos* which had a breadth of meaning in ancient Greek 'to which our standard translation law does not do justice'. Furthermore, Meier writes of the difficulties of trying to grasp Jesus' attitude to the Mosaic Law when each of the four evangelists had his own understanding of the law. He contends that there was much reformulation of what Jesus said on the law by first and second generation Christians, including probable deletion of the law:

> It was this creative and somewhat chaotic matrix that gave birth to the various interpretations of Jesus' approach to the Law that we find in the four Gospels. Here, then, is the nub of the problem: we find in the Gospels not simply Jesus' interpretation of the Law but, first of all, the four evangelists' reinterpretation of Jesus' interpretation of the Law.[51]

Meier adds that 'We must take seriously the possibility that early Christians when they missionized Gentiles simply dropped certain aspects of Jesus' halakhic teaching because these parts were considered unintelligible or irrelevant to the Gentile audience.' He stresses that we must be wary of quoting every pronouncement of Jesus on the law that we find in the Gospels as though it must come from the historical Jesus. One such example is that 'the Gordian knot of Jesus and the law is easily cut by parroting the famous declaration of Matthew 5:17, "Do not think I have come to abolish the Law or the Prophets, I have come not to abolish but to fulfil."' Meier explains how the verb 'fulfil' (*plēroō*) in Matthew's redaction takes on a specific meaning in relation to the law. Whereas other humans 'do', 'keep' or 'observe' the law, it is only Jesus who 'fulfils' the law. Fulfilment takes on a new meaning as this fits in with Matthew's Christology.[52]

Whereas Jesus says nothing about the law being an impulse to sin, the complexity of the law finds a particular tension in the Letters of Paul and the relationship between the law, sin and grace. Paul knows that the law is an expression of the will of God, but he understands the law as 'the embodiment of moral demand'. In his powerful Letter to the Galatians, Paul addresses a particular concern of the law. He is writing to a significant group known as the Judaisers in early Christianity, especially among Jewish Christians, who felt that Christian converts had to observe the Jewish law as well as follow the teachings of Christ, and this applied even to Gentiles. Paul had addressed this issue earlier at the Council of Jerusalem (Acts 15) and had clearly won the day with his argument that Christianity stood on its own and did not need to observe the customs of the Jewish law, such as circumcision and other Mosaic rituals:

> Mark my words! I, Paul, tell you that if you let yourselves be circumcised, Christ will be of no value to you at all. Again I declare to every man who lets himself be circumcised that he is obligated to obey the whole law. You who are trying to be justified by the law have been alienated from Christ; you have fallen away from grace. For through the Spirit we eagerly await by faith the righteousness for which we hope. For in Christ Jesus neither circumcision nor uncircumcision has any value.

> The only thing that counts is faith expressing itself through love (Galatians 5:2–6).

In Galatians 5:14 he states how the law has been fulfilled, bringing to note the love commandment in Leviticus 19:18, 'The whole law has been brought to fulfilment in one sentence, namely "You shall love your neighbour as yourself."'

Paul's dilemma on the law and sin reaches a particular complexity in his Letters to the Romans. In Romans 7:7–14:

> What then shall we say? That the law is sin? By no means! Yet if it had not been for the law, I would not have known sin. For I would not have known what it is to covet if the law had not said, 'You shall not covet.' But sin, seizing an opportunity through the commandment, produced in me all kinds of covetousness. For apart from the law, sin lies dead. I was once alive apart from the law, but when the commandment came, sin came alive and I died. The very commandment that promised life proved to be death to me. For sin, seizing an opportunity through the commandment, deceived me and through it killed me. So the law is holy, and the commandment is holy and righteous and good. Did that which is good, then, bring death to me? By no means! It was sin, producing death in me through what is good, in order that sin might be shown to be sin, and through the commandment might become sinful beyond measure. For we know that the law is spiritual, but I am of the flesh, sold under sin.

Paul refers to human enslavement to sin and writes that even when humankind tries to do moral good by observing the law, people cannot master their passions and desires, and end up doing what they do not want to do. It is sin that brings alienation from creation, for it is sin that brings alienation from God. Sin is the human attempt to establish one's own righteousness through the law, but the law cannot rescue humankind.

In the next section, Romans 7:15–25, which begins with 'I do not understand my own actions, for I do not do what I want but I do the very thing that I hate', Paul is expressing a highly paradoxical account of Christian experience. As a faithful Jew, Paul recognised the law as a blessing from God, but as a Christian he also realised that the law taught what sin is. He is at the same time confident of redemption through Christ but also continues to be aware of the power of sin within him by failing to observe the law: 'Thanks be to God through Jesus Christ our Lord. With my mind I am a slave to the law of God, but with my flesh I am a slave to the law of sin' (Romans 7: 25). It is not entirely clear how this paradox is resolved. The sin inherent in humankind is a barrier to fellowship with God. For Paul, it is in the presence of grace and eternal love as personified in Jesus where redemption lies:

> The Law was our guardian until the Messiah came so we might be justified by faith (Galatians 3:24).
>
> For sin shall not be your master for you are not under law but under grace (Romans 6:14).

For Paul, then, an ethics of law (as duty) must be replaced by an ethics of virtue (enabled by grace). In his Muslim perspective on Paul, Shabbir Akhtar writes that for Paul, 'We need grace to transform us, not only revelation to guide us: what we are by nature can only be rectified by what we may become by grace.'[53] Herein lies a fundamental difference between Christianity and Islam in that the very nature of sin means that guidance alone can never redeem nor restore that which humankind has lost. Sin is not a human act but a human condition in which people are weak and need grace. If prophecy is not enough, neither is guidance, scriptural or otherwise. It is divine grace which must be seen to be active in human life which redeems. From the Muslim perspective, guidance and grace work together not to transform our sinful status but to lead us to God. Paul consistently presents the law as possessing the multiple functions of revealing, transforming, or provoking sin. As Jeffrey Weima writes, 'The Old Testament frequently testifies that the giving of the law to Israel had the effect of bringing to expression the rebelliousness of God's chosen people. In the context of a strong belief in an omnipotent God, the progression from the idea that the law had a given *effect* to the idea that God *intended* it to do so is not a difficult one to make. Paul's statements regarding the causative function of the law are thus hardly illogical but rather are an understandable development of the effect of the law on the people of God as attested in the Old Testament scriptures and validated in everyday experience.'[54]

Rudolf Bultmann interprets Jesus' stance on the Mosaic Law not as one of annulling basic tenets such as ritual cleanness or the Sabbath but in emphasising the ethical demands of the law. He writes:

> The true will of God is set against what is legally right. And, for Jesus, the scribal tradition has the character of law. The mistake of the scribes is their conception of the Old Testament law as a legal code with limited provisions which a man can fulfil by the proper actions. For Jesus, on the other hand, the

> Old Testament has the character of the true will of God which demands of man, not a limited but a radical obedience.[55]

Referring to the Gospel of John, Bultmann does not define sin as consisting in one specific act but states that 'sin is to remain in what one is, in what proves to be darkness now that it is confronted by light'.[56]

In his analysis of Jesus as embodying an 'alternative consciousness' to the social conventions of his time, Walter Brueggemann explains that Jesus' critique of the law 'concerns the fundamental social valuing of his society'. Even if Jesus did not dismantle the social order, he gave voice to the concerns. Brueggemann lists various representative actions that include Jesus' readiness to forgive sin (Mark 2:1–11) which 'evoked amazement, also appeared to be blasphemy, that is to say, a threat to the present religious sanctions'. He writes, 'At one level the danger is that Jesus stood in the role of God and therefore claimed too much but we should not miss the radical criticism of society contained in the act.'[57] Referring to Hannah Arendt who had stated that it was Jesus' 'insistence on his power to forgive even more than his performance of miracles which shocks the people', Brueggemann concludes that 'while the claim of Jesus may have been religiously staggering, its threat to the form of accepted social control was even greater'.[58] In his writings on Jesus and Judaism, E. P. Sanders concludes that Jesus 'did not consider the Mosaic dispensation to be final and absolutely binding'. Sanders suggests that a possible reason for this was that 'It was Jesus' sense of living at the turn of the ages which allowed him to think that the Mosaic law was not final and absolute'.[59]

In the context of historical criticism, Albert Schweitzer viewed the historical Jesus as an 'imperious ruler' in a climate of apocalyptic religion, not as a moral sage offering wisdom for ethical living throughout the ages. Yet, even on Schweitzer's account, it is because of the historical Jesus, not in spite of him, that Christianity yields to an ethical interpretation and demands an ongoing ethical response from the faithful. While people feared that the claims of eschatology would abolish the significance of his words for their time, he writes that these words are based on an eschatological world view and 'contain the expression of a mind of which the contemporary world with all its historical and social circumstances no longer had any existence'. They are appropriate, therefore, to any world, for in every world 'they raise the man who dares to meet their challenge, and does not turn and twist them into meaninglessness, above his world and his time, making him inwardly free, so that he is fitted to be, in his own world and in his own time, a simple channel of the power of Jesus'.[60]

It is worthwhile mentioning here that the sense of Jesus overturning the social order by urging a new moral order is captured in the sayings attributed to Jesus by Muslim saints and scholars. The collection compiled by Tarif Khalidi in his book *The Muslim Jesus* provides resonances to the Biblical Jesus and below is an example of such a saying in which Jesus shows by his own living example the richness and fullness of a life devoted to God:

> If you wish, you may repeat what the Possessor of the Word and the Spirit [of God], Jesus, the son of Mary, used to say: 'Hunger is my seasoning, fear is my garment, wool is my clothing, the light of the dawn is my heat in winter, the moon is my lantern, my legs are my beast of burden, and the produce of the earth is my food and fruit. I retire for the night with nothing to my name. And there is no-one on earth richer than me.'[61]

In medieval thought Thomas Aquinas elaborated extensively on the meaning of law and grace in his *Summa Theologica*. For Thomas, references to the Old Law are to be understood as 'the Torah, the commands and injunctions found in the early books of the Old Testament'.[62] These laws were given at the time of Moses 'as a remedy for human ignorance . . . because "by the Law is the knowledge of sin"' (Romans 3:20).[63] This was required because man had become proud of his knowledge and power. The pride of man's knowledge revealed itself via thinking that 'natural reason could suffice . . . for salvation'.[64] As such, man was left without a written law so that he could appreciate that his reasoning was deficient: 'But, after man had been instructed by the Law, his pride was convinced of his weakness, through his being unable to fulfil what he knew.'[65] Thus Thomas considers the Old Law to have been given to allow man to realise his own inadequacy.[66] This inadequacy is one that cannot be remedied because man, despite having the law, is unable to fulfil it. The only remedy is Christ, for Thomas considers the Old Law to reside 'between the law of nature and the law of grace'.

From an Islamic perspective, Jesus, Paul and their relationship to the law have met with varying responses. Mustansir Mir explains how Jesus may be called the 'seal of the prophets of Israel'. He elaborates that 'Jesus did not intend to violate the law, but only to shock his opponents into the realisation that they had reduced their religion to a set of empty mechanically performed rituals, forgetting and neglecting the spirit of those rituals and upsetting the proper hierarchy of values that they were, to borrow from Matthew 23:24, straining out gnats but swallowing camels.'[67] Taking both themes of ethnicity and election, Ismā'il Farūqi emphasises the importance of works within this historical paradigm by explaining how Islam's concept of good works went further than the Christian concept of the new Israel:

> It is true that in extending election from Israel to the new Israel, the Christian divests it of its Hebraic radicalism and transforms it into an election by faith, and this transformation stands at the root of justification by faith (Romans 4, Galatians 3). In Islam, election and justification are not at all by faith, but by works. Faith in Islam is only a condition, valuable and often necessary, but not indispensable. The Qur'ān counts among the saved not only the ḥanīfs, or the pre-Islamic righteous, but many post-Islamic Christians and Jews and gives as the reason for their salvation, their devoted worship of God, their humility, their charity and their good deeds. Islam may be said to have recaptured the pure Semitic vision, beclouded by the old Hebrew radicalism as well as by the new 'Christianism', of a moral order of the universe in which every human being, regardless of his race or colour – indeed of his religion in the institutionalised sense – gets exactly what he deserves, only what his works and deeds earn for him on an absolute moral scale of justice.[68]

P. S. van Koningsveld has examined various images of Paul as depicted in classical Islamic literature.[69] One of the polemicists in the Andalusian context is Ibn Hazm (d.1064), who accuses Paul of introducing the doctrine of Jesus' divinity to the Christians. But Ibn Hazm also accuses Paul of having prohibited Jewish legal prescriptions, namely circumcision, 'one of the firmest legal prescriptions of the Tawrat'. He ridicules Paul's views on circumcision from the Epistle to the Galatians:

> The cursed Paul says in one of his Epistles, viz. the one to the Galatians, in the sixth chapter, 'We testify to every man who has been circumcised that he is obliged to keep the laws of the *Tawrat* completely.' However, somewhat earlier he writes: 'If you are circumcised, Christ will profit you nothing.' How strange that he prescribed two [different] religions to them!

In more recent times, Syed Qutb, the leading ideologue of the Muslim Brotherhood during the 1950s and 1960s, blamed Paul for promulgating the belief that Jesus Christ is the Son of God. Qutb argued that Jesus had taught unity of God but that not one of the Christian denominations or schools follows God's true religion.[70] 'Ata ur-Rahim also singles out Paul for initiating the process which led to the deification of Jesus and the abolition of circumcision.[71]

Into the complexity of his views on the place of law in the ritual and moral life of the new Christian community, in Galatians 5:16–18 and 22–26, Paul adds the conflict between the flesh and the Spirit:

> So I say, walk by the Spirit, and you will not gratify the desires of the flesh. For the flesh desires what is contrary to the Spirit, and the Spirit what is contrary to the flesh. They are in conflict with each other, so that you are not to do whatever you want. But if you are led by the Spirit, you are not under the law.
>
> But the fruit of the Spirit is love, joy, peace, forbearance, kindness, goodness, faithfulness, gentleness and self-control. Against such things there is no law. Those who belong to Christ Jesus have crucified the flesh with its passions and desires. Since we live by the Spirit, let us keep in step with the Spirit. Let us not become conceited, provoking and envying each other.

For Paul, Christ is not just a teacher who has taught a new concept of God, a new view of the world, a new morality as timeless truth. As Bultmann states, for Paul, Christ is the earthly teacher only for those for whom he is already the exalted Lord.[72] Paul emphasises that judgment is consummated on the cross, 'He who does not let himself be crucified with Christ; he for whom the world is not dead and who is not himself dead to the world; he who does not see that Christ "gave himself for me" so that I have died and now live in faith' (Galatians 2:19).

A Christ-centred soteriology emphasises God's delivering grace and salvific love for all of humanity. Christ expiates and makes reparation for sin in the sense of definitely 'dealing with' the sinful world.[73] The decisive saving act of Christ is his love and Paul experiences that love in obedience to Christ. He admits to being possessed by love and its transformative power in Galatians 2:20:

> I have been crucified with Christ and I no longer live, but Christ lives in me. The life I live, in the body, I live by the faith in the Son of God, who loved me and gave himself for me.

Paul also speaks of the radical presence of love in two different ways:

> Love is patient; love is kind; love is not envious or boastful or arrogant or rude. It does not insist on its own way; it is not irritable or resentful; it does not rejoice in wrongdoing, but rejoices in the truth. It bears all things, believes all things. Hopes all things, endures all things. Love never ends (1 Corinthians 13:4–8).

This complex tension between law and love is largely absent from Islamic thought. Human beings may not observe the law as they are required, but the significance of the law is that it directs towards God. In disobedience to God, humankind does not lose God but must constantly repent in order to find God once again. In God's grace lies our ultimate salvation, but we cannot dispense with the law, for the law is the journey to God irrespective of our constant failure and constant repentance. In fact the foremost theologian of the Islamic world, Abū Ḥāmid al-Ghazālī (1058–1111), considers both love and law to be central tenets of Islam and being a Muslim. He does not see any conditionality in the prior fulfilment of the law, but rather sees observance of the law as the sublime way to show love for God. Al-Ghazālī does not offer any heavy exploration of the Qur'ānic language and concepts of love, but is content to use the most common word for love, *ḥubb*. He begins by describing the mystical states and stations towards God by concluding that the love of God is the highest in rank and the last stage in drawing towards God before repentance and patience. Love is not a means to God, love is the end station, for the acquisition of the love of God is the end. He emphasises that loving God and loving the Prophet are compulsory, that the meaning of faith is the love for God and his Prophet more than anything else. Augustine had stressed that real love is love of God and that the purpose of theological language was to express this proper love:

> True theological language must be the instrument of elevation and purification of the soul. Theological language has no other ultimate purpose than to strip from the mind the material form and content of its thinking about God and to shape the heart in love for God; together these actions constitute the purification of the heart. There is no neutral theological discourse; every

> proper genre of theological discourse – scripture, creeds, liturgy, sermons, exegesis and commentary, letters, dialogues and studies – has the goal of building a proper love for God, that is correctly directed to the true God, or God, as he truly is.[74]

Al-Ghazālī also recognises that true love is love of God and the human endeavour to nourish that love:

> The ultimate rule of perfection of the servant of God is that the love of God Most High triumph in his heart, so that his totality is engulfed (by that). If it is not this, well, it should be more dominant than the love for other things. Coming to understand the true nature of love is so difficult that some of the scholastic theologians have denied it and have said: 'It is not possible to love a person who is not of your kind. The meaning of love is obedience and nothing else.' Whoever thinks this way has no inkling of the basis of religion.[75]

For al-Ghazālī, therefore, love of God 'is the most exalted of the stations'. Those who love God are perfect servants and this love should engulf the totality of one's person – or at least be the dominant aspect of one's personhood. For some, love of God is impossible owing to the perennial *tanzīh–tashbīh* debates. For al-Ghazālī, the scholastic theologian's position that '[t]he meaning of love is obedience and nothing else' is wrong; such thinking is reflective of someone who 'has no inkling of the basis of religion'.[76] This obedience is to be understood as obedience to the law:

> The essence of knowledge is to know what obedience and worship are. Know that obedience and worship are conformity

> to the Lawgiver as regards commands and prohibitions, in both word and deed.[77]

Al-Ghazālī is quite clear that love of God means something more than mere obedience, while equally insisting that Muslims must be obedient. He considers the reward for those who are deemed by God as law-abiding to be the gaining of knowledge that aids the heart in its perennial battle between appetence and anger, thus helping it attain a state of asceticism and detachment from the world:

> And he [i.e. the Messenger] said: 'God Most High floods the heart of whoever eats of the lawful for forty days, without the admixture of anything unlawful, with light and opens the eyes of wisdom in his heart.' One (version of the) Tradition has it that: 'It cuts off the love of the world from his heart.'[78]

The intimacy of law in relation to God is such that Muḥammad is presented as saying, 'Worship has ten parts; nine of those are the seeking of the lawful.'[79] It is possible to say that seeking knowledge (of the un/lawful) is considered by al-Ghazālī to be not only a form of worship, but also *the most important* aspect of worship. For, when one knows *and does* the lawful, one's heart is filled with light and wisdom which will help form the correct character of the intellect, thus determining one's eschatological horizon. This formation helps encourage worldly detachment and orientation toward the divine.

In God we can love the benefactor, we can observe the source of all beauty and finally the issue of affinity. Man loves God because of the affinity between the human soul and God. But how is that so when God is utterly transcendent? It is through those passages in the Qur'ān which say 'I breathed into man of my spirit', or 'I have made you my representative on earth'. The affinity with God lies in the idea that human beings are created in the spiritual not physical image of God. Yet al-Ghazālī concludes that most people love God for selfish reasons.

But al-Ghazālī defines a powerful connection between knowledge and love where precedence is given to knowledge, which is spiritual knowledge. Without spiritual knowledge there can be no love; the stronger the knowledge, the stronger the love, because love is not merely an emotion but the highest form of cognition. Al-Ghazālī quotes the eighth-century scholar Ḥasan al Baṣrī on this: 'He who recognises his Lord, loves him, he who recognises the world adapts to renunciation. The happiest man in the hereafter is the one who has the most love for God during this life.'

But what are the servant's signs of his love for God when obedience to God conflicts with our own desires? Al-Ghazālī admits that we all say we love God, but actually love is a very difficult thing. A true lover will be in harmony with the one he loves, so he refrains from sin and persists in doing good. Another sign is to remember God at all times and to love that which is a sign or blessing from God, such as the Qur'ān or the Prophet, though the mystic Rabia said her love was so great that it did not leave any place even for the messenger.

But wanting love of God comes with its cost. In his collection of Muslim sayings attributed to Jesus, Tarif Khalidi gives an example from al-Ghazālī on the human desire for divine love:

> Jesus passed by a young man who was watering a garden. The young man said to Jesus, 'Ask your God to grant me an atom's weight of love for Him.' Jesus said, 'You cannot bear an atom's weight.' The young man said, 'Then half an atom's weight.' Jesus

> prayed, 'O God, grant him half an atom's weight of love for you.' Jesus then passed on. A long time later Jesus was passing through the place where the young man used to be and, asking about him, was told, 'He has gone mad and left for the mountains.' Jesus prayed to God to reveal his place, and saw him up on the mountains. He found him standing on a rock, staring up at the sky. Jesus greeted him, but the young man did not return his greeting, and so he said, 'I am Jesus.' God then revealed to Jesus, 'How can he whose heart has half an atom's weight of love for me hear the words of human beings? By my glory and might, even if you were to saw him through, he would not be aware of it.[80]

Thus, although our prayer and life should be about wanting nearness to God, such stories reveal that when God returns this love, there is a human cost; we become oblivious to this world and to our life in it.

Death is the key to meeting with God, and for those who think badly of death for fear of separation from family, children and treasure, these are the impediments to the love of God as full love occupies the entire heart. There is a strong sense that the one who loves God does not find consolation in anything else in life. Sin is opposed to full love, but not to basic love. Doing wrong does not mean that love no longer remains in us, but full love does not remain in us; we need to purify our hearts once again to show full love of God.[81] Yet al-Ghazālī claims that sin has two sides. In one sense sin is the decree and will of God to which we have to surrender. The other side of sin is that it is acquired by human beings and therefore their guilt. Thus, 'It is hateful to God and its sign is that God has given you power not to commit it.' If the relationship between a person and God is that of lover and beloved, then 'It is the duty of every lover of God that he should love what God loves and hate what he hates.'[82]

But what of God's love for man? This is a very short extract set against the theme of literal and metaphorical meaning of words. The word *ḥubb* is used for love but does not encapsulate the true sense of God's love for humankind. It is through the goodness and purity of character whereby we approach God. God loves, but God throws into danger and trials the ones he loves. Al-Ghazālī quotes a Prophetic saying that God gives this world to one he loves or doesn't love, but he gives faith only to one he loves. We must not be greedy for God's love as God gives love only by examining people. But if God's love for a servant is doubtful, then how does man know that he is loved by God? Al-Ghazālī says that the Qur'ān is the proof that God loves his servants.[83]

The relationship between law and sin is tied to love of God in a different way from how Paul expresses the dilemma of law and grace. It is not the law in a Pauline sense, but rather laws to which al-Ghazālī refers. Right belief and right action form the path to salvation, but this search for right behaviour is in essence a theological quest, a search for meaning and not confined to legal prescriptions in any narrow sense. There is a paradox implicit in the concept God's law. Law implies a set of rules, a set of precepts imposed upon society, and what came to be known as *sharī'a* is not a superimposed structure on society, it designates religion in its totality, not just duties. This divine legislation comprises both positive law and also ethical behaviour, but by its very nature as God's law it remains ultimately elusive.

But going 'against the law' is part of being human, for human nature is recalcitrant. Adam's disobedience in paradise shows how man's first act of freedom can be seen as man's first act of disobedience. The law is essentially about the believer's struggle and endeavour to understand his relationship to God, but in that struggle humankind will do wrong, for that is the divine expectation. When the Muslim tradition speaks of divine forgiveness and hope, it recognises the inevitability of human wrongdoing which is a consequence of non-observance of the law. Here, the penitent believer can find reassurance in divine mercy:

> According to the tradition, when the servant commits a sin and asks God for pardon, God Almighty says to his angels, 'Look at my servant, he has committed a sin and he knows that he has a Lord who will pardon and take away the sin. I testify to you that I have pardoned him. And according to the tradition, if my servant were to sin so that his sins were to reach the clouds of the skies, I would pardon him in so far as he asked pardon of me and hoped in me.'[84]

In Islam, then, worship of God is law and love of God is also law. Although the tension over how God is close yet distant directed much of Islamic thought to conclude that God is transcendent in his very immanence because to take either position purely is to limit God, there is a distinction between God (*Haqq*) and creation (*khalq*). But God's transcendence and omnipotence within and apart from his creation are not the defining attributes of a distant God. When the human face turns to God, God does not turn away. It is in this turning to God for repentance, for consolation in the dark silence of the universe, where the Muslim encounters the mercy and nearness of the Creator.

In Islamic thought, the theme of God's cosmic love has been most poignantly felt through the rich and wide prism of Ṣūfī literature, even if has not been recognised as an overtly dominant discourse of the Qur'ān itself. Even for the Ṣūfīs, there remained a distinction between how God loves man and how man loves or should love God. Love in its various manifestations is part of the world order, the cosmic order, but there is no particular word which defines the relationship of love between God and man, so that the concept of love carries within it the sense of both the divine and the profane. It was left to the exegetes and the Ṣūfīs to debate not only how God loves but also whether love, which implies a need amongst human beings, can be attributed to a perfect God who has no need. Furthermore, not all Ṣūfīs agreed with the conventional dichotomies posed by the distinction between *ʿishq-i haqīqī* (love directed to God) and *ʿishq-i majāzi* (love directed to human beings). It could be argued that the love verses in the Qur'ān have been interpreted in various ways, that there is no direct teleology between the Qur'ānic verses on love and Ṣūfī love interpretations. However, a mutual understanding of love between God and man can be inferred from the Qur'ān in a verse such as 'O You who believe, whoever from you turns back from your faith, God will soon bring a people whom he loves and they love him' (Q5:54). The emphasis on 'He loves them and they love him' is regarded by many as the focus for the whole of love mysticism in Islamic thought.[85] Unlike al-Ghazālī who connected love of God with obedience, Ibn al-ʿArabī drew a connection between love and worship so that worship of God was not about knowing God or obedience to him, but essentially about loving him. For Ibn al-ʿArabī, love becomes a universal principle encompassing the actions of all creation, the basis by which all phenomena are explicable. Human beings may not be able to attribute a beginning or purpose to God's love, but he writes, 'We came from love, we are created in love.'[86]

The Qur'ānic expression of love is varied, but it is one Qur'ānic motif among many others. God's love is given, but it can also be withheld. The root *ḥabba* and its derivatives best reflect the various dimensions of love, as for example:

> God loves those who keep themselves pure (Q2:222).
>
> Do good, for God loves those who do good (Q2:195).
>
> Say, 'If you love God, follow me, for God will love you and forgive you your sins. God is most forgiving and most merciful' (Q3:31).
>
> Fight in the cause of Allah those who fight you, but do not transgress limits, for God does not love the transgressors (Q2:190).

The language of love, affection or desire appears in various contexts, but a criticism levelled against the Qur'ānic God is that his love is not given freely and that humankind has to earn divine love through good deeds; conditionality is explicit. When one examines Qur'ānic verses where love is expressed in the negative, such as 'God does not love those who do wrong' (Q3:57 and Q3:140), 'God does not love transgressors' (Q2:190) and 'He will cause people to come whom He will love and who will love Him' (Q5:54), one can be left with the image of a God who draws near to man only when man draws near to him. This reading would imply a contingent and bilateral element in God's love, a love which is seemingly earned through right conduct, piety or obedience to divine laws and commands. There is also an element of fear implied in obedience, a fear which does not wipe out love but enforces obedience. This is discussed at some length in al-Ghazālī, who concludes that there should be a balance of fear and hope in one's devotion to God:

> As for the pious person who has forsaken sin, outward and inward, concealed and open, what is most salutary is that his

> hope and fear should be in equilibrium. For that reason it was said, if the fear and hope of the believer were weighed, they would balance each other. And it is reported that ʿAli said to one of his children: Fear God with such a fear as will make you see that, if you brought Him the good deeds of all the people of the earth, he would not accept them from you; and hope in God with such a hope as to make you see that, if you brought Him the evil deeds of all the people of the earth, he would pardon you for them.[87]

Yet one reading of the story of Adam and Eve shows that God has already shown his love in his forgiveness of Adam. Iblīs is cursed as Satan by God for his disobedience in refusing to prostrate in front of Adam, but Adam is forgiven by God for eating from the forbidden tree. Adam's sense of guilt and shame at his behaviour causes him to ask Gabriel that after one parting glance at paradise, he be allowed to flee from paradise:

> When Adam had one foot outside the gate, the voice of God called, 'Gabriel, stop him at the gate of paradise.' Then the mighty one called saying, 'O Adam, I created you to be a thankful servant, not an unbelieving slave.' 'O Lord,' cried Adam, 'by your splendour I beg you to restore me to the dust from which you created me, and I shall be dust as I first was.' 'O Adam,' said God, 'how can I restore you to dust when I have known for all eternity that I would fill the earth and hell from your loins.' And Adam was silent.[88]

The universal significance's of Adam's action does not entail universal guilt but rather a different destiny for man. Adam and humanity as a whole are now to multiply and fill the earth, but this must be done in the presence of God, with hope in God, with all of our human failings; we cannot hide from God in sin and nor are we condemned for our sins. In continuing to worship God we continue to love him, and our sins rather than any ontological sin are cleansed by the good that we do. It can be argued that sin is a reflection of unbelief, but in his collection of the sayings of Jesus Khalidi cites a saying attributed to Jesus who makes a distinction, 'You disciples are afraid of sin, we prophets are afraid of unbelief.'[89]

What matters is continued belief and hope in God, not the sins we commit. We don't need to be saved from sin but rather from unbelief. Being open to God's love is part of this journey and humankind has to take only one step towards God to feel his love:

> God the Almighty has said, 'Whoever shows enmity to a friend of mine, I shall be at war with him. My servant does not draw near to me with anything more loved by me than what I have made obligatory upon him and my servant continues to draw near to me with supererogatory works so that I shall love him. When I love him I am his hearing with which he hears, his seeing with which he sees, his hand with which he strikes and his foot with which he walks. Were he to ask (something) of me, I would surely give it to him; and were he to ask me for refuge, I would surely grant him it.[90]

The concept of trying to draw near to God evokes God as a God in waiting, a God almost desperate to respond to human longing. He does not just listen to us, he becomes the ears with which we listen, the sight with which we see, the hand with which we strike and the foot with which we walk. One of the ways of being close to

God is through prayer, as in Q40:62, 'Pray and I will answer.' Annemarie Schimmel writes of the famous Ṣūfī, al-Makki:

> 'To be deprived of prayer (*duʿā*) would be for me a much greater loss than to be deprived of being heard and granted.' This word of Abū Hāzim al-Makki, an early Ṣūfī, is the keynote for an understanding of the moderate Ṣūfic point of view concerning prayer. Prayer is an intimate conversation between man and God which consolates the afflicted heart even if it is not immediately answered.[91]

The mystics want to pray, but prayer itself could be seen as a sign of ingratitude, a lack of complete self-surrender. On the other hand, some mystics argued that God longs for our prayers and afflicts man so that he can hear his prayers, his voice. Schimmel writes that it was Rūmī who interpreted mystical prayer in the most perfect manner. 'Being asked "Is there any way to God nearer than the ritual prayer?" he replied in his work *Fihi ma Fihi* (*In it what is in it*): "No, but prayer does not consist in forms alone. . . . Prayer is the drowning and unconsciousness of the soul, so that all these forms remain without. At that time there is no room even for Gabriel, who is pure spirit. One may say that the man who prays in this fashion is exempt from all religious obligations, since he is deprived of his reason. Absorption in the Divine Unity is the soul of prayer."'[92]

While the varying notions of love contained in the Qur'ān through the vocabulary of *ḥubb* or *wadd* allude to God's love, these concepts on their own are only a partial reflection of God's relationship with this creation. The love vocabulary complements that which lies at the core of divine engagement with creation. The fundamental term which allows us a glimpse of God's nature is in the principle of *raḥma* – mercy or loving compassion. Muslim tradition is full of the language of compassion as the defining essence of God:

> And according to a tradition, truly God possesses a hundred mercies. From these, he has put away ninety-nine beside himself and revealed only one mercy in this world. By virtue of it people show compassion to each other and the mother is compassionate to her child, and the beast is humane with its offspring. On the day of resurrection God will join this mercy to the ninety-nine and will spread them out over the whole of his creation and every single mercy will be in conformity with the heavens and the earth.[93]

This overwhelming mercy is a mystery, for it is essentially a plea from God to humankind not to despair of God's mercy. In al-Ghazālī's *Book of Fear and Hope*, there is a tradition, 'There was a man of the children of Israel who was inducing despair in men and was being hard on them. So God said to him, "The day of Resurrection will be a day on which I will make you despair of my mercy as you have made my creatures despair of it."' Another tradition, attributed to Imam 'Ali, says, 'The knowledgeable person is simply he who does not make people despair of the mercy of God and does not make them feel secure from the stratagems of God.'[94]

Mercy, unlike love, is not bilateral – human beings cannot have mercy on God, but God chooses, indeed desires to be merciful to human beings. Al-Ghazālī also quotes a tradition where a believer implores God to keep him away from sin. God's response is, 'All my believing servants ask this from me. But if I should keep them away from sin, upon whom will I bestow my blessings and to whom will

I grant forgiveness?'[95] God expects, I would argue, indeed wants human beings to commit sin so that he can forgive; herein lies a mutual dependency between the divine and the human, between love and law.

At its most basic understanding, the Qur'ān speaks of a merciful God who always responds to a free but disobedient humanity. Our relationship with God is defined by this mutual hope, human hope in God and God's hope in us. But the Qur'ān does not speak of one act by God nor one defining expression of God's love. Perhaps this is Islam's biggest parting with Christian doctrine in that it does not have those defining moments of both alienation from God as in the Fall and subsequent reconciliation with God, redemption through the death and resurrection of Christ. Christianity emphasises grace through Christ, which shows that God's love is spontaneous and has no expectations of us. Love not only refers to the nature of God, but as a consequence must therefore be the basis for all human relationships. The double love commandment proclaimed by Jesus in the Gospels of Matthew, Mark and Luke are central to the Christian belief:

> You shall love the Lord your God with all your heart, and with all your soul, and with all your mind. This is the greatest and first commandment. And a second is like it: You shall love your neighbour as yourself (Matthew 22.37–39; cf. Mark 12.29–31; Luke 10.27–28).

The most fundamental doctrine for *agape* love for most Christians lies in a Trinitarian understanding of God, where the manifestation of divine love precedes the polemics of divine unity. Nevertheless, this doctrine poses a dilemma. Christians have analysed the problematics of Latin Trinitarianism which looked on God as a single personal being, in relation to how and whom God loves. Brian Hebblethwaite argues that the model of a single individual person does create difficulties for theistic belief. It presents us with the picture of one who despite his infinite attributes, is unable to enjoy the excellence of personal relations unless he first creates an object for his love:

> Monotheistic faiths have not favoured the idea that creation is necessary to God, but short of postulating personal relations in God, it is difficult to see how they can avoid it.[96]

However this Godhead is defined, it is both in the Trinity and the Cross where we encounter the essence of divine love and the mystery of human salvation. It is here that we see relational love, the loving relationship between the Father, Son and the Holy Spirit, and sacrificial love. In this relational love lies the expression of God's love when no creation yet existed. But God's love is also eternal, that is, he is love before the existence of creation; his love is not contingent on creation even if it is given to creation:

> And in this love he has done all his works, and in this love he has made all things profitable to us, and in this love our life is everlasting. In our creation we had beginning, but the love in which he created us was in him from without beginning. In this love we have our beginning, and all this shall we see in God without end.[97]

Divine love is central to Christianity, the defining element of the Christian faith. In Christianity, God is a God of love, indeed God is love (1 John 4:8). Even though theologians have wrestled with what is meant by 'God is love', there remains in Christianity a fundamental conviction that neither God nor humanity can be understood outside the pluriform expressions of divine love. How God loves humankind has dominated Christian theology. In his classic work *Agape and Eros*, Anders Nygren argued that God's love is a gift, prompted by the very nature of God to love:

> We have therefore every right to say that *agape* is the centre of Christianity. . . . *Agape* comes to us as a quite new creation of Christianity. It sets its mark on everything in Christianity. Without it, nothing that is Christian would be Christian. Agape is Christianity's own original basic conception.[98]

For Nygren, God's spontaneous love is for all, not a love merited only by the righteous or those who pertain to godliness; God loves generously and unconditionally. It is this love which defines us and our value and worth come from God loving us and not from our experiences. Whereas human beings struggle to love, there is no end to God's love. As Rowan Williams writes, the true meaning of *agape* is that God's love never comes to an end: 'The good news of Christianity is that if God suffers human pain, since God is the victim of human injury, then there is beyond all our sin a love that is inexhaustible. God's love for this creation never comes to a point when it can take no more.'[99]

If God loves us unconditionally, then our love for neighbour is also unconditional and impartial. Here, Nygren has problems with the Johannine concept of love where one detects a tension between universalist aspirations and community limitations. While a fellowship and intimacy of love can be found in the Christian community's faith in God, Nygren saw in John's neighbourly love a particularistic love, a love for those who share the Christian faith. Nygren writes that love in John 'loses something of its original, all-embracing scope; it becomes love for those who bear the Christian name'.[100] *Agape* cannot become a preferential love, it must retain its universal expression. God's love in Christianity is reflected ultimately not in law nor in a book but in the story of divine presence in Christ, the self-revelation of God:

> The New Testament neither is able nor intends to give information about how we are to conceive the being of God beyond the history of revelation, about whether it really is a being only in the philosophical sense. It intends rather to report the great event of God's revelation in Christ. The reticent allusions to something beyond revelation are made on the periphery of the New Testament witness and serve solely to point to the simultaneous distinction and unity of the Father and the Son, and thus to remind us all that Christology is *Heilsgeschichte*.[101]

If human beings acknowledge that God lives in Jesus, that Jesus Christ is God in his self-revelation, they must also acknowledge in word and deed the life Jesus led. Herein lies the transformative power of the life of Christ and by implication the law of Christ. As Cullmann writes, 'The faith which regards Jesus Christ as the Revealer as such implies of course also a statement not only about his work but also about his person. But it does so in such a way that one can speak of his person only in connection with his work.'[102]

In Christianity and Islam the modes of God's disclosure are dramatically different. In both religions God's relating to humankind says something about the nature of God and the human condition. In the Gospels it is the primacy of God's love which is repeated as our earthly paradigm. The primary interpretation of Christ's death is the association with sin and its forgiveness, but it has also been understood to have something to say about the problem of human suffering. If traditional Christian theology had for many years taught that God is impassible so as to keep apart God from the suffering of his creatures, modern theology increasingly recognises that human suffering is the most searching challenge to theistic faith and that God must in some ways be 'involved'. God may not suffer as human beings do, but God responds to the suffering of his creatures. God has shown this by entering into the dereliction of the human Jesus on the cross.[103] However wretched the human condition is, redemption through Christ's death means that Christianity is ultimately about hope in tragedy.

At some level the attempt to draw any comparison between the redemptive, kenotic love exemplified in Christ's crucifixion and resurrection, and the various dimensions of divine love as reflected in the Qur'ān, is flawed. For in the Incarnation, Christ moved into a solidarity with all human beings; the divine took on human form and became the essential structure at the very basis of a Christian understanding of God, creation and redemption. This can be found in Barth's formulation of love and grace:

> The Love of God is grace. Grace is the distinctive mode of God's being in so far as it seeks and creates fellowship by its own free inclination and favour, unconditioned by any merit or claim in the beloved, but also unhindered by any unworthiness or opposition in the latter, able on the contrary to overcome all unworthiness and opposition. It is in this distinctive characteristic that we recognise the divinity of God's love.[104]

While both Islam and Christianity talk of a loving God, Islam relying on the concept of mercy for a more comprehensive and expansive definition of love, in my view there is a profound structural difference in the way love is conceptualised in both religions. By focusing primarily on its human manifestation in Christ, love in Christianity is a redemptive act and becomes visible on the cross and its power in the paradox of the weakness of the cross (2 Corinthians 13:4). Salvation does not come about through our best efforts; it is not some happy state to which we can lift ourselves; it is an utterly new creation into which we are brought by our death in Jesus' death and our resurrection in his. In Islam, however, there is no divine Incarnation, nor is prophecy messianic, nor is Muḥammad the redeemer. God's love is manifest through the risk he takes in humanity by giving man both faith and freedom to work towards a moral life. Humanity has the choice to use both to transform itself to a state of higher consciousness. However, humankind is not damned by the impossibility of overcoming sin, for there is no sinless place to which we can return, only a better place which we can create. We may know some limited truths in this life, but the ultimate truth awaits us. Until then, the Qur'ānic command to 'enjoin what is right and forbid what is wrong' remains morally imperative for human flourishing and the earthly order, even though our ultimate salvation lies with God alone.

CHAPTER 6

CONCLUSION

REFLECTIONS ON THE CROSS

The concept of the word God has become unclear. The renowned Catholic theologian Karl Rahner stated that the word God has become as enigmatic for us as a blank face.[1] To this point Wolfhart Pannenberg wrote that while the word God can seem to be an embarrassment for Christian proclamation, without this word an appeal for faith in Jesus of Nazareth loses its foundation:

> If Jesus is just one man among others, and merely a man for all the uniqueness of his life and teaching, then we cannot believe in him in the sense of primitive Christian preaching, and above all we cannot exhort others to believe in him, especially when many of his traditional sayings and even his understanding of himself seem to be odd and to have been outdated by the march of history. Thus Christian proclamation and faith cannot give up the word 'God' which underlies what Jesus says concretely about his 'Father', the one being unintelligible without the other. How can we gain new access, however, to what the blank face of God covers and conceals?[2]

This book has been the search for another meaning for God, another way to understand why the word God remains so powerful in my own life and in the lives of many Christian and Muslim friends. It has been a personal and a spiritual journey for me. I have been engaged in Christian–Muslim dialogue for many years as an ethical and intellectual imperative which has directed me to explore and understand my own Muslim faith from various perspectives. It is true that the word dialogue is laden with all kinds of contested meanings, but I use the word in a very personal capacity; for me dialogue is learning. Christian theology and its perspectives on Islamic thought have been invaluable to this journey. In my conversations with my Christian colleagues, in my reading of Christian theology, I have been fortunate enough to listen and I have learnt in greater depth how to talk of God.

In this work I have tried to show some glimpses of the history of this theological encounter, how the two faiths have talked of Jesus Christ who remains central to continued conversations between the two faiths. I agree with Oddbjorn Leirvik's reflection on Bakhtin's 'dialogic imagination' as a way of approaching intertextuality and monologism/dialogism in the history of Christian–Muslim theology. Bakhtin writes that however monological an utterance may be,

> It cannot but be in some measure, a response to what has already been said about the given topic on the given issue, even though this responsiveness may not have assumed a clear-cut external expression.... The utterance is filled with dialogic overtones, and they must be taken into account in order to fully understand the style of the utterance.[3]

Throughout the book it is the status and images of Jesus Christ as understood and debated by certain Christian and Muslim thinkers which have been the main focus of study. I have not ventured into political, sociological and civilisational aspects of the Muslim or Christian world because Christological doctrines are in my mind, the most disputed and perhaps the most intriguing area of Christian–Muslim debate. Leirvik himself writes that 'A Christology of today needs to be a Christology in dialogue, and the image of Christ in world religions should be recognised as a necessary aspect of systematic theology. Like in the first encounters with Islam, the challenge from Islamic Christologies will be a challenge not only to reaffirm, but also to re-examine the classical controversies and dogmatic resolutions of the Church itself.'[4]

The reader will note that I have as yet not given much prominence to the crucifixion and cross, for many the most poignant image in Christianity, the image of the dying and suffering Jesus. For Christians Jesus crucified is God crucified. Rowan Williams writes, 'This cross is a unique, terrible, extreme act of violence, a summary of all sin. It represents the human rejection of love.'[5] The radical criticism embodied in the crucifixion can be discerned in the passion announcements of Mark's Gospel:

> The Son of man will be delivered into the hands of men, and they will kill him; and when he is killed, after three days he will rise (Mark 9:31).
>
> Behold, we are going up the Jerusalem; and the Son of man will be delivered to the chief priests and the scribes, and they will condemn him to death, and deliver him to the gentiles; and they will mock him, and spit upon him, and scourge him, and kill him; and after three days he will rise (Mark 10:33–34).

Walter Brueggemann explains that 'There is no more radical criticism than these statements, for they announce that the power of God takes the form of death and that real well-being and victory only appear after death.'[6] Humanity is encouraged to be like Jesus:

> Who, being in very nature God, did not consider equality with God something to be used to his own advantage; rather, he made himself nothing by taking the very nature of a servant, being made in human likeness. And being found in appearance as a man, he humbled himself by becoming obedient to death, even death on a cross. (Philippians 2:4–8)

Brueggemann adds:

> The crucifixion of Jesus is not to be understood simply in good liberal fashion as the sacrifice of noble man, nor should we too quickly assign a cultic, priestly theory of atonement to the event. Rather we might see the crucifixion of Jesus as the ultimate act of prophetic criticism in which Jesus announces the end of a world of death and takes that death into his own person.[7]

Conversely from the Islamic perspective, Ali Merad says:

> In the Qur'ān everything is aimed at convincing the believer that he will experience victory over the forces of evil. Islam refuses to accept this tragic image of the Passion, not simply because it has no place for the dogma of redemption but because the Passion would imply in its eyes that God had failed.[8]

Lamin Sanneh writes passionately about the 'deadlock' between Muslims and Christians on this issue, saying, 'Muslims are adamant that the weakness and humiliation of the crucifixion are unworthy of God and fatal to the success of God's will and design for the social order. That is the scandal, the affront, of the cross: a scandal to the Muslim religious temper, and a scandal to worldly wisdom.'[9]

It is true that from the Islamic perspective the cross has little religious significance of either death or suffering as Jesus' death by crucifixion is largely denied. Although Muslim exegetes debated this point at some length, a quote from the twelfth-century exegete Fakhr al-Dīn al-Rāzī (d.1209) encapsulates a general tone of disbelief among many of the writers, 'Whether they say that God is this visible bodily person, or that God fully incarnated in him, or [speak of] three parts, [each of these beliefs is] false (*bāṭil*). If the God of the world were this body, then when the Jews killed him they in fact killed the God of this world. How could the world survive without a God?'[10]

T. E. Hughes wrote in the *Dictionary of Islam* that 'The cross of Christ is the missing link in the Muslim's creed: for we have in Islam the great anomaly of a religion which rejects the doctrine of a sacrifice for sin, whilst its great central feast is a *Feast of Sacrifice*.' Samuel Zwemer laments the absence of Jesus Christ in the life of the Muslim:

> As in a total eclipse of the sun the glory and the beauty of the heavenly orb are hidden, and only the corona appears on the edge, so in the life and thought of Mohammedans their own Prophet has almost eclipsed Jesus Christ. Whatever place He may occupy in the Koran – and the portrait there given is a sad caricature; whatever favourable critics may say about Christ's honourable place among the Moslem prophets, it is nevertheless true that the large bulk of Mohammedans know extremely little and think still less, about Jesus Christ. He has no place in their hearts nor in their lives.[11]

I do not intend to go into the doctrinal debates in this chapter nor the linguistic challenges posed by the Qur'ānic verses; they have been exhausted by numerous scholars. Most recently, Todd Lawson's book *The Crucifixion and the Qur'ān* will take the interested reader through a variety of classical and modern commentaries.[12] There are, however, four Qur'ānic verses which speak of the crucifixion and/or the 'death' of Jesus. Here the verb *tawaffā* has been translated 'to die' but it has been placed in quotation marks to show that the verb can be understood in other ways:

> [God said]: 'O Jesus, I am causing you to "die" [*mutawaffika*] and raising you to myself, and cleansing you of those who do not believe, and causing those who follow you to be above those who do not believe until the Day of Resurrection.' (Q3:55)
>
> [The Jews'] saying: 'We killed Christ Jesus the son of Mary, the messenger of God.' And they did not kill him, and they did not crucify him, but it was made to appear so to them [*shubbiha lahum*]. And those who have differed about it are in doubt about it: they do not have knowledge about it, but only the following of supposition. They did not kill him for certain. (Q4:157)
>
> [Jesus said to God]: 'I was a witness over them as long as I was among them, and when you caused me to "die" [*tawaffaytani*], you were their Overseer, and you are Witness over everything.'(Q5:117)
>
> [Jesus said]: 'Peace was on me the day I was born, and will be on me the day I die [*amutu*], and the day I am raised to life again[*ub'athu*].'[13]

Lawson has taken Q4:157, 'They did not kill him and they did not crucify him, rather it only appeared to them', as the only verse that mentions the crucifixion of Jesus. He follows this with an interesting comment about how the crucifixion of Jesus is bound up with the cultural identity of western Christianity:

> This is the only verse in the Qur'ān that mentions the crucifixion of Jesus. It has been understood both by Muslims and in some ways, more interestingly, by Christians as a denial of the historical and, to many, irrefutable 'fact' of the crucifixion of Jesus. Obviously, such a doctrinal position serves as a great obstacle separating Muslims and Christians on the grounds of belief. But more importantly, such belief frankly serves to diminish Islam in the eyes of Christians and so called 'Westerners' whose cultural identity is bound up, whether they are believers or not, with the axiomatic and unquestionable 'myth' of the death and resurrection of Jesus.[14]

Nevertheless, if the cross is part of the cultural identity of the west, it can be argued that Christianity in the west 'seems to have somewhat lost sight of the symbolic character of the cross and come to regard it as no longer anything but the sign of an historical event'.[15] The cross means little without belief in the crucifixion and death of Christ. Kenneth Cragg summarises the Muslim perspective which disputes not that the Jews desired to crucify Jesus, but that God saved him. For Cragg this poses another question:

> What are we to say of the nature of a God who behaves in this way or of the character of a Christ who permits another – even if a Judas – to suffer the consequences of an antagonism his own teaching has raised against himself? Christian history believes that Christ suffered the full length of that hostility, and that he

> did so willingly, as the price of loyalty to his own message . . . not rendering evil for evil, nor encountering hatred with guile.[16]

While reference is made to Jesus' death in the Qur'ān, Muslim belief has tended to read this as a *future death*, after his Second Coming. Some Muslims like Muḥammad ʿAbduh and Rashid Riḍā rejected the view that Jesus was taken up from this world without dying. They maintained that Jesus did die on the cross but that his soul was taken up to heaven. The issue is that even if Muslims came to believe that Jesus did die on the cross before he was raised, in the Qur'ānic frame of references this death has no atoning significance and would not be seen as the decisive event in the redemptive plan for humankind.

But the story does not end with either the crucifixion and death or the crucifixion and non-death. The Messianic hope was of course transformed by the crucifixion, but the resurrection affirmed the divinity of Christ, for in the post-Easter phenomenon lies the genuine Christian faith. In the resurrection lies the hope for the liberation of humanity and the world. While Brian Hebblethwaite analyses why the resurrection is held to constitute sufficient evidence for belief in Christ's divinity, he says, 'It was the resurrection that both opened up the way to an understanding of the soteriological significance of a Crucified Messiah and made possible and necessary the high Christology of the Johannine prologue and eventually the Chalcedonian definition.' It is the transforming power of the risen Christ which makes all things new, it also enables the faithful to be drawn into incarnate love assuring us that such love will 'in the end be all in all'.[17]

In Islam, there is no paschal mystery and Jesus is simply gone, however his ascension is understood. Although he will return at the end times, neither the story of the crucifixion nor his return indicates a divine nature, redemption or salvation for humankind; even in his second coming he remains God's messenger only, a sign of formidable events to come. Mahmoud Ayoub tries to portray what I call the 'something more' in Jesus:

> Like the Christ of Christian faith and hope, the Jesus of the Qur'ān and later Muslim piety is much more than a mere human being, or even simply the messenger of a Book. While the Jesus of Islam is not the Christ of Christianity, the Christ of the Gospel often speaks through the austere, human Jesus of Muslim piety. Indeed, the free spirits of Islamic mysticism found in the man Jesus are not only the example of piety, love and asceticism which they sought to emulate, but also the Christ who exemplifies fulfilled humanity, a humanity illumined by God.[18]

But from the Christian viewpoint the Islamic understanding of God acting through Jesus Christ is not only erroneous, it is a scandal to God's love for all of humanity and the plan of reconciling all his creature to him. The Christian story insists on the radical transformation of both God and man in Christ where the crucifixion becomes the radical event. As Brueggemann writes:

> That tradition of radical criticism is about the selfgiving emptiness of Jesus, about dominion through the loss of dominion, and about fullness coming only by self-emptying. The crucifixion then, is not an odd event in the history of faith, although it is the decisive event. It is rather the full expression of dismantling that has been practised and insisted upon in the

> prophetic tradition since Moses confronted Pharaoh. The cross is the ultimate metaphor of prophetic criticism because it means the end of the old consciousness that death brings on everyone. The crucifixion articulates God's odd freedom, his strange justice, and his peculiar power.[19]

We have noted before that this self-emptying of God or *kenosis* has no real place in Muslim theology, because the stories of human sin and alienation from God are different in both religions. In the Christian tradition there is a sense of the tragedy of the human situation which among other things asserts that sinful man has lost the knowledge of God against whom he has sinned and that God frees us from this ignorance and reveals to us both who he is and who we are. The human condition is one of a certain 'lostness' in which humanity does not know how to save itself. Thus, 'The character, acts and teaching of Jesus, are seen as God's own revelatory and loving acts for our salvation.'[20] While the Church Fathers held a variety of views on human salvation and atonement, there was an underlying sense that since all humanity is part of the corporate personality of the first Adam, all human beings share in Adam's guilt. Salvation therefore entails 'being relieved of this corporate guilt and this is done through the fact that Christ paid the price on behalf of all humanity on the cross'.[21] Maurice Wiles points out that while the Fathers did not work out any systematic theory on the atonement, they needed to make God the agent of salvation: 'If it is God who has to be reconciled, it is God also who is the reconciler.'[22]

I conclude this part of my own journey sitting in front of a cross in a local church and wondering what this symbol means to me as a Muslim. I have witnessed dramatic and beautiful paintings of the cross, sat in churches and cathedrals with the cross in front of me. I have seen a wooden, chipped cross lying amidst piles of paper on the table of a close colleague, but I don't think I have truly reflected on why the cross remains so powerful. Maybe it is unsettling, for it blurs the boundaries between God and humanity.

When thinking of how to end this book, I had asked a number of my Christian friends (who remain anonymous) to tell me briefly what they think and feel when they look at a cross or a crucifix. I realise that if traditional theologies of the cross are primarily concerned with sin and atonement, the redemption of human sins through the punishment of the Son, modern theologies look at the social and political significance of the cross and the vulnerability of the human condition, the suffering of God in a godless world. Did my friends see the same thing when they reflected on this symbol and on this question? I wanted to know how they felt inside and what they felt about their faith as they gazed upon this symbol. Did God crucified make sense? One friend's reply came late; he had been thinking of this request every day for three weeks. I am indebted to them all for their honesty and their time. Their responses are below quoted verbatim:

> Looking at the crucifix is the moment when I can cope with the evening news. Every night another mother is grieving the loss of her child; every night a natural disaster leads to untold suffering; and every night human ingenuity expresses itself in imaginative ways of inflicting harm on each other. The crucifix is the visual reminder that God has embraced and entered into this grizzly and unpleasant existence. Whatever reason God has for suffering is less important than my understanding that God knows what it is to suffer. The crucifix is the mechanism that helps me cling to faith, when everything else seems to point against it.

The cross is both holy and overabundant with meaning, a site where God and humanity, suffering and redemption meet. Every word I put down seems inadequate, wrong by being only partly right, likely to be misread and, as has happened so often, misused, badly misused. Whatever I write, I want to un-write, explain, qualify, balance out . . . and quickly I end up with a tome that I still think is inadequate.

I think of the cross as a symbol of Christianity, and thus of Jesus Christ and of the church. I think of the cross as a place of suffering and death, taken on by God incarnate for us in Jesus Christ. I think of the cross as empty: that suffering and death have ultimately been overcome by resurrection.

Most times when I see a cross I just think of it as a sort of wallpaper, background, i.e. I don't really think about it. But occasionally it makes an impact – e.g. the rather stark tree/cross on the cover of my human rights book, or the accidentally broken wooden cross in my Edinburgh study – these suggest the cost to God of love and justice.

I suppose in the end my thoughts usually come back to Grünewald's Isenheim Altarpiece. I think, in the end, I would be what most of my colleagues would call a 'death-of-God-theologian' and thus the cross affirms the death as actual and real. At the same time, in the spirit of the *coincidentia oppositorum*, Grünewald's is the greatest image of Christ in glory. The two are one moment.

Looking at the cross is looking in front of a brand name (I seem not to look in it or beyond it) or a very successful marketing symbol and seeing nothing (an absent presence or a present absence?). It is so prevalent in the culture (in my profession) that I begin to see nothing – much like looking at rows of soft drink labels and deciding on what to drink. What liquid will go into the cup? Coke or Pepsi – it holds no difference – the taste is the same. And yet, there is that small nudge that tells me it is something somewhere in me and in the world.

When I look at the Catholic crucifix I see compassion and arguably sadness. This may have to do with how the actual body of Christ is positioned and 'the look' on his face. Compassion, because Jesus lived a life of compassion and love even towards those who were seemingly undeserving of it. And yet, ironically, Jesus was ultimately shown no compassion/love in the manner of his death. As such, there is a certain juxtaposition of compassion and non-compassion for me when I look at the cross (love can equally be put in here instead of compassion). I also feel sadness because at a fundamental level I suppose there is an awareness that I have the capacity to persecute/treat others as Jesus was treated. And this is reflected in the preceding compassion sentence by noting that Jesus showed love to those who were seemingly undeserving of it. No one is undeserving of love; that (for me) is the main point of the gospel. And yet that is our vocation, to love all regardless, the (extreme) inability to do so being the manifestation of the ultimate compassion and loving person being executed on a cross. If this is how we treat a man of Christ's calibre, what does this say about how we treat others? People just like us full of imperfections? Do we respond with love and compassion or non-love and non-compassion? Are we the crucifier or are we the crucified? What role are we playing presently in the 'Jesus narratives'? And I suppose with every self-negation or instance of choosing the other over ourselves, we are 'sacrificing' some part/desire of ourselves. In giving you the last biscuit, I crucify myself (to an extent)! I guess that is what I see/feel when I look at the cross but generally don't attempt to articulate it!

> I see four things when I look at a cross: First, I see a call to love and reconciliation – that Jesus Christ loved us so much that he overcame our enmity and violence and rejection by willingly laying down his life in forgiving love to reconcile us, and that he calls me to willingly give myself in love for others. Second, I see a call to solidarity with all who suffer – that Jesus' self-giving on the cross is the ultimate expression of God's solidarity with all innocent victims of violence and oppression, and that God calls us to live out that solidarity ourselves. Third, I see a call to repentance – that Jesus suffered in my place to atone for my sins, and that this challenges me to turn from my sin and to live in love for God and for others. Fourth, I see a reminder of failure – that Christians in the Crusades distorted the cross into a symbol of violence, so that for countless Muslims and Jews the cross signifies not a call to Christians to give their lives for others in love, but rather a banner under which Christians have killed others out of hate. This means that I look upon the cross with a mixture of sorrow and joy, sorrow over my own sin and the sin of the Christian community, but joy in God's love and forgiveness expressed in Jesus Christ.

In these personal reflections, I see a range of views. The cross is nothing, a 'marketing symbol', the cross is a symbol of conquest, compassion, and in the cross one witnesses the suffering of God. Does the cross draw the believer nearer to God and if so what kind of God does the cross reflect? The impact of the cross is not just as a visual image; it represents a truth which is both terrible and hopeful, death and triumph. It is a symbol inspiring a kind of wonder that leaves many struggling for words. Some have tried to convey the experience of suffering and victory on the cross, the agony of Jesus, the wretchedness of humanity, but also the power of love and hope in this redemptive death. All the various meanings of the cross still point to one truth, which is that at the centre of the Christian faith is the passion and death of Christ on the cross. The cross is at the heart of the Christian faith and the very focus of its sacramental *anamnesis* in 'the bread and wine' of the Eucharist.[23]

Nothing in Islam compares to this and, if anything, Muslims have either rejected or ignored the significance of the cross. I am reminded of the Indian Muslim philosopher Muḥammad Iqbal in whose religious symbolism Christ held no special status but who called Christ 'the lamp of all creation whose light lit up the world'. Yet Iqbal was in fundamental disagreement with the basic point of orthodox Christianity: 'No religious system can ignore the moral value of suffering', but 'the error of the builders of Christianity was that they based their religion on the factor of suffering alone, and ignored all the other factors.'[24] It seems to me that Iqbal may have been right to use the model of Jesus in rejecting the asceticism and renunciation which he saw in his people, but he misses a fundamental point. The higher purpose of this suffering has been ignored, which is the reconciling of the creature with the creator, of an ultimate triumph.

It is true that for many Christians, the cross represents Christ's broken body and a brutal death. But in Jesus' death, eternal death is wiped out. The German-American theologian and commentator Reinhold Niebuhr (1892–1971) saw this suffering in the larger framework of man's most basic needs and the imperilled nature of the human enterprise. For Niebuhr, the most basic human need of the human spirit is the need for security and the most fundamental problem of religion is meeting this need. He writes that 'In a true religion, faith in the ultimate meaningfulness of existence, grounded in a God who transcends the caprices and contingencies of the physical order and who is capable of overcoming the chaos created by human sin, is the final security of the human spirit. In false religion this ultimate security is prematurely appropriated and corrupted so that it assures man peace in his sins and not through the forgiveness of his sins.'[25] For Niebuhr, all power leads to pride and injustice, and pride as a consequence of power gives man a false security.

Niebuhr's main message is that Christianity is a religion transcending tragedy. He wrote that the Saviour truly says, 'Weep not for me', for the Saviour is a revelation of the goodness of God. If Christ is defeated in history, 'that very defeat proves that he cannot be ultimately defeated', because God's nature is to 'swallow up evil in Himself and destroy it'. The cross is not the tragedy but the resolution of tragedy. For Niebuhr, the crucifixion points to that which transcends human striving, and without this revelation, 'that which is beyond tragedy in life could not have been apprehended'. Without the cross, people are 'beguiled by what is good in human existence into a false optimism and by what is tragic into despair'. His views of the suffering servant acting in the realms of eternity explain the nature of the cross event and the suffering servant as one of ultimate victory:

> The basic plan of life cannot be finally defeated. The will of God prevails even when the Son of God is crucified. In that very crucifixion God has absorbed the contradictions of historic existence into Himself. Thus Christianity transmutes the tragedy of history into something which is not tragedy. God is revealed as not only the ground but as the goal of human existence and man's rebellion against God is proved to be an abortive effort which cannot finally prevail. The suffering servant is the son of man.[26]

Yet the more I read personal accounts of the cross, the more I am convinced that for most people the cross reveals a surprising truth about the way God really is, a God for whom no rejection is final. The cross addresses what people are rather than what they do. For Doug Frank, the process of imagining a demanding and judgemental God is similar to the process of imagining, 'in our embarrassment and shame, that the people around us have unkindly eyes towards us, even when they may only wish us well. It seems that invariably, humans project onto God their own self-contempt, and then they suffer in the unkindly gaze of this unlovable, imaginary God.' For Frank, the Jesus on the cross, naked, bound, wounded and willingly powerless, is still compassionate towards those who hung him there. Genuine faith begins in that moment of shock when, as Frank states, we realise that God is not a figure of power and glory but 'more truly present to us as one who is vulnerable, seemingly powerless, and infinitely forgiving'. Jesus on the cross reveals our own human selves as 'shame loosens its hold on us and we begin to wear our nakedness more openly'.[27]

If Muslim theological reflection on the cross has been wanting, I have discovered that many Muslim writers (not just Arabs and Persians) have used Jesus as a symbol of healing but also as a symbol of suffering and hope. J. S. Addleton provides a useful review of this literature from which I have made a brief selection. The eighteenth-century Urdu poet Mir Hasan, for example, reflects the widely held view of the asceticism and spirituality of Jesus:

> If Jesus lives in heaven, it is because
> For years he roamed the desert lands of love.[28]

A somewhat similar image appears in the poetry of Kushal Khan Khattak, another seventeenth-century Pushto poet:

If winged words could have carried me
In their flight up to the skies
I'd be seated now in the heavenly sphere
Where the prophet Jesus is.[29]

When we come to the poet philosopher Muḥammad Iqbal, Annemarie Schimmel notes, 'The person of Christ takes no important place in his religious symbolism.' Whosoever has read Oriental poetry knows how widely spread the symbol of the life-giving breath of Christ is. In Iqbal, he is scarcely mentioned, and in a typical strain, turned against the Europeans. Schimmel also states:

> The figures of Adam, Abraham, and Moses are used, in Iqbal's poetry, with more or less important variations, as models of life and behaviour for every faithful Muslim. But the figure of Jesus Christ is handled quite differently in his work, and the picture of Christianity is dark and full of bitter criticism.[30]

Drawing on Annemarie Schimmel's work, Addleton provides a short verse by the Sindhi poet Mirza Qalich Beg, a near contemporary of Iqbal's whom Addleton describes as giving an almost unique and heretofore unprecedented presentation of Christ:

> All you readers have had this news, Ponder on whatever you read.
>
> You know the full account of Jesus; you know also all his deeds. He had loved the world greatly always, suffered and sacrificed for the world. He gave teaching, preached everywhere; in every way he expressed the truth. The ones who believe will live joyfully, and have salvation hereafter.[31]

The great Urdu literary genius of the twentieth century Faiz Ahmed Faiz touches not so much on the *moral* value as on the *redemptive* possibilities of suffering in his poem from his prison. The scene is a prison in 1954:

> In my barred window is hung many a cross
> Each colored with the blood of its own Christ,
> Each craving to hug tight a divine form.
>
> On one the heaven's spring cloud is sacrificed,
> On one the radiant moon is crucified,
> On one is torn asunder the trance-filled grove,
> And on another the delicate breeze has died.
>
> Daily these kind and beautiful godlike things
> Come weltering in their blood to my bitter cell;
> And day by day before my watching eyes
> Their martyred bodies are raised up and made well.[32]

In this poem there is a flicker of the sentiment which Jürgen Moltmann refers to in the healing of sicknesses and griefs: 'In the image of the crucified God the sick and dying can see themselves, because in them the crucified God recognizes himself.'

The cross is powerful and the crucifixion is sorrowful. But as I sit here I feel that while the cross speaks to me, it does not draw me in. Its mystery is moving, but I cannot incline towards what it says about a God in form, a God who undergoes this inexplicable agony for an inexplicable act of mercy. It is not the language of redemption which I cannot understand, it is the necessity of God's self-revelation for this act of redemption. Why does the fall become the paradigm of human life, making the cross the ultimate paradox of death and new life? There are other ways to come to redemption even if this means looking at the world in a dramatically different way. This is a world in which the intimacy of human relations with God does not rest on an event that has occurred but on our constant movement towards him in the hope of events which are about to occur. Forgiveness is not a given, it has not happened yet, not because it needs to be earned but simply because we have not witnessed it yet.

Among postmodern philosophers, Slavoj Žižek questions the excesses of God's mercy, the strangeness of this love and the sacrifice of his Son 'in order to bind us to himself through love'. But Žižek saw in this love which does not demand anything from us, an act of perversion:

> When the falsely innocent Christlike figure of pure suffering and sacrifice for our sake tells us, 'I don't want anything from you!', we can be sure that this statement conceals a qualification, '. . . except *your very soul*.' When somebody insists that he [*sic*] wants nothing that we have, it simply means that he has his eye on what we *are*, on the very core of our being.[33]

However, Žižek offers other explanations which do not demand that we see Christ's death as a sacrifice. In the coming of Christ, we have 'the descent of the Sublime Beyond to the everyday level', which does not mean that we renounce transcendence completely but that in Him, the transcendent realm becomes accessible as 'immanent transcendence'.[34] Christianity is the religion of love, for God does not remain in the Sublime Beyond. As he writes, Christ is God and with his coming the 'God of Beyond' has died. God is a mystery for himself and this culminates in the words of Jesus on the cross,

'Father, why did you forsake me?' For Žižek, 'At that moment God is completely abandoned by God and shares the human experience of being abandoned by God.' On the cross, God abandons himself totally and in this way the absolute identity of God and humankind is realised.[35]

Thomas J. J. Altizer spoke of the end of God's transcendence in the Incarnation in his *The Gospel of Christian Atheism.* Altizer argued that after the Incarnation there is no transcendent God. Christians do not take the Incarnation seriously as long as they combine the doctrine of the Incarnation with a belief in a 'transcendent, a sovereign, and an impassive God'. He writes:

> Thus the radical Christian reverses the orthodox confession, affirming that 'God is Jesus' rather than 'Jesus is God'. Before the Incarnation can be understood as a decisive and real event, it must be known as effecting a decisive and real event, it must be known as effecting a real change or movement in God himself: God becomes incarnate in the Word, and he becomes fully incarnate, thereby ceasing to exist or to be present in his primordial form. To say that 'God is Jesus' is to say that God has become the Incarnate Word, he has abandoned or negated his transcendent form; or rather, he remains present and real in his original form only where faith itself refuses to become incarnate.[36]

For Altizer, the Crucifixion meant that the Word has 'finally died to its original form, losing its transcendent glory and its primordial holiness, while fully becoming flesh'.[37] Even if Altizer is criticized for not offering a positive view of divinity, it is Altizer who emphasizes that the Incarnation is a kenotic movement in which it was God himself who took the initiative to empty himself.

It seems to me that the structural differences between Islam and Christianity through the Incarnation, death and resurrection of Jesus Christ are so great that one could be forgiven for wondering what do Islam and Christianity have in common? Even God seems to be so different. Furthermore, where is the meeting ground around ideas of love and hope? In Christianity, love is understood primarily through the divine *kenosis*, hope is renewed in the mystery of the resurrection. If the Qur'ān alludes to Christians and Christianity, it does not allude to the 'software' of these theologies – love, suffering and redemption, how Christians have developed meaning and consolation from these doctrines

Islam has a different concern. It lifts God back into the transcendent, not in the sense of a distant God but a God who chooses to retain the secrets of his Self. Prophecy points to the transcendent, but prophecy can only guide to the divine, it cannot assume the divine. The vocabulary of God's nearness is radically different because there is always a separation between God and man. But this separation is in doctrine only, not in experience. The absence of the cross does not diminish divine love, it is replaced by a different longing for God. I have a copy of the Qur'ān always at my bedside table. I try to read at least a couple of lines before I leave the house every day. I do not see God physically in this reading but I feel his presence. To feel God's gaze in this action is powerful, consoling, even moving, although I carry no physical image of a God whose dramatic death revealed his dramatic love.

But does this mean that the Christian understanding of Jesus Christ is meaningless for me? If I don't accept the totality of the Christian message, am I missing out on hope and love? Karl Barth wrote that 'If we do not have Christ, we do not have at all, but utterly lack the fullness of God's presence. If we separate ourselves from Him, we are not even on the way to this richness, but are slipping back into an impoverishment in which the omnipresent God is not known.'[38] Christians dwell on God by reflecting on Christ. But I feel I cannot agree with Barth's statement, because God's nature must always be full, it can never be less or more, it is not contingent on events in time or our belief in him, rather, it remains full irrespective of human recognition, worship or indeed love. If it is only through the belief in the Incarnation and the redemptive role of Christ that I can understand God, then as a Muslim what meaningful relationship can I have with the one worshipped as the Son of God?

In this church there is silence, space and me. People have come in, sat down, prayed and left. I have been witness to their presence but not shared in their devotion. I have watched them in their reverence as they prayed in silence, as they suffered in silence and I have been moved. The cross in front of me speaks to me personally, emotionally and intellectually. I am drawn to its starkness and emptiness, and yet I don't desire it. Is this because I don't understand its depth or because I have confined my understanding of God to something which does not unsettle me? I am moved by the Christian theology of love, its radical implication of a God that dies so that man can live. But I am not sure that I see the complexities of this theology as meaningful in my life. I don't understand the radical nature of this love which makes God man and man God. If this is tied to the truth of the human condition, the brokenness of humanity, then I too see that humankind is weak, vulnerable, and that sin and suffering are as much part of our earthly paradigm as love and hope. I know that God watches over me, guides me, indeed loves me, but I also know that I must go to him eventually, that he has not already come, the descent of the sublime.

If the most profound message of the cross is about God's power of love and forgiveness reaching out to all humanity, this is a message that I cannot ignore. I need to be able to forgive more easily. It has taken me a long time to understand that the ability to forgive others is a precious gift because the inability to forgive damages your soul. The anger and the hurt never really goes, it just lingers. But I also need to pray for forgiveness for the wrong that I do because my faith resides not only in my hope in God, rather in his hope in me. My Christian friend may well say that it is not what we do, but the brokenness of what we are wherein lies the existential dilemma of the human condition; we cannot reconcile ourselves to God, only God can reconcile us to him. Herein lies the Christian story, powerful, transformative and enriching.

Maybe my own view of God is too definite of him as a 'being beyond', even though I want a glimpse of him in this life, so that I cannot understand him in the Christ-God theophany. A suffering God is a moving thought but I know that God must feel my pain, for he is a God desperately waiting for my prayers.

In my journey through this book, I have tried to understand how Christians and Muslims have talked to each other using their own doctrines. Christians have been baffled as to why Muslims refuse to accept the Incarnation and salvific role of Christ, while Muslims are baffled at the complex nature of the Christian God. Yet I do not think that Muslims and Christians worship a different God, whatever that question means to some. God is God and no amount of poetical or philosophical language can exhaust any definition of him. I also know that I do not have an adequate appreciation of what it is to love and worship God or indeed to be loved by him till the very end. I live always with the dual reality of the wrongfulness of my deeds but hope in God's infinite mercy. This is a challenge for

Muslims who try to balance human temptation with hope in God's ultimate forgiveness. I cannot read the Qur'ān without being moved by God's plea that humankind does not despair of his divine mercy. It seems to me that in spite of all the legalistic models and interpretations of Islam, the language of divine mercy dominates. My Christian friends see their relationship with God in a different way. It is not the wrongfulness of our individual actions and our failures that needs divine forgiveness. Rather, the human condition itself is broken and needs restoring. It is in our woundedness that the risen Christ came with the message of peace, love and forgiveness so that the deeper emptiness of our lives becomes a privileged place where we can encounter God. In both religions, it seems to me that our journey in life rests on these immeasurable realities of suffering and hope.

However differently Christians and Muslims define God and their relationship to God, God remains the deepest presence in our lives. For me, he lives in my thoughts and prayers, in the lives of my children, and in my most fragile hopes. In this respect I am convinced that whenever and wherever I turn to God, I share this humbling but joyful relationship with all who turn to him in faith.

NOTES

Chapter 1 The End of Prophecy

1. For a short but useful introduction to this literature, see Roberto Tottoli, 'Narrative Literature' in Andrew Rippin (ed.), *The Blackwell Companion to the Qur'ān*, Blackwell Publishing, 2006, 467–80. See also the reference to Brinner in W. M. Brinner, 'Arā'is al-majālis fī qisas al-anbiyā' or "Lives of the Prophets" as Recounted by Abū Ishāq Ahmad ibn Muḥammad ibn Ibrāhīm al-Tha'labī', Leiden: E. J. Brill, 2002.
2. Christopher Buck, 'Discovering', in Rippin, *Blackwell Companion to the Qur'ān*, p. 27.
3. Graham Houston, *Prophecy Now*, Leicester: Intervarsity Press, 1989, 30.
4. Houston, *Prophecy*, 31.
5. Frederick E. Greenspahn, 'Why Prophecy Ceased', *Journal of Biblical Literature*, 108:1, 1989, 37–49.
6. Sten H. Stenson, 'Prophecy, Theology and Philosophy', *Journal of Religion*, 44:1, 1964, 17–28.
7. Oscar Cullmann, *The Christology of the New Testament*, London: SCM Press, 1957, 22.
8. Cullmann, *Christology*, 25.
9. Ibn Sīnā, *The Metaphysics of the Healing*, translated by M. E. Marmura, Provo, UT: Brigham Young University Press, 2005, 365–78.
10. Frank Griffel, 'Muslim philosophers' rationalist explanation', in Jonathan E. Brockopp (ed.), *The Cambridge Companion to Muhammad*, Cambridge: Cambridge University Press, 2010, 173. This is a useful article summarising some of the main philosophical debates.
11. Griffel, 'Muslim philosophers', 175.
12. Fazlur Rahman, *Prophecy in Islam*, London: George Allen and Unwin, 1958, 96.
13. The idea of *'iṣma* was first articulated by the Shī'ites, who applied the doctrine not to prophets but to their imāms. See also Daniel Brown, *Rethinking Tradition in Modern Islamic Thought*, Cambridge: Cambridge University Press, 1996, 61–80.
14. Wadad, 'What is Prophecy?' in Michael Ipgrave (ed.), *Bearing the Word: Prophecy in Biblical and Qur'ānic Perspective*, Church House Publishing, 2005, 47.
15. Jane McAuliffe, 'The Abrogation of Judaism and Christianity in Islam', in Hans Küng and Jürgen Moltmann (eds), *Islam: A Challenge for Christianity*, London: SCM Press, 1994, 117.
16. H. A. R. Gibb, *Islam: An Historical Survey*, 2nd edn, Oxford: Oxford University Press, 1970.
17. For an accessible overview of these debates, see Fred M. Donner, 'The Qur'ān in Recent Scholarship', in Gabriel Reynolds (ed.), *The Qur'ān in its Historical Context*, New York: Routledge, 2008, 29–50.

18. For a comprehensive view of this subject, see Aliza Shnizer in 'Sacrality and Collection', in Rippin, *Blackwell Companion*, 159–71.
19. This is a theme running throughout the Qur'ān and one which has been carefully analysed in Daniel A. Madigan, *The Qur'ân's Self Image*, Princeton, New Jersey: Princeton University Press, 2001.
20. François de Blois, 'Naṣrānī and ḥanīf: Studies on the Religious Vocabulary of Christianity and Islam', *Bulletin of the School of Oriental and African Studies*, 65:1, 2002, 1–30.
21. Jewish Christians means those Christian sects who followed the law of the Jews, especially in regard to circumcision and observation of the Sabbath.
22. Jaroslav Pelikan, *Mary Through the Centuries: Her Place in the History of Culture*, New Haven: Yale University Press, 1998, 76.
23. M. Sharon, 'People of the Book', in J. McAuliffe (ed.), *The Encyclopaedia of the Qur'ān*, vol. 4, Leiden: Brill, 2004, 42–3.
24. D. Marshall, 'Christianity in the Qur'ān', in Lloyd Ridgeon (ed.), *Islamic Interpretations of Christianity*, Curzon Press, 2001, 24–5.
25. Basit Bilal Koshul, 'Studying the Western Other', in Muhammad Suheyl Umar (ed.), *The Religious Other: Towards a Muslim Theology of Other Religions in a Post-Prophetic Age*, Lahore: Iqbal Academy Pakistan, 2008, 195.
26. For a brief history of the concept of *taḥrīf*, see Martin Accad, 'Corruption and/or Misinterpretation of the Bible: The Story of the Islamic Usage of *Taḥrīf*', *The Near East School of Theology Theological Review*, 24, 2003, 67–97.
27. J. Windrow Sweetman, *Islam and Christian Theology*, Part One, vol. 2, London: Lutterworth Press, 1947, 140.
28. Adolfo Gonzales Montes, 'The Challenge of Islamic Monotheism: a Christian View', in Hans Küng and Jürgen Moltmann (eds), *Islam: A Challenge for Christianity*, London: SCM Press, 1994, 69–70.
29. Josef van Ess, 'Verbal Inspiration', in Stefan Wild (ed.), *The Qur'ān as Text*, Leiden: E. J. Brill, 1996, 187.
30. See Wild's useful analysis of *nuzūl* etc. in Stefan Wild, 'We Have Sent Down to Thee The Book', in Wild, *The Qur'ān*, 137–8.
31. Van Ess, 'Verbal Inspiration', 194.
32. Van Ess, 'Verbal Inspiration', 179.
33. F. E. Peters, 'The Quest of the Historical Muhammad', *International Journal of Middle-Eastern Studies*, 23:1991, 291–315.
34. http://www.religion-online.org/showchapter.asp?title=452&C=364. Sallie McFague, *Speaking in Parables*, Philadelphia: Fortress Press, first published, 1975.
35. Peters, 'Quest', 291–2.
36. Van Ess, 'Verbal Inspiration?', 178.
37. James D. G. Dunn, *Christianity in the Making, Vol. 1, Jesus Remembered*, Grand Rapids: William B. Eerdmans Publishing Company, 2003, 661.
38. C. H. Dodd, 'Jesus as Teacher and Prophet', in G. K. A. Bell and A. Deissmann (eds), *Mysterium Christi*, London: Longmans, 1930, 53–66.
39. Dunn, *Christianity*, 665.
40. Vincent Taylor, *The Names of Jesus*, London: Macmillan, 1953, 17.
41. Walter Brueggemann, *The Prophetic Imagination*, Philadelphia: Fortress Press, 1978, 16–17.
42. Brueggemann, *Prophetic*, 80–1 and 82–3.
43. Cullmann, *Christology*, 46.
44. *Abba* is the Aramaic for father.
45. Taylor, *Names*, 55.
46. Gerald O'Collins, S.J., *Christology*, Oxford: Oxford University Press, 1995,123.
47. James Barr, 'Abbā Isn't "Daddy"', in *Journal of Theological Studies*, 39:1, 1988, 28–47.
48. Barr, 'Abba', 28–47.

49. James Dunn, *Christology in the Making*, London: SCM Press, and Philadelphia: Westminster Press, 1980, 60.
50. Dunn, *Christology*, 31
51. Dunn, *Christianity*, 724
52. John Macquarrie, *Jesus Christ in Modern Thought*, London: SCM Press, 1990, 42.
53. John Macquarrie, *Christology Revisited*, London: SCM Press, 1998, 17.
54. Søren Kierkegaard, *Philosophical Fragments*, Princeton: Princeton University Press, 1985, 104. This analysis can be found in John Hick, *The Metaphor of God Incarnate* (2nd edn), London: SCM Press, 150–60.
55. Wolfhart Pannenberg, *The Apostles' Creed in the Light of Today's Questions*, London: SCM Press, 1972, 70.
56. Sarah Stroumsa, 'The Signs of Prophecy: The Emergence and Early Development of a Theme in Arabic Theological Literature', *The Harvard Theological Review*, 78:1. 1985, 101–14.
57. Frithjof Schuon, *Islam and the Perennial Philosophy*, World of Islam Festival Publishing Company Ltd, 1976, 20.
58. Neal Robinson, 'Jesus and Mary in the Qur'ān: Some Neglected Affinities', *Religion*, 1990: 20, 161–75. It is worth citing in full Robinson's footnote to this. 'It is possible that as a result of typological exegesis or confusion Jesus is here portrayed as the Old Testament figure of Joshua. The whole passage seems odd to us but would have made sense to Muhammad's audience because of the Byzantine Christians' conquest of Palestine.' See John Bowman, 'The Debt of Islam to Monophysite Syrian Christianity', *Nederlands Theologisch Tijdschrift*, 19 (1964–5), pp. 177–201.
59. In 1 John 2:1 'Paraclete' is used to describe the intercessory role of Jesus who pleads to the Father on our behalf. And in John 14:16 Jesus says 'Another Paraclete' will come to help his disciples, implying Jesus is the first and primary Paraclete. According to some Muslim commentators, the concept of 'Another Paraclete' in John 14:16 refers to Muḥammad, though Christians do not recognise this.
60. http://www.tertullian.org/fathers/timothy_i_apology_01_text.htm. The translation is by Alphonse Mingana
61. Ibn Qayyim al-Jawziyya, *Hidāyat al-hayārā fī ajwibāt al-Yahūd wa-'l-Nasārā*, ed. By Ahmad Hijazi al-Saqqa, Cairo, 1980, 37. This translation comes from Martin Accad, 'Muhammad's Advent As The Final Criterion', in Barbara Roggema, Marcel Poorthuis, Pim Valkenberg (eds), *The Three Rings*, Utrecht: Thomas Instituut, 2005, 223.
62. The original letter is edited and translated in French by Paul Khoury, *Paul d'Antioche, Évêque melkite de Sidon (X11 s.)*, Beirut, 1964, 58–83 (Arabic) and 169–87 (French). For analysis of the history and content of this *Letter* see D. Thomas, 'Paul of Antioch's Letter to a Muslim Friend and the Letter from Cyprus', in D. Thomas (ed.), *Syrian Christians under Islam: The First Thousand Years*, Leiden: E. J. Brill, 2001.
63. See also Herman Teule, 'Paul of Antioch's Attitude Towards the Jews and the Muslims', in *The Three Rings*, 91–110.
64. This translation can be found on www.salafitranslation.com
65. Rudolf Bultmann, *Faith and Understanding*, translated by Louise Pettibone Smith, 1969, London: SCM Press, 283.
66. Bultmann, *Faith*, 291.
67. Bultmann, *Faith*, 308.
68. Adolf von Harnack, *What is Christianity? Sixteen lectures delivered in the University of Berlin during the Winter Term, 1899–1900*, translated by Thomas Bailey Saunders, London, Edinburgh and Oxford: Williams and Northgate; New York: G.P. Putnam's Sons, 1901, 204–5.
69. Heikki Räisänen is cited in Oddbjørn Leirvik, *Images of Jesus Christ in Islam*, 2nd ed., London: Continuum, 2010, 29.
70. Tarif Khalidi, *The Muslim Jesus*, Cambridge, Massachusetts: Harvard University Press, 2003, 12.

71. Wild 'We Have Sent', 137.
72. Carmelo Dotolo, *The Christian Revelation, Word, Event and Mystery*, translated by Cavallo Domenica, 2006, The Davies Group Publishers, 2006, i–ii.
73. The response by Daniel Madigan S. J. to *A Common Word*, www.acommonword.com/response
74. Mahmoud Ayoub, 'Towards an Islamic Christology II', in Irfan Omar (ed.), *A Muslim View of Christianity: Essays on Dialogue by Mahmoud Ayoub*, Maryknoll, New York : Orbis Books, 2007, 156.
75. Heikki Räisänen, 'The Portrait of Jesus in the Qur'ān: Reflections of a Biblical Scholar', *Muslim World*, 7000:2, 1980, 122–33.
76. Cullmann, *Christology*, 47.
77. Kenneth Cragg, '"My Tears Into Thy Bottle", Prophethood and God', *The Muslim World*, 88: 3–4, 1998, 238–55.
78. Hans Küng, 'Christianity and World Religions: The Dialogue with Islam as One Model', *The Muslim World* 77:2, 1987, 80–95.
79. Jürgen Moltmann, *The Way of Jesus Christ*, London: SCM Press Ltd, 1990, 33.

Chapter 2 God as One: Early Debates

1. John Moorhead, 'The Earliest Christian Theological Response to Islam', *Religion*, 1981:11, 265–74.
2. Moorhead, 'Earliest Christian', 266.
3. A comprehensive approach to Sebeos's work can be found in *The Armenian History Attributed to Sebeos*, translated with notes by R. W. Thomson, historical commentary by James Howard Johnston, Assistance from Tim Greenwood, vol. 2, Liverpool Hope University Press, 1999, p. 1i.
4. Thomson, Johnston and Greenwood, *Armenian History*, 1i.
5. Pseudo-Dionysius of Tell Mahre, *Chronique de Denys de Tell Mahre, quatrième part*, ed. and trans. J. B. Chabot, Paris, 1895, 4, and quoted in Moorhead, 'Earliest Christian', 267.
6. Sidney H. Griffith, *The Church in the Shadow of the Mosque: Christians and Muslims in the World of Islam*, Princeton: Princeton University Press, 2008, 176.
7. Mariamna Fortounatto and Mary B. Cunningham, 'Theology of the icon', in Mary B. Cunningham and Elizabeth Theokritoff (eds), *The Cambridge Companion to Orthodox Christian Theology*, Cambridge: Cambridge University Press, 2008, 136.
8. Fortounatto and Cunningham, 'Theology', 141.
9. Bibliographical material and translations are taken largely from Daniel J. Sahas, *John of Damascus on Islam: The Heresy of the Ishmaelites*, Leiden: E. J. Brill, 1972. The precise dates of John's birth and death are unknown, but Sahas states that most scholars place his date of birth as 675, though there is some dispute, making 652 also a possibility (pp. 38–9). His death has been dated c.748. John's family name was Mansūr, which he inherited from his father, and his ancestors held high hereditary public office with the Umayyad Muslim rulers of Damascus. According to the Arabic and Greek sources, John too became an advisor/minister of public affairs, though it is not clear from the sources what exactly his public duties were, 7ff.
10. Griffith, *The Church*, 40–1.
11. Whether John was a Sabaite monk has recently been brought into question by Marie-France Auzépy. See 'Les Sabaites et L'iconoclasme', in J. Patrich (ed.), *The Sabaite Heritage in the Orthodox Church from the Fifth Century to the Present*, Leuven, 2001, 305.
12. Sahas, *John of Damascus*, 52.
13. Sidney Griffith, 'John of Damascus and the Church in Syria in the Umayyad Era: The Intellectual and Cultural Milieu of Orthodox Christians in the World of Islam', *Hugoye: Journal of Syriac Studies*, vol. 11:2, 2008, online at http://syrcom.cua.edu/Hugoye/Vol11No2/HV11N2Griffith.html.

14. Sahas, *John of Damascus*, 133–9.
15. Adelbert Davids and Pim Valkenberg, 'John of Damascus, The Heresy of the Ishmaelites', in Barbara Roggema, Marcel Poorthuis, Pim Valkenberg (eds), *The Three Rings*, Utrecht: Thomas Instituut, 2005, 78.
16. Sahas, *John of Damascus*, 69.
17. John Merrill, 'Of the Tractate of John of Damascus on Islam', *The Moslem World*, vol. XL1, 88–99.
18. http://www.arian-catholic.org/arian/arius.html
19. A detailed study of Arius can be found in the revised edition of Rowan Williams, *Arius, Heresy and Tradition*, Eerdmans Publishing, 2002. Williams argues that Arius was declared a heretic when in fact he was a theological conservative driven by a concern to defend the free and personal character of the Christian God. Williams also asserts that in that pluralist Christian world there were political motivations behind the impulse to declare Arianism a heresy.
20. Gerald O'Collins, *Christology: A Biblical, Historical and Systematic Study of Jesus*, Oxford: Oxford University Press, 1995, 237–8.
21. Sahas, *John of Damascus*, 133.
22. Sahas, *John of Damascus*, 133.
23. Sahas, *John of Damascus*, 135.
24. Davids and Valkenberg, 'John of Damascus', in *The Three Rings*, 87.
25. Sahas, *John of Damascus*, 75–82.
26. *Opusculum* XX, PG 97:1545C, in Daniel J. Sahas, '"Holosphyros"? A Byzantine Perception of "The God of Muhammad"' in Y. Haddad and W. Haddad (eds), *Christian–Muslim Encounters*, Gainsville, 1995, 109–25. Also, Davids and Valkenberg, 'John of Damascus', *The Three Rings*, 89.
27. Sahas, *John of Damascus*, 76.
28. Sidney Griffith, 'The View of Islam from the monasteries of Palestine in the Early 'Abbāsid Period: Theodore Abū Qurrah and the *Summa Theologiae Arabica, Islam and Christian–Muslim Relations*, 7:1, 1996, 9–28. This short overview of the rise of Arabic Christian literature is derived from Sidney Griffith's article.
29. John C. Lamoreaux, *Theodore Abū Qurrah*, Library of the Christian East, Brigham University Press, 2005, xxix. The book has a very useful introduction looking at the most recent findings on the works attributed to Theodore.
30. The full title is 'Refutations of the Saracens by Theodore Abū Qurrah, the Bishop of Ḥarrān, as Reported by John the Deacon', in Lamoreaux, *Theodore Abū Qurrah*, 211.
31. Lamoreaux, 'Refutations'.
32. Lamoreaux, 'Refutations', 224.
33. Lamoreaux, 'Refutations', 227.
34. Lamoreaux, 'Refutations', 144.
35. Mahmud Ayoub, 'Jesus the Son of God', in Yvonne Yazbeck Haddad and Wadi Z. Haddad (eds), *Christian–Muslim Encounters*, University Press of Florida: Gainesville, 1195, 65–81. In the Qur'ān the term *ibn* occurs only once with reference to Jesus as son of God. The term *walad* occurs 15 times, although only two refer to Jesus directly.
36. Lamoreaux, 'Refutations', 143–4.
37. Lamoreaux, 'Refutations', 23.
38. Lamoreaux, 'Refutations', 22–3.
39. For a useful introduction to this genre of writing, see the Introduction by Sandra Toenies Keating, *Defending the 'People of Truth' in the Early Islamic Period: The Christian Apologies of Abū Rā'iṭah*, Brill: Leiden, 2006, 1–81. This is a well-researched introduction to Abū Rā'iṭah books and all translations are from Keating's work where the original Arabic is next to the English translation.
40. Keating, *Defending*, 27.
41. Keating, *Defending*, 45.
42. Keating, *Defending*, 66–7.

43. Although Christians and Jews remained in high positions of government, their freedoms and equal rights with Muslims were becoming limited. Their official status as *dhimmīs* meant that the gap between Muslims and non-Muslims widened and may well have provided the incentive to many to convert to Islam.
44. Keating, *Defending*, 107–9. *Ousia* is the translation of the Arabic *jauhar* meaning intrinsic or essence as well as jewel or gem. The Arabic for hypostaseis is *aqānīm* (sing. *uqnūm*).
45. Uri Rubin, 'Pre-Existence and Light', *Israel Oriental Studies*, 5, 1975, 62–119. See also Gerhard Bowering, 'The Light Verse: Qur'ānic Text and Ṣūfī Interpretation', *Oriens*, 36:2001, 113–44.
46. Rubin, 'Pre-Existence', 66.
47. W. Gairdner, *Al-Ghazzali's Mishkāt al-Anwār*, A Translation with Introduction, Royal Asiatic Society, 1924, 88.
48. Keating, *Defending*, 115.
49. Keating, *Defending*, 175–7
50. Keating, *Defending*, 225–7.
51. Keating, *Defending*, 235.
52. Mark Beaumont, *Christology in Dialogue with Muslims*, Regnum, 2005, 57.
53. Keating, *Defending*, 241.
54. Keating, *Defending*, 249. The Arabic word for divine, godhead is *lāhūt*.
55. Beaumont, *Christology*, 98.
56. Jane McAuliffe, *Qur'ānic Christians*, Cambridge, Cambridge University Press, 1991, 93.
57. Peter Adamson, *Al-Kindī*, Oxford University Press, 2007, 55–6.
58. David Thomas, *Early Muslim Polemic against Christianity: Abū 'Īsā al-Warrāq's 'Against the Incarnation'*, Cambridge, Cambridge University Press, 58.
59. See above, note 58. Thomas provides a good overview of the debates between Muslims and Christians during this time and a very informative introduction to Abū 'Īsa's life and other bibliographical material, including the various editions of his writing. The book then follows a similar format to that of the other two Arabic/English texts we have looked at, with the Arabic on one page and the English translation facing. All references will simply begin *Early Muslim*.
60. Thomas, *Early Muslim*, 97.
61. Thomas, *Early Muslim*, 103–5.
62. Thomas, *Early Muslim*, 155.
63. Thomas, *Early Muslim*, 157.
64. Alphonse Mingana, *Timothy I: Apology for Christianity*, 1928, 16–90. Full text can be found on http://www.tertullian.org/fathers/timothy_i_apology_00_intro.htm.
65. J. Windrow Sweetman, *Islam and Christian Theology*, Part One, vol. 2, London: Lutterworth Press, 1947, 17.

Chapter 3 Scholastic, Medieval and Poetic Debates

1. Mustapha Shah, 'Trajectories in the Development of Islamic Legal Thought: the Synthesis of *Kalām*', *Religion/Compass*, 1:4, 2007, 430–54; this is a very useful overview of theories around the origins, nature and expansion of *kalām*. See the author's references to Shlomo Pines, 'A Note on an Early Meaning of the Term *Mutakallim*', *Israel Oriental Studies*, 1, 1971, pp. 224–40, esp. pp. 236–7. Also, Sarah Stroumsa, *Freethinkers of Medieval Islam: Ibn al-Rawandi, Abū Bakr al-Rūzī and their Impact on Islamic Thought*, Leiden: E. J. Brill, 1999.
2. Joseph van Ess. 'Wrongdoing and Divine Omnipotence in the Theology of Abū Ishāq al-Nazzām', in T. Rudavsky (ed.), *Divine Omniscience and Omnipotence in Medieval Philosophy*, Dordrecht, 1985, 53–67.
3. See his entry in Daniel Gimaret, 'Mu'tazila', in the *Encyclopaedia of Islam*, Leiden: E. J. Brill, 2nd edn, 783–93.

4. Guy Monnot, *Penseurs musulmans et religions iraniennes: Abd al-Jabbar et ses devanciers*, J. Vrin: Paris, 1974, 101. See also D. Gimaret, 'Mu'tazila', in H. A. R. Gibb et al. (eds), *The Encyclopaedia of Islam, New Edition*, Leiden: E. J. Brill, 1960–2002, V11, 783–93.
5. See Wadi Z. Haddad, 'Al-Bāqillānī', in Yvonne H. Haddad and Wadi Z. Haddad (eds), *Christian–Muslim Encounters*, Florida: University Press of Florida, 1995, 82–94.
6. See Shah, 'Trajectories', 440.
7. W. Montgomery Watt, *The Formative Period of Islamic Thought*, Edinburgh: Edinburgh University Press, 1973, 209–11.
8. 'Ali Rabbān al-Ṭabarī, *Kitāb al-dīn wa-l-dawla, The Book of Religion and Empire*, translated by A. Mingana, Manchester: Manchester University Press, 1922, 3.
9. Al-Ṭabarī, *Book of Religion*, 15–16.
10. Al-Ṭabarī, *Book of Religion*, 157.
11. Al-Ṭabarī, *Book of Religion*, 159.
12. All references to al-Jāḥiz are from Joshua Finkel, 'A Risāla of Al-Jāḥiz', *Journal of the American Oriental Society*, vol. 47, 1927, 311–34. Finkel provides an interesting introduction to al-Jāḥiz and mentions those who considered him as being a skeptic, but also duplicitous for 'blowing hot and cold in the same breath; this included Mas'ūdī' (316). The translation begins at p. 322.
13. Al-Jāḥiz, *Al-Risāla*, 332.
14. Al-Jāḥiz, *Al-Risāla*, 333–4.
15. Al-Jāḥiz, *Al-Risāla*, 321.
16. David Thomas, 'Early Muslim Relations with Christianity', *Anvil*, 6:1, 1989, 23–31.
17. Wadi Z.Haddad, 'Al-Bāqillānī', 82–94.
18. David Thomas, *Christian Doctrines in Islamic Theology*, Brill: Leiden, 2008. Extract taken from 'Abū Bakr al-Bāqillānī', 169–71. Thomas provides a useful introduction to the intellectual period of the writers as well as a synopsis of their main arguments
19. Thomas, *Christian*, 173–7.
20. Thomas, *Christian*, 132.
21. Thomas, *Christian*, 193–5.
22. Margaretha Heemskerk, 'A Mu'tazilite Refutation of Christianity and Judaism', in *The Three Rings*, as above, 186–7. Heemskerk provides some brief but useful biographical details. See also Joel L. Kraemer, *Humanism in the Renaissance of Islam: The Cultural Revival during the Būyid Age*, Leiden, E. J. Brill, 1986.
23. For a helpful introduction and overview to the life and works of 'Abd al-Jabbār, see *'Abd al-Jabbār, Critique of Christian Origins*, edited, translated and annotated by Gabriel Said Reynolds and Samīr Khalīl Samīr, Utah: Brigham Young University Press, 2010, xvi–xxv.
24. Thomas, *Christian*, 207–8.
25. See Gabriel Reynolds, as above.
26. 'Abd al-Jabbār, *Critique*, 161.
27. 'Abd al-Jabbār, *Critique*, 7–8. Translations are taken largely from Reynolds.
28. 'Abd al-Jabbār, *Critique*, 151.
29. 'Abd al-Jabbār, *Critique*, 166–7.
30. See also on this S. M. Stern's article ''Abd al-Jabbār's Account of how Christ's Religion was falsified by the Adoption of Roman Customs', *Journal of Theological Studies*, 1968:XIX(1), 128–85. Here 'Abd al-Jabbār proposes to show that whereas Jesus himself and his disciples had observed the law of Moses, the Christians had subsequently changed the law and adopted the customs and institutions of the pagan Romans. The corruption began soon after the disappearance of Jesus, but the chief culprits were Paul, and later Constantine.
31. See James Waltz, 'Muhammad and the Muslims in St Thomas Aquinas', *The Muslim World*, vol. LXV1, 1976:2, 81–95. Waltz informs us in footnote 10 that Thomas's early years are presented in unusual fullness in James A. Weisheipl, *Friar Thomas d'Aquino*

(New York: Doubleday, 1974), pp. 6–20; one of Thomas's brothers accompanied Emperor Frederick II on the 'crusade' of 1228–9.

32. Waltz, 'Muhammad and the Muslims', 88.
33. Iogna-Prat, Dominique, Graham Robert Edwards and Barbara H. Rosenwein, *Order and Exclusion: Cluny and Christendom Face Heresy, Judaism, and Islam, 1000–1150*, New York: Cornell University Press, 2002, 326.
34. John V. Tolan, *Sons of Ishmael: Muslims through European Eyes in the Middle Ages*, Gainsville, Florida: University Press of Florida, 2008, 113–23.
35. William Montgomery Watt, *Muslim–Christian Encounters: Perceptions and Misperceptions*, New York: Routledge, 1991, 88.
36. James Kritzeck, *Peter the Venerable and Islam*, Princeton, New Jersey: Princeton University Press, 1964, 36.
37. Richard William Southern, *Western Views of Islam in the Middle Ages*, Cambridge, Mass.: Harvard University Press, 1962, 37.
38. Kritzeck, *Peter*, 132.
39. Kritzeck, *Peter*, 142–3.
40. Kritzeck, *Peter*, 143.
41. Norman Daniel, *Islam and the West: The Making of an Image*, Oxford: Oneworld, paperback edition 2009, 209.
42. Henk Schoot, 'Christ Crucified Contested: Thomas Aquinas', in Barbara Roggema, Marcel Poorthuis, Pim Valkenberg (eds), *The Three Rings*, Utrecht: Thomas Instituut, XI, 2005, 142–3.
43. Schoot, 'Christ Crucified', 141. Waltz (note 31 above) has a useful footnote on p. 2, cited here, explaining the background to this work: 'Furthermore, strongly desiring the conversion of unbelievers, Raymond [of Peñafort] asked an outstanding Doctor of Sacred Scripture, a Master in Theology, Brother Thomas of Aquino of the same Order, who among all the clerics of the world was considered in philosophy to be next to Brother Albert, the greatest, to compose a work against the errors of unbelievers, by which both the cloud of darkness might be dispelled and the teaching of the true Sun might be made manifest to those who refuse to believe. The renowned Master accomplished what the humility of so great a Father asked, and composed a work called the Summa Contra Gentiles held to be without equal in its field.'
44. Thomas Aquinas, *Summa contra Gentiles*, Book1:2. All extracts are taken from the online translation http://dhspriory.org/thomas/ContraGentiles1.htm#2.
45. *SCG*, Book 6:1.
46. *SCG*, Book 1:6.
47. *SCG*, Book 4:83.
48. Frithjof Schuon, *Islam and the Perennial Philosophy*, World of Islam Festival Publishing Company, 1976, 19.
49. SCG, Book 1:5.
50. Joseph Kenny O.P. has translated *De Rationibus Fidei*; the Latin text is on one side, with the English translation facing. All extracts from *DRF* are taken from Kenny's online translation at http://josephkenny.joyeurs.com/CDtexts/Rationes.htm
51. *DRF*, Chapter 1.
52. Robert Hammond, *The Philosophy of Al-Farābi and its Influence on Medieval Thought*, New York: Hobson Book Press, 1947. The book gives extensive citations in parallel columns from al-Farābī and Thomas showing the latter's almost verbatim dependence on the former.
53. Kenny, *DRF*, Chapter 3.
54. Kenny, *DRF*, Chapter 5.
55. This theme of the violence of Christ's death as an act which burdened humankind with guilt has been re-ignited by several postmodern thinkers, including Slavoj Žižek.

56. Christopher M. Bellitto, *The General Councils: A History of the Twenty-one Church Councils from Nicaea to Vatican II*, New York: Paulist Press, 2002, 82.
57. Nicholas Rescher, 'Nicholas of Cusa on the Qur'ān' *The Muslim World*, 55:3, 1965, 195–202.
58. Inigo Bocken, 'Nicholas of Cusa and the Plurality of Religions', in *The Three Rings*, 163.
59. http://jasper-hopkins.info/CAII-12–2000.pdf *Cribratio Alkorani II, 19.*
60. http://jasper-hopkins.info/CAIII-12–2000.pdf, *Cribratio Alkorani* III:15. This is a rejection of Qur'ān 3:67, 'Abraham was neither a Jew nor a Christian, he was upright [true in faith]'.
61. http://jasper-hopkins.info/CAII-12–2000.pdf, *Cribratio Alkorani* II,19.
62. *Nicholas of Cusa's De pace fidei and Cribratio Alkorani*, translation and analysis by Jasper Hopkins (2nd edn), Minneapolis: Banning Press, 1994. This section relates to paragraphs 25/26.
63. http://jasper-hopkins.info/CAII-12–2000.pdf *Cribratio Alkorani* II, 4–5.
64. Gregory J. Miller, 'Luther on the Turks and Islam', *Lutheran Quarterly*, 14:1, 2000, 79–97.
65. Robert O. Smith, 'Luther, the Turks and Islam', *Currents in Theology and Mission*, 34:5, 2007, 351–64. Smith also provides a list of Luther's major writings on Islam: *On War Against the Turk* (1529), intended to help Christians fight against thc threat with good conscience *(LW* 46:157–205): *Heerpredigt wider den Türken (Military Sermon Against the Turks.* 1529), with an exposition of Daniel 7. Luther attempted to explain the Turkish threat in all its seriousness *(WA* 30/2:160–97), *Vorwort zu dem Libellus de rhu et moribiis Turcorum* (Preface to *Libellus de ritu et moribus Turcorum*, 1530). This is a preface to a small book written around 1481 to detail the religion and customs of the Turks: such information was in great demand given the Ottoman threat to Vienna *(WA* 30/2:205): *Admonition to Prayer against the Turks* (1541), in which Luther's concern for Christian penitence and prayer to counteract foreign military threat finds fullest expression *(LW* 43:215–41): *Verlegung des Alcoran Bruder Richardi, Prediger Ordens (Refutation of the Alcoran of Brother Richard, Preaching Order.* 1542). Luther's German translation of a popular medieval polemical tract against Islam *(WA* 53:272–396); and the *Vorrede zu Theodor Biblianders Koranausgabe (Preface to Theodor Bibliander's Edition of the Quran*), 1543.
66. Smith, 'Luther', 352. He contrasts Luther with John Calvin.
67. Miller, 'Luther', 79.
68. For a good overview of Riccoldo's methodology and style, see Thomas Burman, 'How an Italian friar read his Arabic Qur'an', in *Dante Studies, with the Annual Report of the Dante Society*, 125, 2007, 93–109. Burman writes: 'We are used to reading the extensive medieval literature of religious disputation as it appears to us in finished products: treatises against one or another religion, imagined literary dialogues between members of two or three religious communities, carefully edited summaries of actual religious disputations. In these texts, religious disputants generally have the appearance of unchanging types whose positions and beliefs are static and seemingly inborn. The interactive process that we glimpse in Riccoldo's Qur'an reading and anti-Islamic writing provides us with a very different picture. Here we see time-consuming consultation of earlier works and philological sophistication in handling the Qur'an. We see the physical Qur'an itself used as a notebook on which to sketch out polemical ideas. We see, in short, an engaged, serious intellectual working through difficult problems. Even if we find his work distasteful, he is no longer a tedious type; he is now an energetic, many-sided human. Modern scholars of medieval religious polemic, apologetic, and disputation have generally focused on questions either of fact – who had what accurate knowledge of another religion? when? how? – or functionality – how does a text (mis)represent the religiously other in ways that

allow communal boundaries or political hegemony to be maintained? In watching Riccoldo read his Arabic Qur'an, I suggest, we may have an opportunity to move beyond these two (admittedly fruitful) lines of inquiry, for it strikes me that there is more of interest here than can be grasped by asking about levels of knowledge and mechanisms of social control.'

69. Francisco citing *Verlegung* in *Martin Luther*, 208.
70. Smith, 'Luther', 358.
71. Fred P. Hall, 'Martin Luther and Islam', *Missio apostolica*, 13:1, 2005, 49–57.
72. For a translation of Luther's works, I have used Adam S. Francisco, *Martin Luther and Islam: A Study in Sixteenth-Century Polemics and Apologetics*, E. J. Brill: Leiden, 2007, 113–16.
73. Francisco, Enarratio Psalmi II, WA, 121.
74. Luther's *Verlegung* cited and translated by Francisco, *Martin Luther*, 116. The term means 'refutation' and refers to Luther's *Verlegung des Alcoran*, the translation in German of Riccoldo da Monte di Croce's *Confutatio Alcorani*.
75. Francisco, *Martin Luther* (Vorwort, WA), 177.
76. Luther's *Verlegung* cited and translated by Francisco, *Martin Luther*, 115.
77. For a broad view of the medieval views of Islam, see Norman Daniels, *Islam and the West: The Making of an Image*, Edinburgh: Edinburgh University Press, 1960.
78. Gregory J. Miller, 'Luther on the Turks and Islam', *Lutheran Quarterly*, 14:1, 2000, 79–97.
79. See James Royster, 'Personal Transformation in Ibn al-'Arabī and Meister Eckhart', in Yvonne Y. Haddad and Wadi Z. Haddad (eds), *Christian–Muslim Encounters*, Florida: University Press of Florida, 1995, 158–79.
80. Toshihiko Isutzu, 'Ibn al-'Arabī', *The Encyclopaedia of Religion*, Mircea Eliade, ed.-in-chief, Macmillan, 1987.
81. Royster, 'Ibn al-'Arabī', 162.
82. Ibn al-'Arabī, *Fusūs al-hikām, The Bezels of Wisdom*, translated by R. W. J. Austin, New York: Paulist Press, 1980, 174–8. For a helpful overview of select Ṣūfī writings on Jesus, see Oddbjørn Leirvik, *Images of Jesus Christ in Islam*, 2nd edn, London: Continuum, 2010, 83–106.
83. Sorour S. Soroudi, 'On Jesus' Image in Modern Persian Poetry', *The Muslim World*, vol. 69:4, 221–8.
84. R. Nicholson cited in James Roy King, 'Jesus and Joseph in Rūmī's *Mathnawi*', *The Muslim World*, 80:2, 1990, 81–95.
85. Afzal Iqbal, *The Life and Work of Rūmī*, 4th edn. Lahore: Institute of Islamic Culture, 1978. The verses are from the section entitled 'The Message of the Mathnavi', 189–90.
86. Annemarie Schimmel, 'Jesus and Mary in Rūmī's Verse', in Haddad and Haddad, *Christian–Muslim Encounters*, 144 and 147.
87. A. J. Arberry, *Mystical Poems of Rumi*, Chicago: University of Chicago Press, 1968, 78.
88. King, 'Jesus', 89.
89. Tarif Khalidi, *The Muslim Jesus*, Cambridge, Mass.: Harvard University Press, 2003, 45.
90. Khalidi, [Abū Bakr ibn Abī al-Dunya d.894], 110.
91. Khalidi, [Ibid.], 118.
92. Khalidi, [al-Ghazālī, d.11], 176.
93. Khalidi, [Abū Nu'aym al-Isbahāni, d.1038], 159.
94. Khalidi, [Al-Abshīhi, d.1487], 211.

Chapter 4 Reflections on Mary

1. The quote is from Jane Smith and Yvonne Haddad, 'The Virgin Mary in Islamic Tradition', *The Muslim World*, vol. 79:3–4, 1989, 161–87. This is a helpful and detailed

article on Mary. See also Barbara F. Stowasser, *Women in the Qur'ān: Traditions and Interpretation*, Oxford, New York: Oxford University Press, 1994, 67–82. The name Maryam is the same as that used in the Greek in the Bible and in Syriac.

2. R. J. McCarthy, 'Mary in Islam', in Alberic Stacpoole (ed.), *Mary's Place in Christian Dialogue*, Wilton, Connecticut: Moorhouse-Barlow, 1982, 205–8.
3. Bartholomew of Edessa, *Refutation of the Hagarene*, in Jaroslav Pelikan, *Mary Through the Centuries*, New Haven: Yale University Press, 1996, 77.
4. Smith and Haddad, 'The Virgin', 162.The other biblical references to Mary are: Galatians 4:4 (Jesus was born of a woman); Mark 6:3 (Mary is Jesus' mother); Mark 3:31ff., Matthew 12:46ff., Luke 8:19ff. (Jesus says that his real family is those who do the will of God); John 2:3–5 (wedding at Cana – Mary asks Jesus for more wine).
5. Smith and Haddad, 'The Virgin',163.
6. *Sūra* Maryam has been the subject of considerable exegetical and scholarly attention. Besides Qur'ānic commentaries, *sūra* Maryam has also benefited from separate, individual treatment. It has been the object of special attention by modern western scholars, in particular those of comparative religion and of Christianity, whose attention has centred largely on the virtue and piety of Mary, on the miraculous nature of the birth of Jesus, on Jesus' ministry, and on how Jesus' time on Earth came to an end. In addition, this section of the Qur'ān is a favourite with the interfaith community.
7. Annemarie Schimmel, 'Jesus and Mary in Rūmī's Verse', in Haddad and Haddad, *Christian–Muslim Encounters*, 143–57.
8. Anthony McRoy, 'The Christ of Shi'a Islam', *Evangelical Review of Theology*, 30:4, 339–51.
9. Hans Urs von Balthasar and Joseph Cardinal Ratzinger, *Mary: The Church at the Source*, translated by Adrian Walker, Ignatius Press: San Francisco, 1980, 87–9.
10. Balthasar and Ratzinger, *Mary*, 119–20.
11. Balthasar and Ratzinger, *Mary*, 140.
12. Mary Thurkill, *Mary and Fatima in Medieval Christianity and Shī'ite Islam*, Notre Dame, Indiana: University of Notre Dame Press, 2007, 44.
13. Smith and Haddad, 'The Virgin', 187.
14. Rachel Sered, 'Rachel, Mary and Fatima', *Cultural Anthropology*, 6:2, 1991, 131–46.
15. W. Montgomery Watt, *Islam and Christianity Today: A Contribution to Dialogue*, London: Routledge and Kegan Paul, 1982, 101–2.
16. Thurkill, *Chosen Among*, 13.
17. Jürgen Moltmann, *The Way of Jesus Christ*, London: SCM Press, 1990, 83.
18. Moltmann, *The Way*, 85.
19. Balthasar and Ratzinger, *Mary*, 29.
20. 'Abd al-Jabbār, *Critique of Christian Faith*, 10–11.
21. See chapter on Tissa Balasuriya in Philip Kennedy, *Twentieth-Century Theologians*, London: I.B.Tauris, 2010, 261–70.
22. Balthasar and Ratzinger, *Mary*, 99.
23. Sered, 'Rachel, Mary and Fatima', 139.
24. Wolfhart Pannenberg, *The Apostles' Creed*, London: SCM Press, 1972, 77.

Chapter 5 Monotheism and the Dialectics of Love and Law

1. Hendrik Kraemer, *The Christian Message in a Non-Christian World*, Grand Rapids Michigan: Kregel Publications, 1956 (3rd edn), 217. Hendrik Kraemer was a Dutch Reformed missiologist, lay theologian and ecumenical leader. He studied Javanese in Leiden before working for the Dutch Bible Society in Indonesia (1922–37). His most influential writing is a *Christian Message in a Non-Christian World* (1938) prepared for

the International Missionary Council meeting in Madras. Kraemer states in this work that 'In its main, genuine structure Islam is a simple religion' and its admirers see none of the 'intricate subtleties of the Christological dogmas'.
2. Kraemer, *Christian Message*, 217.
3. Kraemer, *Christian Message*, 218.
4. Samuel Zwemer, *The Disintegration of Islam*, London: Fleming H. Revell Company, 1916. The book is based on a series of lectures Zwemer gave at Princeton, the purpose of the lectures being 'distinctly missionary', 9–10.
5. Zwemer, *Disintegration*, 10.
6. Zwemer, *Disintegration*, 185.
7. Kenneth Cragg, 'Each Other's Face, Some Thoughts on Muslim–Christian Colloquy Today', *The Muslim World*, 45:2, 1955, 172–82.
8. Karl Barth, *Church Dogmatics*, 2:1, Edinburgh: T&T Clark, 1957, 447–8.
9. Barth, *Dogmatics*, 448.
10. Barth, *Dogmatics*, 448.
11. Barth, *Dogmatics*, 448.
12. Barth, *Dogmatics*, 448.
13. Barth, *Dogmatics*, 319. Barth is presumed to be referring to Islam among these heathen religions.
14. Barth, *Dogmatics*, 1:2, Edinburgh: T&T Clark, 1956, 301 and 329.
15. Maurice Wiles, *The Remaking of Christian Doctrine*, London: SCM Press, 1974, 59.
16. Paul Tillich quoted in Wiles, *Remaking*, 56.
17. Frithjof Schuon, *The Fullness of God*, Indiana: World Wisdom, 1974, 115.
18. Badi'al-Zamān Foruzanfar, *Āḥadīth-Masnavi*, reprint, Tehran: Amir Kabir, 1987, 29.
19. Rowan Williams, *Resurrection: Interpreting the Easter Gospel*, London: Darton, Longman and Todd, 1982, 29.
20. Barth, *Dogmatics*, 2:1, 274.
21. Wolfhart Pannenberg, *Systematic Theology*, vol. 1, Grand Rapids Michigan: William B. Eerdmans Publishing Company, 1988, 445.
22. Frithjof Schuon, *The Fullness*, 1.
23. Ibn al-'Arabī, *The Bezels of Wisdom*. Translated by R. W. J. Austin, New York, Paulist Press, 1980, 75.
24. Schuon, *Fullness*, 2.
25. Gustave E. von Grunebaum, 'Observations on the Muslim Concept of Evil', *Studia Islamica*, no. 31, 1970, 117–34. I have developed Islamic and Christian approaches to evil and love in greater detail in my monograph, *The Good Muslim: Reflections on Classical Islamic Law and Theology*, Cambridge: Cambridge University Press, 2012.
26. For an interesting take on the legacy of Augustine's theology of original sin, see Charles T. Mathewes, 'Original Sin and the Hermeneutics of Charity: A Response to Gilbert Meilaender', *The Journal of Religious Ethics*, vol. 29:1, Spring 2001, pp. 35–42. Mathewes writes, 'We ought to bury Augustine, not praise him . . . burial would recognise Augustine's humanity. Like us he struggled with clarity, changed his mind and operated within a fairly limited set of intellectual options whose parameters he did not set. Like us, that is, he worked under conditions of original sin. . . . Ironically enough, it may be the extremity of our respect for antique minds that traps us in the habit of scolding them for not being more like us.'
27. Jean Baudrillard, *The Intelligence of Evil or the Lucidity Pact*, translated by Chris Turner, Oxford: Berg Publishers, 2005, 160.
28. Ghazālī, Abū Ḥāmid Muḥammad b. Muḥammad, *Iḥyā 'ulūm al-dīn*, vol. 4, Ālim al-Kutub, Damascus, date unknown, p. 2.
29. Mahmoud Ayoub, *A Muslim View of Christianity: Essays on Dialogue by Mahmoud Ayoub*, Irfan A. Omar (ed.), Maryknoll, New York: Orbis Books, 2007, 94.

30. *Ḥadīth* 25 related by al-Bukhāri and 34 related by al-Tirmidhī respectively, cited in Ezzeddin Ibrahim and Denys Johnson Davies, *Forty Hadīth Qudsī*, Islamic Texts Society, Cambridge, 1997, 126.
31. Maurice Wiles, *The Remaking of Christian Doctrine*, London: SCM Press, 1974, 61.
32. Gerald O'Collins, Christology, *A Biblical, Historical and Systematic Study of Jesus*, Oxford: Oxford University Press, 1995, 280–1.
33. Reinhold Niebuhr, *The Nature and Destiny of Man*, vol.1, *Human Nature*, New York: Scribners, 1941, 16.
34. Ng Kam Weng, 'Being Human', in Michael Ipgrave and David Marshall (eds), *Humanity, Texts and Contexts*, Washington DC: Georgetown University Press, 2011, 7.
35. Shabbir Akhtar, *The Quran and the Secular Mind*, London and New York, Routledge, Taylor and Francis, 277.
36. Reinhold Niebuhr, *Beyond Tragedy*, London: Nisbet and Co. Ltd, 1938, 18–19.
37. Wiles, *The Remaking*, 66.
38. Sandra Toenies Keating, 'Let us leave the past aside', in Caterina Belo and Jean-Jacques Pérennès (eds), *Mission in Dialogue: Essays in Honour of Michael L. Fitzgerald*, Louvain: Peeters, 2012, 167.
39. Albert Hofstadter, *Reflections on Evil*, The Lindley Lecture, University of Kansas, 1973, p. 3. This is explored further in Jovan Babić, 'Toleration vs Doctrinal Evil in Our Times', *The Journal of Ethics*, vol. 8, no.3 (2004), 225–50.
40. Slavoj Žižek, *Violence*, London: Profile Books, 2009, 56.
41. Žižek, *Violence*, 56.
42. Jean Baudrillard, *The Intelligence of Evil or the Lucidity Pact* (translated by Chris Turner), Oxford: Berg, 2005, 156–7.
43. Baudrillard, *Intelligence*, 157.
44. Peter Dews, '"Radical Finitude" and the Problem of Evil', in María Pía Lara (ed.), *Rethinking Evil*, University of California Press, 2001, 46–7.
45. Maeve Cook, 'Moral Evil and Moral Identity', in Lara (ed.), *Rethinking Evil* (above), 115.
46. Frederiek Depoortere, *Christ in Postmodern Philosophy*, London: T&T Clark, 2008, 114.
47. The Holy Scriptures, revised and edited by Harold Fisch, Jerusalem: Koren Publishers, 1998.
48. G. Vajda, *L'Amour de Dieu dans la Théologie Juive du Moyen Age*, Paris, 1957, 51.
49. David Zeidan, 'A comparative Study of Selected Themes in Christian and Islamic Fundamentalist Discourses', *British Journal of Middle Eastern Studies*, 30:1, 2003, 43–80.
50. L. E. Browne, 'The Law and the Gospel', *The Muslim World*, 29:2 (1939), 125–9.
51. John P. Meier, *Jesus, A Marginal Jew*, vol. 4, New Haven: Yale University Press, 2010, 40–1.
52. Meier, *Jesus*, 40–1.
53. Akhtar, *The Quran*, 277.
54. Jeffrey A. D. Weima, 'The Function of the Law in Relation to Sin: An Evaluation of the View of H. Räisänen', *Novum Testamentum*, 32: 3, 1990, 219–35.
55. Rudolf Bultmann, *Faith and Understanding*, London: SCM Press, 1969, 224–5.
56. Bultmann, *Faith*, 169.
57. Walter Brueggemann, *The Prophetic Imagination*, Philadelphia: Fortress Press, 1978, 83.
58. Brueggemann, *The Prophetic*, 83.
59. E. P. Sanders, *Jesus and Judaism*, London: SCM Press, and Philadelphia: Fortress Press, 1985, 267.
60. Albert Schweitzer, *The Quest of the Historical Jesus: A Critical Study of its Progress from Reimarus to Wrede*, William Montgomery (trans.), London: A. & C. Black, 1910, 402. This is a translation of the first German edition: *Von Reimarus zu Wrede: eine Geschichte der Leben-Jesu-Forschung*, Tübingen: J. C. Mohr, 1906.

61. Khalidi, *The Muslim Jesus*, 159.
62. Davies, B., *The Thought of Thomas Aquinas*, Oxford: Clarendon Press, 1993, p. 257. Thomas Aquinas's main treatise on law is found in *Summa Theologica* [*ST*], the First Part of the Second Part [FS] QQ 90–108. I have used the online translation http://www.sacred-texts.com/chr/aquinas/summa/sum229.htm
63. *ST* I/II.98.6.
64. *ST* I/II.98.6.
65. *ST* I/II.98.6.
66. In relation to why the Old Law was given at a particular point in history as opposed to immediately after the fall, Thomas states the following: 'It was not fitting for the Old Law to be given at once after the sin of the first man: both because man was so confident in his own reason, that he did not acknowledge his need of the Old Law; because as yet the dictate of the natural law was not darkened by habitual sinning'. Another reason Thomas gives for the multiplicity of, in this instance, ceremonial law, is that: 'it was necessary . . . to lay many obligations on such like men, in order that being burdened, as it were, by their duties to the Divine worship, they might have no time for the service of idols', *ST* I/.II.101.3.
67. Mustansir Mir, 'Islamic Views on Jesus', in Gregory A. Barker (ed.), *Jesus in the World's Faiths*, Maryknoll, New York: Orbis Books, 2005, 121.
68. Ismail al-Faruqi, *Islam and Other Faiths*, Ataullah Siddiqui (ed.), The Islamic Foundation: Leicester, The International Institute of Islamic Thought: Virginia, 1998, 116–17.
69. P. S. van Koningsveld, 'The Islamic Image of Paul and the Origin of the Gospel of Barnabas', *Jerusalem Studies in Arabic and Islam*, 20, 1996, 200–28. Owing to restrictions of space, I do not offer any thoughts on the Gospel of Barnabas in Christian–Muslim relations. A useful overview of past and present issues arising from this document can be found in Oddbjørn Leirvik, *Images of Jesus Christ in Islam*, 2nd edn, London: Continuum, 2010, 132–9. Leirvik writes that 'the alleged Gospel is regarded by many Muslims as going back to a manuscript from early Christianity, whereas western scholars take it for granted that it was produced either in the late Middle Ages or in the early modern period'. A primary accusation in this Gospel is against Paul, who preached that Jesus is the son of God.
70. Neal Robinson, 'Syed Qutb's attitude towards Christianity', in Lloyd Ridgeon (ed.), *Islamic Interpretations of Christianity*, Surrey: Curzon, 2001,167.
71. 'Ata ur Rahim, *Jesus – A Prophet of Islam*, New Delhi: Taj Printers, 1979, and London: MWH London Publishers, 1st edn, 1977.
72. Bultmann, *Faith*, 239.
73. Collins, *Christology*, 287.
74. Michel Rene Barnes, 'Latin Trinitarian Theology', in Peter C. Phan (ed.), *The Cambridge Companion to the Trinity*, Cambridge: Cambridge University Press, 2011.
75. Al-Ghazālī, *On Love, Longing and Contentment*, translated by Muhammad Nur Abdus Salam, Illinois, Chicago: Great Books of the Islamic World, 2002, 15.
76. Al-Ghazālī, *On Love*, 15. See also page 38 in which he describes the scholastic theologians as 'the escort of the belief of the unlettered' and being useful for warding off heresy but ultimately lacking insight.
77. Al-Ghazālī, *Letter to a Disciple (Ayyuhā 'l-Walad)*, translated and introduced by Tobias Mayer, Cambridge: The Islamic Texts Society, 2005, 22.
78. Al-Ghazālī, *On the Lawful, the Unlawful and the Doubtful*, translated by Muhammad Nur Abdus Salam, Illinois, Chicago: Great Books of the Islamic World, Inc, 2002, 8.
79. Al-Ghazālī, *On the Lawful*, 8.
80. Khalidi, *The Muslim Jesus*, 184–5.

81. Maulana Fazul-ul-Karim, *Imam Gazzali's Ihya Ulum-Iddin*, Book 4, Lahore: Sind Sagar Academy, 1971, 340–1.
82. Karim, *Imam Gazzali*, 374–5.
83. Karim, *Imam Gazzali*, 335–6.
84. William McKane, *Al-Ghazālī's Book of Fear and Hope*, Leiden: E. J. Brill, 1962,14.
85. See the writings of William Chittick including *Sufism: A Short Introduction*, Oxford: Oneworld Publications, 2000.
86. Muḥammad ibn 'Alī Muh'yī al-Dīn Ibn al-'Arabī, *Tarjumān al'Ashwāq: A Collection of Mystical Odes by Muhyiuddīn ibn al-'Arabī*, vol. 2, ed. and trans. Reynold A. Nicholson, London: Oriental Translation Fund, 1911, 318. Ibn al-'Arabī defines God's love for man as *al-ḥubb al-Ilāhī*.
87. McKane, *Al-Ghazālī's*, 46.
88. 'Abd Allah al-Kisā'ī, *Qiṣaṣ al-anbiyā', Tales of the Prophets*, translated by Wheeler Thackston Jr, Great Books of the Islamic World, 1997, 43–4.
89. Khalidi, *The Muslim*, 174.
90. Ezzedin Ibrahim and Denys Johnson Davies (translators), *An-Nawawi's Forty Hadith*, The Holy Koran Publishing House, 1976, Hadith 31,104.
91. Annemarie Schimmel, 'Some Aspects of Mystical Prayer in Islam', *Die Welt des Islam*, 2:2, 1952, 112–25.
92. Schimmel, 'Some Aspects', 122.
93. McKane, *Al-Ghazālī's*, 18.
94. McKane, *Al-Ghazālī's*, 9 and 10.
95. McKane, *Al-Ghazālī's*, 19.
96. Brian Hebblethwaite, *The Incarnation: Collected Essays in Christology*, Cambridge: Cambridge University Press, 1987, 14.
97. Julian of Norwich, *Showings*, Edmund Colledge and James Walsh (trans.), New York: Paulist Press, 1978, 342–3.
98. Anders Nygren, *Agape and Eros*, Translation by Philip S. Watson, New York: Harper and Row, 1969, 85.
99. Rowan Williams, 'The Forgiveness of Sins', in Mark D. Baker (ed.), *Proclaiming the Scandal of the Cross*, Grand Rapids, Michigan: Baker Academic, 2006, 80.
100. Nygren, *Agape*, 154.
101. Oscar Cullmann, *The Christology of the New Testament*, London: SCM Press, 327.
102. Cullmann, *The Christology*, 325.
103. Philip Kennedy, *Twentieth-Century Theologians*, London: I.B.Tauris, 2010, 201–2.
104. Karl Barth, *Church Dogmatics*, vol. 2:1, Edinburgh: T&T Clark, 1957, 353.

Chapter 6 Conclusion

1. Karl Rahner, *Foundations of Christian Faith*, New York, 1978, 46.
2. Wolfhart Pannenberg, *Systematic Theology*, vol. 1, translated by Geoffrey Bromiley, Grand Rapids Michigan: Eerdmans Publishing, 1988, 64.
3. Leirvik, *Images of Jesus Christ in Islam*, London: Continuum, 2010, 15. M. M. Bakhtin, *Speech Genre and Other Late Essays*, Austin: University of Texas Press, 1996.
4. Leirvik, *Images*, 4.
5. Rowan Williams, 'The Forgiveness of Sins', in Mark D. Baker (ed.), *Proclaiming the Scandal of the Cross*, Grand Rapids Michigan: Baker Academic, 2006, 80.
6. Walter Brueggemann, *The Prophetic Imagination*, Philadelphia: Fortress Press, 1978, 92.
7. Walter Brueggemann, *The Prophetic Imagination*, 91.
8. M. A. Merad, 'Christ according to the Qur'ān', 1980, *Encounter*, 69.
9. Lamin Saneh's Foreword in David Emmanuel Singh (ed.), *Jesus and the Cross*, Eugene, Oregon: Wipf & Stock, 2008, viii.

10. Fakhr l-Dīn al-Rāzī, *Mafātīḥ al-Ghayb, Keys to the Unknown*, cited in Gordon Nickel, '"Self-evident truths of reason": Challenges to clear thinking in the *Tafsīr al-Kabīr of Fakhr al-Dīn al-Rāzī*', *Islam and Christian–Muslim Relations*, 22:2, 2011, 161–72.
11. Samuel Zwemer, *The Disintegration of Islam*, London: Fleming H. Revell Company, 1916, 181–2.
12. Todd Lawson, *The Crucifixion and the Qur'ān: A Study in the History of Muslim Thought*, Oxford: Oneworld, 2009.
13. I am grateful to Joseph Cumming from Yale Divinity School for sending me his paper on this subject.
14. Lawson, *The Crucifixion*, 1.
15. René Guénon, *The Symbolism of the Cross*, translated by Angus Macnab, Hillsdale: New York: Sophia Perennis, 3.
16. Kenneth Cragg, *The Call of the Minaret*, Oxford: Oxford University Press, 1956, 294.
17. Brian Hebblethwaite, 'The Resurrection and the Incarnation', in Paul Avis (ed.), *The Resurrection of Jesus Christ*, London: Darton, Longman and Todd, 1993, 155–70.
18. Mahmoud Ayoub, 'Towards an Islamic Christology', in Irfan A. Omar (ed.), *A Muslim View of Christianity*, Maryknoll, New York: Orbis Books, 2007, 152.
19. Brueggemann, *The Prophetic*, 94–5.
20. Brian Hebblethwaite, *The Incarnation: Collected Essays in Christology*, Cambridge: Cambridge University Press, 1987, 63.
21. Vincent Brümmer, *Atonement, Christology and the Trinity*, Hampshire: Ashgate, 2005, 69.
22. Maurice Wiles, *The Christian Fathers*, London: SCM Press, 1977, 103.
23. Kenneth Cragg, 'The Qur'ān and the Cross – Less Absent than You Think', in David Emmanuel Singh (ed.), *Jesus and the Cross: Reflections of Christians from Islamic Contexts*, Oregon: Wipf and Stock Publishers, 2008, 177.
24. Annemarie Schimmel, *Gabriel's Wing: A Study into the Religious Ideas of Sir Muhammad Iqbal*, Leiden: E. J. Brill, 1963, 264.
25. Reinhold Niebuhr, *Beyond Tragedy*, London: Nisbet and Co., 1938, 94–5.
26. Niebuhr, *Beyond*, 192–3.
27. Doug Frank, 'Naked but Unashamed', in Mark Baker (ed.), *Proclaiming*, 130–3.
28. Mir Hasan in Ralph Russell and Khurshidul Islam, *Three Moghul Poets*, Cambridge, Massachusetts: Harvard University Press, 1968, p.15. Hasan is quoted in J. S. Addleton, 'Images of Jesus in the Literatures of Pakistan', *The Muslim World*, 80:2, 1990, 96–106.
29. D. N. MacKenzie, *Poems from the Diwan of Khushal Khan Khattak*, London: George Allen & Unwin, 1965, 109.
30. Schimmel, *Gabriel's Wing*, 264.
31. See Addleton, 'Images', 102.
32. V. G. Kiernan, *Poems by Faiz*, London: George Allen & Unwin, 1971, 205, 207, cited in Addleton, 'Images'. http://www.columbia.edu/itc/mealac/pritchett/00urdu/3mod/kiernan_faiz/index.html
33. Slavoj Žižek, *The Puppet and the Dwarf: The Perverse Core of Christianity*, Cambridge, Massachusetts: MIT Press: Short Circuits, 2003, 170.
34. See the analysis of Žižek's work in Frederiek Depoortere, *Christ in Postmodern Philosophy*, London and New York: T&T Clark, 2008, 114.
35. Slavoj Žižek, *The Parallax View*, Cambridge, Massachusetts: MIT Press: Short Circuits, 2006, cited in Depoortere, *Christ*, 115.
36. Thomas J. J. Altizer, *The Gospel of Christian Atheism*, Philadelphia: The Westminster Press, 1966, 41.
37. Altizer, *The Gospel*, 54.
38. Karl Barth, *Church Dogmatics*, vol. 2:1, Edinburgh: T&T Clark, 1957, 320.

Select Glossary

Abadan: eternal

Abba: father

Aḥad: the pure and absolute one

Ahl al-Kitāb: the People of the Book or 'scriptures', a general term to denote both Jews and Christians

Aqānīm: hypostases

Banī Isrā'il: the children of Israel

Bāṭil: false, void (in legal sense)

Falāḥ: success

Furqān: distinguisher between right and wrong (a name for the Qur'ān)

Ḥanīf: upright

Ḥikma: wisdom

Hudā: guidance

Ibn: of/son

Injīl: Good News; refers most commonly to the Gospels

'Isā: Jesus

'Iṣma: protection and immunity

Jisd: body

Jibrīl: Gabriel

Jisdun Abadan: eternal body

Kalām: speculative theology
Kalimat: word
Khayr: good
Kitāb ḥakīm: the book of wisdom
Kitāb: book
Lāhūt: divine
Lauḥ al-maḥfūz: Heavenly/Preserved Tablet
Masā'il: questions
Miḥna: Inquisition
Mukhālifūn: opponents
Munāẓara: a way of debating to arrive at the truth rather than to display mastery of rhetoric alone.
Mushrikūn: those who associate others with God
Naṣārā: Arabic form of the name Nazarene, often referring to Christians
Naskh: abrogation
Nubuwwa: prophecy
Nuzūl: coming down, sending down (refers mostly to the descent of the Qur'ān)
Qāḍī: judge in a court of law
Qiṣaṣ al-anbiyā': stories of the prophets
Qiyās: analogy
Qur'ānic Sūras: Qur'ānic chapters
Raḥīq: non-intoxicating wine (in paradise)
Raḥma: mercy
Risālah: letter
Rūḥ Allah: spirit of God
Ṣamad: eternal
Sā'a: the appointed hour

Sharr: evil

Shirk: associating another with God

Shubbiha lahum: it was made to appear so to them

Taḥrīf al-lafz: accusation of textual corruption

Taḥrīf: corruption

Tanzīh: elimination of anthropomorphic elements from God, the otherness/transcendence of God.

Tanzīl: sending down (of divine revelation/inspiration)

Tashbīh: anthropomorphisation of God, the immanence of God

Tasnīm: non-intoxicating drink (in paradise)

Tathlīth: make three, usually referring to the doctrine of the Trinity

Tawaffa: To die

Tawḥīd: unity/doctrine of oneness of God

Umm al-Kitāb: The Mother of the Book

Uqnūm/aqānīm: hypostasis/hypostases, divine person within the Trinity

Waḥy: revelation

Walada: engender, to give birth

Bibliography

Accad, Martin. 'Corruption and/or Misinterpretation of the Bible: The Story of the Islamic Usage of *Taḥrīf*', *The Near East School of Theology Theological Review* 24, 2003.

Accad, Martin. 'Muḥammad's Advent as the Final Criterion', in Barbara Roggema, Marcel Poorthuis, Pim Valkenberg (eds), *The Three Rings*, Utrecht: Thomas Instituut, 2005.

Adamson, Peter. *Al-Kindī*, Oxford: Oxford University Press, 2007.

Addleton, J. S. 'Images of Jesus in the Literature of Pakistan', *The Muslim World*, 80:2, 1990, 96–106.

Akhtar, Shabbir. *The Quran and the Secular Mind*, London and New York: Routledge, Taylor and Francis, 2008.

Al-Faruqi, Ismail. *Islam and Other Faiths*, Ataullah Siddiqui (ed.), Leicester: The International Institute of Islamic Thought, Virginia, 1998.

Al-Ghazālī, Abū Ḥāmid Muḥammad b. Muḥammad. *Iḥyā' ulūm al-dīn*, vol. 4, Damascus: Ālim al-Kutub, no date.

Al-Ghazālī, Abū Ḥāmid Muḥammad b. Muḥammad. *Letter to a Disciple* (*Ayyuhā l-Walad*), translated and introduction by Tobias Mayer, Cambridge: The Islamic Texts Society, 2005.

Al-Ghazālī, Abū Ḥāmid Muḥammad b. Muḥammad. *On Love, Longing and Contentment*, translated by Muhammad Nur Abdus Salam, Chicago: Great Books of the Islamic World, 2002.

Al-Ghazālī, Abū Ḥāmid Muḥammad b. Muḥammad. *On the Lawful, the Unlawful and the Doubtful*, translated by Muhammad Nur Abdus Salam, Chicago: Great Books of the Islamic World, 2002.

Al-Jawziyya, Ibn Qayyim. *Hidāyat al-hayārā fī ajwibāt al-Yahūd wa-'l-Nasārā*, Ahmad Hijazi al-Saqqa (ed.), Cairo, 1980.

Al-Kisā'ī, 'Abd Allah. *Qiṣaṣ al-anbiyā', Tales of the Prophets*, translated by Wheeler Thackston Jr, USA: Kazi Publications, 1997.

Altizer, Thomas J. J. *The Gospel of Christian Atheism*, Philadelphia: The Westminster Press, 1966.

Arberry, A. J. *Mystical Poems of Rumi*, Chicago: University of Chicago Press, 1968.

Auzépy, Marie-France. 'Les Sabaites et L'iconoclasme', in J. Patrich (ed.), *The Sabaite Heritage in the Orthodox Church from the Fifth Century to the Present*, Leuven: Peeters, 2001.

Ayoub, Mahmoud. 'Towards an Islamic Christology', in Irfan A. Omar (ed.), *A Muslim View of Christianity*, Maryknoll: New York: Orbis Books, 2007.

Ayoub, Mahmud. 'Jesus the Son of God', in Yvonne Yazbeck Haddad and Wadi Z. Haddad (eds), *Christian–Muslim Encounters*, Gainesville: University Press of Florida, 1995.

Babić, Jovan. 'Toleration vs Doctrinal Evil in Our Times', *The Journal of Ethics*, vol. 8:3, 2004.
Baker, Mark D. *Proclaiming the Scandal of the Cross: Contemporary Images of the Atonement*, Grand Rapids, Michigan: Baker Academic, 2006.
Bakhtin, M. M. *Speech Genre and Other Late Essays*, Austin: University of Texas Press, 1996.
Balthasar, Hans Urs von, and Ratzinger, Joseph Cardinal. *Mary: The Church at the Source*, translated by Adrian Walker, San Francisco: Ignatius Press, 1980.
Barnes, Michel Rene. 'Latin Trinitarian Theology', in Peter C. Phan (ed.), *The Cambridge Companion to the Trinity*, Cambridge: Cambridge University Press, 2011.
Barr, James. 'Abbā Isn't "Daddy"', *Journal of Theological Studies*, 39:1, 1988.
Barth, Karl. *Church Dogmatics*, vol. 2:1, Edinburgh: T&T Clark, 1957.
Bartholomew of Edessa. *Refutation of the Hagarene*, quoted in Jaroslav Pelikan, *Mary Through the Centuries*, New Haven: Yale University Press, 1996.
Baudrillard, Jean. *The Intelligence of Evil or the Lucidity Pact*, translated by Chris Turner, Oxford: Berg, 2005.
Beaumont, Mark. *Christology in Dialogue with Muslims*, Oxford: Regnum, 2011.
Bellitto, Christopher M. *The General Councils: A History of the Twenty-One Church Councils from Nicaea to Vatican II*, New York: Paulist Press, 2002.
Blois, François de. 'Naṣranī and *ḥanīf*: Studies on the Religious Vocabulary of Christianity and Islam', *Bulletin of the School of Oriental and African Studies*, 65:1, 2002.
Bocken, Inigo. 'Nicholas of Cusa and the Plurality of Religions', in Barbara Roggema, Marcel Poorthuis, Pim Valkenberg (eds), *The Three Rings*, Utrecht: Thomas Instituut, 2005.
Bowering, Gerhard. 'The Light Verse: Qur'ānic Text and Ṣūfī Interpretation', *Oriens*, 36, 2001.
Bowman, John. 'The Debt of Islam to Monophysite Syrian Christianity', *Nederlands Theologisch Tijdschrii*, 19,1964.
Brinner, W. M. 'Arā'is al-majālis fī qiṣaṣ al-anbiyā' or "Lives of the Prophets" as recounted by Abū Isḥāq Aḥmad ibn Muḥammad ibn Ibrāhīm al-Tha'lābī'. Leiden: E. J. Brill, 2002.
Brown, Daniel. *Rethinking Tradition in Modern Islamic Thought*, Cambridge: Cambridge University Press, 1996.
Browne, L. E. 'The Law and the Gospel', *The Muslim World*, 29:2, 1939.
Brueggemann, Walter. *The Prophetic Imagination*, Philadelphia: Fortress Press, 1978.
Buck, Christopher. 'Discovering', in Andrew Rippin (ed.), *Blackwell Companion to the Qur'ān*, Wiley–Blackwell, 2006.
Bultmann, Rudolf. *Faith and Understanding*, translated by Louise Pettibone Smith, London: SCM Press, 1969.
Chittick, William. *Sufism: A Short Introduction*, Oxford: Oneworld, 2008.
Cook, Maeve. 'Moral Evil and Moral Identity', in Maria Pia Lara (ed.), *Rethinking Evil*, London: University of California Press, 2001.
Cragg, Kenneth. 'Each Other's Face, Some Thoughts on Muslim–Christian Colloquy', *The Muslim World*, 45:2, 1955.
Cragg, Kenneth. '"My Tears Into Thy Bottle," Prophethood and God', *The Muslim World*, 88:3–4, 1998.
Cragg, Kenneth. *The Call of the Minaret*, Oxford: Oxford University Press, 1956.
Cullman, Oscar. *The Christology of the New Testament*, London: SCM Press, 1957.
Daniel, Norman. *Islam and the West: The Making of an Image*. Oxford: Oneworld, 2009.
Daniel, Norman. *Islam and the West: The Making of an Image*. Edinburgh: Edinburgh University Press, 1960.
Davids, Adelbert, and Valkenberg, Pim. 'John of Damascus, the Heresy of the Ishmaelites', in Barbara Roggema, Marcel Poorthuis, Pim Valkenberg (eds), *The Three Rings*, Utrecht: Thomas Instituut, 2005.
Davies, Brian. *The Thought of Thomas Aquinas*, Oxford: Clarendon Press, 1993.

Depoortere, Frederiek. *Christ in Postmodern Philosophy*, London and New York: T&T Clark, 2008.

Dews, Peter. '"Radical Finitude" and the Problem of Evil', in Marìa Pìa Lara (ed.), *Rethinking of Evil*, London: University of California Press, 2001.

Donner, Fred M. 'The Qur'ān in Recent Scholarship', in Gabriel Reynolds (ed.), *The Qur'*ān *in its Historical Context*, New York: Routledge, 2008.

Dodd, C.H. 'Jesus as Teacher and Prophet', in G. K. A. Bell and A. Dessmann (eds), *Mysterium Christi*, London: Longmans, 1930.

Dotolo, Carmelo. *The Christian Revelation: Word, Event and Mystery*, translated by Cavallo Domenica, Aurora, CO: The Davies Group, 2006.

Dunn, James D. G. *Christianity in the Making. Vol. 1, Jesus Remembered*, Grand Rapids: William B. Eerdmans, 2003.

Dunn, James. *Christology in the Making*, London: SCM Press and Philadelphia: Westminster Press, 1980.

Ess, Josef van. 'Verbal Inspiration', in Stefan Wild (ed.), *The Qur'ān as Text*, Leiden: E. J. Brill, 1996.

Ess, Josef van. 'Wrongdoing and Divine Omnipotence in the Theology of Abū Ishāq al-Nazzām', in T. Rudavsky (ed.), *Divine Omniscience and Omnipotence in Medieval Philosophy*, Dordrecht: D. Reidel Publishing, 1985.

Finkel, Joshua. 'A Risāla of Al-Jāḥiz', *Journal of the American Oriental Society*, vol. 47, 1927.

Fisch, Harold. *The Holy Scriptures*, Jerusalem: Koren, 1998.

Fortounatto, Mariamna, and Cunningham, Mary B. 'Theology of the icon', in Mary B. Cunningham and Elizabeth Theokritoff (eds), *The Cambridge Companion to Orthodox Christian Theology*, Cambridge: Cambridge University Press, 2008.

Foruzanfar, Badi'al-Zamān. *Āḥādīth-Masnavi*, Tehran: Amir Kabir, 1987.

Francisco, Adam S. *Martin Luther and Islam: A Study in Sixteenth-Century Polemics and Apologetics*, Leiden: E. J. Brill, 2007.

Gairdner, W. *Al-Ghazzali's Mishkāt al-Anwār*, A Translation with Introduction. London: Royal Asiatic Society, 1924.

Gibb, H. A. R. *Islam: A Historical Survey*, 2nd edn, Oxford: Oxford University Press, 1986.

Gimaret, Daniel. 'Mu'tazila', in H. A. R Gibb (ed.), *The Encyclopaedia of Islam,* Leiden: E. J. Brill, 1960–2002.

Gonzales, Adolfo. 'The Challenge of Islamic Monotheism: a Christian View', in Hans Küng and Jürgen Moltmann (eds), *Islam: A Challenge for Christianity*. London: SCM Press, 1994.

Greenspahn, Frederick E. 'Why Prophecy Ceased', *Journal of Biblical Literature*, 108, 1989.

Griffel, Frank. 'Muslim philosophers' rationalist explanation', in Jonathan E. Brockopp (ed.), *The Cambridge Companion to Muḥammad*, Cambridge: Cambridge University Press, 2010.

Griffith, Sidney H. *The Church in the Shadow of the Mosque, Christians and Muslims in the World of Islam*, Princeton: Princeton University Press, 2008.

Griffith, Sidney. 'John of Damascus and the Church in Syria in the Umayyad Era: The Intellectual and Cultural Milieu of Orthodox Christians in the World of Islam', *Hugoye: Journal of Syriac Studies*, vol. 11:2, 2008.

Griffith, Sidney. 'The View of Islam from the monasteries of Palestine in the early 'Abbāsid Period: Theodore Abū Qurrah and the *Summa theologiae arabica*', *Islam and Christian–Muslim Relations*, 7:1, 2007.

Grunebaum, Gustave E. von. 'Observations on the Muslim Concept of Evil', *Studia Islamica*, 31,1970.

Guénon, René. *The Symbolism of the Cross*, translated by Angus Macnab, Hillsdale, NJ: Sophia Perennis, 2004.

Haddad, Wadi Z. 'Al-Bāqillānī', in Yvonne H. Haddad and Wadi Z. Haddad (eds), *Christian–Muslim Encounter*, Gainesville: University Press of Florida, 1995.

Hall, Fred P. 'Martin Luther and Islam', *Mission apostolica*, 13:1, 2005.
Hammond, Robert. *The Philosophy of Al-Farābi and its Influence on Medieval Thought*, New York: Hobson Book Press, 1947.
Hebblethwaite, Brian. 'The Resurrection and the Incarnation', in Paul Avis (ed.), *The Resurrection of Jesus Christ*, London: Darton, Longman and Todd, 1993, 155–70.
Heemskerk, Margaretha. 'A Muʿtazilite Refutation of Christianity and Judaism', in Barbara Roggema, Marcel Poorthuis, Pim Valkenberg (eds), *The Three Rings*, Utrecht: Thomas Instituut, 2005.
Hick, John. *The Metaphor of God Incarnate*, 2nd edn, Louisville, Kentucky: Westminster John Knox Press, 2006.
Hofstadter, Albert. *Reflections on Evil, The Lindley Lecture*, University of Kansas, 1973.
Hopkins, Jasper. *Nicholas of Cusa's De Pace Fidei and Cribratio Alkorani*, 2nd edn, Minneapolis: Banning Press, 1994.
Houston, Graham. *Prophecy Now*, Leicester: Intervarsity Press, 1989.
Ibn al-ʿArabī Muḥammad ibn ʿAlī Muḥī al-Dīn. *Fusūs al-hikām, The Bezels of Wisdoms*, translated by R. W. J. Austin, New York: Paulist Press, 1980.
Ibn al-ʿArabī Muḥammad ibn ʿAlī Muḥī al-Dīn. *Tarjumān al ʿAshwāq: A Collection of Mystical Odes by Muḥyiuddīn ibn al-ʿArabī*, vol. 2, ed. and trans. by Reynold A. Nicholson, London: Oriental Translation Fund, 1922.
Ibn Sīnā. *The Metaphysics of the Healing*, translated by M. E. Marmura, Provo, UT: Brigham Young University Press, 2005.
Ibrahim, Ezzedin, and Denys Johnson Davies. *Forty Hadīth Qudsī*, Cambridge: Islamic Texts Society, 1997.
Ibrahim, Ezzedin and Denys Johnson Davies. *An Nawawi's Forty Hadith*, Damascus: The Holy Koran Publishing House, 1976.
Iqbal, Afzal. *The Life and Work of Rumi*, 4th edn, Lahore: Institute of Islamic Culture, 1978.
Isutzu, Toshihiko. 'Ibn al-ʿArabī', in Mircea Eliade (editor in chief), *The Encyclopaedia of Religion*, New York: Macmillan, 1987.
Julian of Norwich, *Showings*, translated by Edmund Colledge and James Walsh, New York: Paulist Press, 1978.
Kadi, Wadad. 'What is Prophecy?' in Michael Ipgrave (ed.), *Bearing the Word: Prophecy in Biblical and Qur'ānic Perspective*, Church House Publishing, 2005.
Keating, Sandra Toenies. 'Let us leave the past aside', in Caterina Belo and Jean-Jacques Pérennès (eds), *Mission in Dialogue: Essays in Honour of Michael L. Fitzgerald*, Louvain: Peeters, 2012.
Keating, Sandra Toenies. *Defending the 'People of Truth' in the Early Islamic Period: The Christian Apologies of Abū-Rā'itah*, Leiden: Brill, 2006.
Khalidi, Tarīf. *The Muslim Jesus*, Cambridge, MA: Harvard University Press, 2001.
Khoury, Paul. *Paul d'Antioche, Évêque melkite de Sidon*, Beirut, 1964.
Kierkegaard, Søren. *Philosophical Fragments*, Princeton: Princeton University Press, 1985.
Kiernan, V. G. *Poems by Faiz*, London: George Allen & Unwin, 1971.
King, James Roy. 'Jesus and Joseph in Rūmī's Mathnawi', *The Muslim World*, 80:2 1990.
Koningsveld, P.S. van. 'The Islamic Image of Paul and the Origin of the Gospel of Barnabas', *Jerusalem Studies in Arabic and Islam*, 20, 1996.
Koshul Basit, Bilal. 'Studying the Western Other', in Muhammad Suheyl Umar (ed.), *The Religious Other: Towards a Muslim Theology of Other Religions in a Post-Prophetic Age*, Lahore: Iqbal Academy Pakistan, 2008.
Kraemer, Hendrik. *The Christian Message in a Non-Christian World*, 3rd edn, Grand Rapids, Michigan: Kregel, 1956.
Kraemer, Joel L. *Humanism in the Renaissance of Islam: The Cultural Revival during the Būyid Age*, Leiden: E. J. Brill, 1986.

Kritzeck, James. *Peter the Venerable and Islam*, Princeton, New Jersey: Princeton University Press, 1964.

Küng, Hans, and Moltmann, Jürgen (eds), *Islam: A Challenge for Christianity*, London: SCM Press, 1994.

Lamoreaux, John C. *Theodore Abū Qurrah*, Library of the Christian East. Brigham Young University Press, 2005.

Lawson, Todd. *The Crucifixion and the Qur'ān: A Study in the History of Muslim Thought*, Oxford: Oneworld, 2009.

Leirvik, Oddbjørn. *Images of Jesus Christ in Islam*, 2nd edn, London: Continuum, 2010.

McAuliffe, Jane. 'The Abrogation of Judaism and Christianity in Islam', in Hans Küng and Jürgen Moltmann (eds), *Islam: A Challenge for Christianity*, London: SCM Press, 1994.

McKane, William. *Al-Ghazālī's Book of Fear and Hope*, Leiden: E.J. Brill, 1962.

MacKenzie, D. N. *Poems from the Diwan of Khushal Khan Khattak*, London: George Allen & Unwin, 1965.

Macquarrie, John. *Christology Revisited*, London: SCM Press, 1998.

Macquarrie, John. *Jesus Christ in Modern Thought*, London: SCM Press, 1990.

Madigan, Daniel A. *The Qur'ân's Self Image*, Princeton, New Jersey: Princeton University Press, 2001.

Marshall, D. 'Christianity in the Qur'ān', in Lloyd Ridgeon (ed.), *Islamic Interpretations of Christianity*, Richmond: Curzon Press, 2001.

Mathewes, Charles T. 'Original Sin and the Hermeneutics of Charity: A Response to Gilbert Meilaender', *The Journal of Religious Ethics*, 29:1, 2001.

McAuliffe, Jane. *Qur'ānic Christians*, Cambridge: Cambridge University Press, 1991.

McCarthy, R. J. 'Mary in Islam' in Alberic Stacpoole (ed.), *Mary's Place in Christian Dialogue*, Wilton, Connecticut: Moorhouse-Barlow, 1982.

McFague, Sally. *Speaking in Parables*, Philadelphia: Fortress Press, 1975.

McRoy, Anthony. 'The Christ of Shi'a Islam', *Evangelical Review of Theology*, 30:4, 2006.

Meier, John P. *Jesus, A Marginal Jew: Law and Love*, New Haven: Yale University Press, 2010.

Merrill, John. 'Of the Tractate of John of Damascus on Islam', *The Moslem World*, XLI, 1951.

Miller, Gregory J. 'Luther on the Turks and Islam', *Lutheran Quarterly*, 14:1, 2000.

Mir, Mustansir. 'Islamic Views on Jesus', in Gregory A. Barker (ed.), *Jesus in the World's Faiths*, Maryknoll, New York: Orbis Books, 2005.

Monnot, Guy. *Penseurs musulmans et religions iraniennes: Abd al-Jabbar et ses devanciers*, Paris: J. Vrin, 1974.

Moorhead, John. 'The Earliest Christian Theological Response to Islam', *Religion*,11, 1981.

Nickel, Gordon. 'Self-evident truths of reason: Challenges to clear thinking in the *Tafsīr al-Kabīr* of Fakhr al-Dīn al-Rāzī', *Islam and Christian-Muslim Relations*, 22:2, 2011.

Niebuhr, Reinhold. *Beyond Tragedy*, London: Nisbet, 1938.

Niebuhr, Reinhold. *The Nature and Destiny of Man*, vol. 1, *Human Nature*, New York: Charles Scribner's Sons, 1941.

Nygren, Anders. *Agape and Eros*, translated by Philip S. Watson. New York: Harper and Row, 1969.

O'Collins, Gerald. *Christology: A Biblical, Historical, and Systematic Study of Jesus*. Oxford: Oxford University Press, 2nd edn, 2009.

Pannenberg, Wolfhart. *Systematic Theology*, vol. 1, translated by Geoffrey Bromiley, Grand Rapids, Michigan: Eerdmans, 1988.

Pannenberg, Wolfhart. *The Apostles' Creed in the Light of Today's Questions*, London: SCM Press, 1972.

Pelikan, Jaroslav. *Mary Through the Centuries: Her Place in the History of Culture*, New Haven: Yale University Press, 1998.

Peters, F. E. 'The Quest of the Historical Muḥammad', *International Journal of Middle Eastern Studies*, 23, 1991.

Pines, Shlomo. 'A Note on an Early Meaning of the Term *Mutakallim*', *Israel Oriental Studies*, 1, 1971.

Prat, Igona Dominique, Graham Robert Edwards and Barbara H. Rosenwein. *Order and Exclusion: Cluny and Christendom Face Heresy, Judaism, and Islam, 1000–1150*, New York: Cornell University Press, 2002.

Rahim, 'Ata Ur. *Jesus, A Prophet of Islam*. New Delhi: Taj Printers, 1979 and London: MWH London Publishers, 1st edn, 1979.

Rahner, Karl. *Foundations of Christian Faith: An Introduction to the Idea of Christianity*, translated by William V. Dych, New York: Seabury Press, 1978.

Räisänen, Heikki. 'The Portrait of Jesus in the Qur'ān: Reflections of a Biblical Scholar', *The Muslim World*, 70:2 1980.

Rescher, Nicholas. 'Nicholas of Cusa on the Qur'ān', *The Muslim World*, 55:3, 1965.

Robinson, Neal. 'Jesus and Mary in the Qur'ān: Some Neglected Affinities', *Religion*, 20, 1990.

Robinson, Neal. 'Syed Qutb's attitude towards Christianity', in Lloyd Ridgeon (ed.), *Islamic Interpretations of Christianity*, Richmond: Curzon Press, 2001.

Royster, James. 'Personal Transformation in Ibn al-'Arabī and Meister Eckhart', in Yvonne Y. Haddad and Wadi Z. Haddad (eds), *Christian–Muslim Encounters*, Gainesville: University Press of Florida, 1995.

Rubin, Uri. 'Pre-Existence and Light', *Israel Oriental Studies*, 5, 1975.

Russell, Ralph, and Khurshidul Islam. *Three Moghul Poets*, Cambridge, MA: Harvard University Press, 1968.

Sahas, Daniel J. '"Holosphyros"? A Byzantine Perception of "The God of Muhammad"', in Yvonne Y. Haddad and Wadi Z. Haddad (eds), *Christian–Muslim Encounters*, Gainesville: University Press of Florida, 1995.

Sahas, Daniel J. *John of Damascus on Islam, The Heresy of the Ishmaelites*, Leiden: E. J. Brill, 1972.

Sanders, E. P. *Jesus and Judaism*, London: SCM Press and Philadelphia: Fortress Press, 1985.

Saneh, Lamin. Foreword in David Emmanuel Singh (ed.), *Jesus and the Cross*, Eugene, Oregon: Wipf & Stock, 2008.

Schimmel, Annemarie. 'Some Aspects of Mystical Prayer in Islam', *Die Welt des Islam*, 2:2, 1952.

Schimmel, Annemarie. 'Jesus and Mary in Rūmī's Verse', in Yvonne Y. Haddad and Wadi Z. Haddaad (eds), *Christian–Muslim Encounters*, Gainesville: University Press of Florida, 1995.

Schimmel, Annemarie. *Gabriel's Wing: A Study into the Religious Ideas of Sir Muhammad Iqbal*, Leiden: E. J. Brill, 1963.

Schoot, Henk. 'Christ Crucified Contested: Thomas Aquinas', in Barbara Roggema, Marcel Poorthuis, Pim Valkenberg (eds), *The Three Rings*. Utrecht: Thomas Instituut, XL, 2005.

Schuon, Frithjof. *Islam and the Perennial Philosophy*, London: World of Islam Festival Publishing, 1976.

Schuon, Frithjof. *The Fullness of God*, Indiana: World Wisdom, 1974.

Schweitzer, Albert. *The Quest of the Historical Jesus: A Critical Study of its Progress from Reimarus to Wrede*, translated by William Montgomery. London: A & C Black, 1910.

Sered, Rachel. 'Rachel, Mary and Fatima', *Cultural Anthropology*, 6:2, 1991.

Shah, Mustapha. 'Trajectories in the Development of Islamic Legal Thought: the Synthesis of *Kalām*', *Religion/Compass*, 1:4, 2007.
Sharon, M. 'People of the Book', in J. McAuliffe (ed.), *The Encyclopaedia of the Qur'ān*, vol. 4, Leiden: E. J. Brill, 2004.
Shnizer, Aliza. 'Sacrality and Collection', in Andrew Rippin (ed.), *Blackwell Companion to the Qur*'ān, Wiley–Blackwell, 2008.
Siddiqui, Mona. *The Good Muslim: Reflections on Classical Islamic Law and Theology*, Cambridge: Cambridge University Press, 2012.
Smith, Jane, and Haddad, Yvonne. 'The Virgin Mary in Islamic Tradition', *The Muslim World*, 79: 3–4, 1989.
Smith, Robert O. 'Luther, the Turks and Islam', *Currents in Theology and Mission*, 34:5, 2007.
Soroudi, Sorour S. 'On Jesus' Image in Modern Persian Poetry', *The Muslim World*, 69:4, 1979.
Southern, Richard William. *Western Views of Islam in the Middle Ages*, Cambridge, MA: Harvard University Press, 1962.
Stenson, Sten H. 'Prophecy, Theology and Philosophy', *Journal of Religion*, 44:1, 1964.
Stern, Samuel M. ''Abd al-Jabbār's Account of how Christ's Religion was falsified by the Adoption of Roman Customs', *Journal of Theological Studies*, 8:19, 1996.
Stowasser, Barbara F. *Women in the Qur'ān, Traditions, and Interpretation*, New York: Oxford University Press, 1994.
Stroumsa, Sarah. 'The Signs of Prophecy: The Emergence and Early Development of a Theme in Arabic Theological Literature', *The Harvard Theological Review*, 78:1, 1985.
Stroumsa, Sarah. *Freethinkers of Medieval Islam: Ibn al-Rawandi, Abū Bakr al-Rūzī and their Impact on Islamic Thought*, Leiden: E. J. Brill, 1999.
Sweetman, J. Windrow. *Islam and Christian Theology*, Part One, vol. 2, London: Lutterworth Press, 1947.
Ṭabarī, Rabbān al. *Kitāb al-dīn wa-l-dawla, the Book of Religion and Empire*, translated by A. Mingana, Manchester: Manchester University Press, 1922.
Taylor, Vincent. *The Names of Jesus*, London: Macmillan, 1953.
Teule, Herman. 'Paul of Antioch's Attitude Towards the Jews and the Muslims', in Barbara Roggema, Marcel Poorthuis, Pim Valkenberg (eds), *The Three Rings*, Utrecht: Thomas Instituut, 2005.
Thomas, David. 'Early Muslim Relations with Christianity,' *Anvil*, 6:1, 1989.
Thomas, David. 'Paul of Antioch's Letter to a Muslim Friend and the Letter from Cyprus', in D. Thomas (ed.), *Syrian Christians under Islam: The First Thousand Years*, Leiden: E. J. Brill, 2001.
Thomas, David. *Christian Doctrines in Islamic Theology*, Leiden: E. J. Brill, 2008.
Thomas, David. *Early Muslim Polemic against Christianity: Abū 'Īsā al-Warrāq's "Against the Trinity"*, Cambridge: Cambridge University Press, 1982.
Thomson, R. W., Howard, James Johnston, Greenwood, Tim (eds), *The Armenian History*, vol. 2, Liverpool: Liverpool Hope University Press, 1999.
Thurkill, Mary. *Mary and Fatima in Medieval Christianity and Shī'ite Islam*, Notre Dame, Indiana: University of Notre Dame Press, 2007.
Tolan, John V. *Sons of Ishmael: Muslims through European Eyes in the Middle Ages*, Gainesville: University Press of Florida, 2008.
Tottoli, Roberto. 'Narrative Literature', in Andrew Rippin (ed.), *The Blackwell Companion to the Qur'ān*, Wiley–Blackwell, 2006.
Vajda, G. *L'Amour de Dieu dans la Théologie Juive du Moyen Age*, Paris: Librairie Philosophique J. Vrin, 1957.
Waltz, James. 'Muhammad and the Muslims in St Thomas Aquinas', *The Muslim World*, 66:2, 1976.

Watt, W. Montgomery. *Islam and Christianity Today: A Contribution to Dialogue*, London: Routledge and Kegan Paul, 1983.
Watt,W. Montgomery. *The Formative Period of Islamic Thought*, Edinburgh: Edinburgh University Press, 1973.
Watt,W. Montgomery. *Muslim–Christian Encounters: Perceptions and Misperceptions*, New York: Routledge, 1991.
Weima, Jeffery A. D. 'The Function of the Law in Relation to Sin: An Evaluation of the View of H. Räisänen', *Novum Testamentum*, 32:3, 1990.
Weisheipl, James A. *Friar Thomas d'Aquino*, New York: Doubleday, 1974.
Weng Ng Kam. 'Being Human', in Michael Ipgrave and David Marshall (eds), *Humanity, Texts and Contexts*, Washington DC: Georgetown University Press, 2001.
Wild, Stefan. 'We Have Sent Down to Thee The Book', in S. Wild (ed.), *Qur'ān as Text*, Leiden: E. J. Brill, 1996.
Wiles, Maurice. *The Remaking of Christian Doctrine*, London: SCM Press, 1974.
Williams, Rowan. *Arius, Heresy and Tradition*, Grand Rapids, Michigan: Eerdmans, 2002.
Williams, Rowan. *Resurrection: Interpreting the Easter Gospel*, London: Darton, Longman and Todd, 1982.
Zeidan, David. 'A Comparative Study of Selected Themes in Christian and Islamic Fundamentalist Discourses', *British Journal of Middle Eastern Studies*, 30:1, 2003.
Žižek, Slavoj. *The Parallax View*, Cambridge, MA: MIT Press, Short Circuits, 2006.
Žižek, Slavoj. *The Puppet and the Dwarf: The Perverse Core of Christianity*, Cambridge, MA: MIT Press, Short Circuits, 2003.
Zwemer, Samuel. *The Disintegration of Islam*, London: Fleming H. Revell, 1916.

Electronic sources

http://dhspriory.org/thomas/ContraGentiles1.htm
http://jasper-hopkins.info/CAII-12-2000.pdf
http://josephkenny.joyeurs.com/DCtexts/Rationes.htm
http://salafitranslation.com
http://syrcom.cua.edu/Hugoye/Vol11No2/HV11N2Griffith.html.
http://www.arian-catholicorg/arian/arius.html
http://www.religion-online.org/showchapter.asp?title=452&C=364
http://www.sacred-texts.com/chr/aquinas/summa/sum229.htm
http://www.tertullian.org/father/timothy_i_apology_01_text.htm
http://www.tertullian.org/fathers/timothy_i_apology_00_intro.htm

INDEX